Collins

Cascade 7

A SKILL-BASED COURSE IN SOCIAL STUDIES

Archna Golcha
Urmi Chakraborty
Swati Shukla

Components of DigiSuite

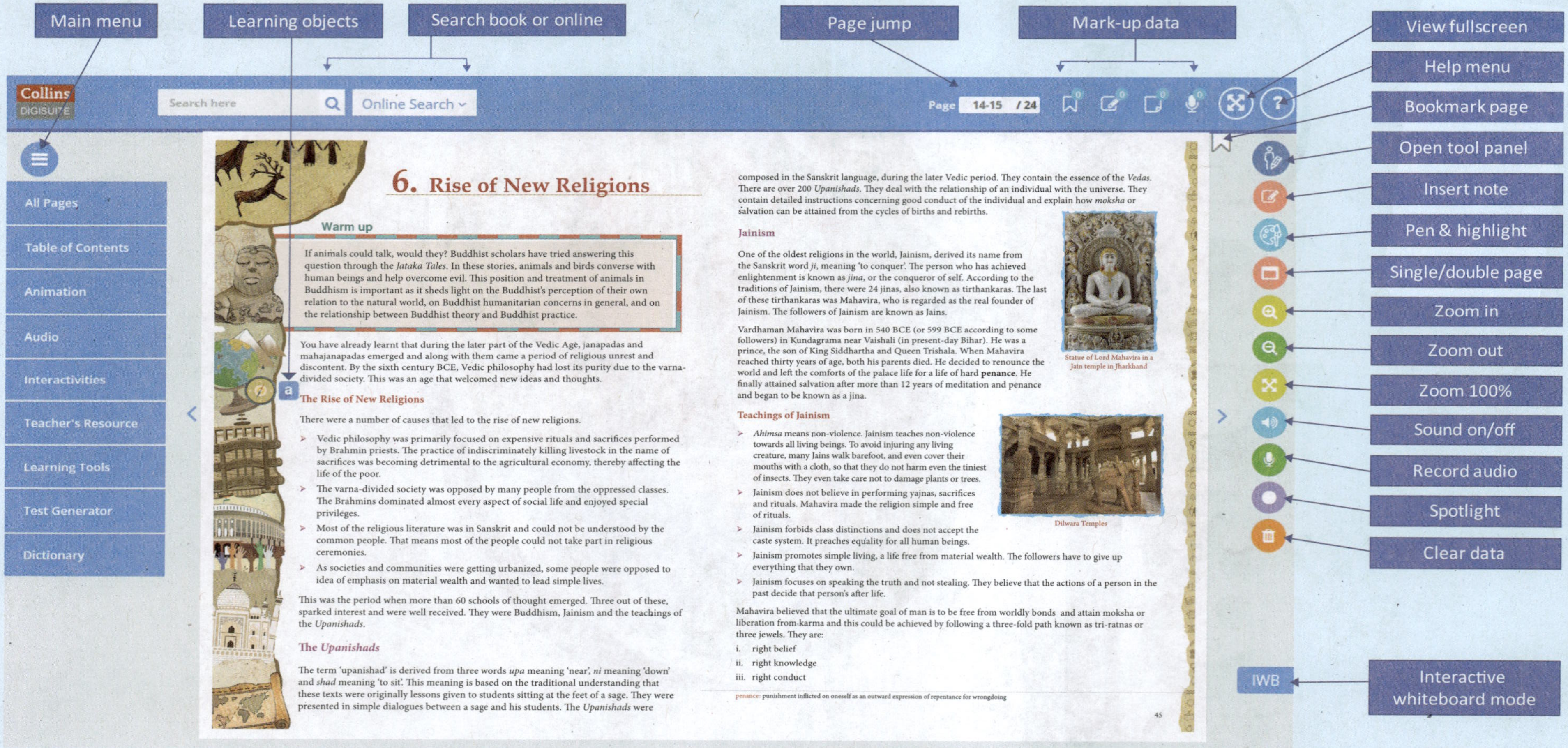

Student + Teacher

- a — animations
- ilt — instructor-led tutorials
- ia — activities
- w — worksheets
- audio
- g — games
- v — videos

Teacher-only

- lp — lesson plans
- w — worksheets
- tn — teacher's notes
- ak — answer keys

PREFACE

Cascade is a skill-based course on Environmental Studies and Social Studies for the foundational, preparatory and middle stages. This series for classes 1 to 8 is aligned to the National Education Policy, 2020. Taking into account the multidisciplinary nature of Environmental Studies and Social Studies, the series follows an interactive approach through a variety of tasks and stimulating content. This series deals with the study of human behaviour, relationships, resources and institutions in local as well as global contexts, all of which are fundamental to our conception of society.

Cascade and the NEP

Based on an interactive pedagogy, the books focus on:

- Conceptual development encouraging students to learn how to learn through Constructivist learning tasks
- Thinking critically, solving problems and learning essential life skills to imbibe 21st century learning
- Creative skills aimed at developing all capabilities of learners and to increase individual happiness from childhood
- Multidisciplinary teaching which aligns to the NIPUN initiative for young learners
- Inquiring, analyzing and absorbing new information in a world of increasing interconnections through inferential and experiential tasks
- Sustainable Development Goals that hold the key to the future of mankind sensitizing young learners through a gradual study that builds environmental and social awareness
- The promotion of Indian arts and culture to inculcate a sense of identity as well as an appreciation of other cultures and identities
- Competency-based Structured Assessments For Analyzing Learning (SAFAL)

About the authors

Archna Golcha is a resource person for CBSE and a master trainer. She has conducted several training programmes for educators and students. She also has been an observer CBSE for NEET and JEE exams on several occasions. She is presently working with Manikgarh Cement English School as the principal.

Urmi Chakraborty has over three decades of teaching experience. She has taught in Sardar Patel Vidyalaya, New Delhi, Welham Girls' School, Dehradun and The Shriram Millennium, Noida. She has been selected as a mentor by The Council for Secondary Education.

Swati Shukla has over two decades of teaching experience. She is currently teaching in Sanskriti School, New Delhi.

KEY FEATURES

Cascade offers features that focus on essential skills to assist learners achieve holistic learning through a multidisciplinary approach. In so doing, the series is aligned with the guidelines given in the National Education Policy, 2020.

Learning

Warm up has pre-reading tasks for discovery-based learning

Conceptual Development

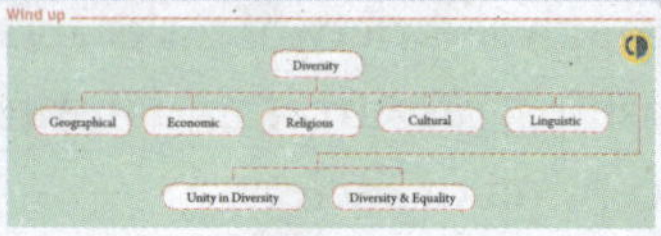

Wind Up has concept maps to assist in learning

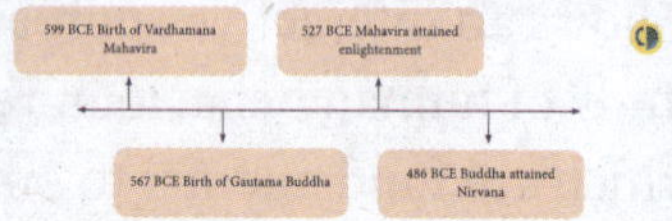

Timeline helps learners understand the chronology of events

Extended learning

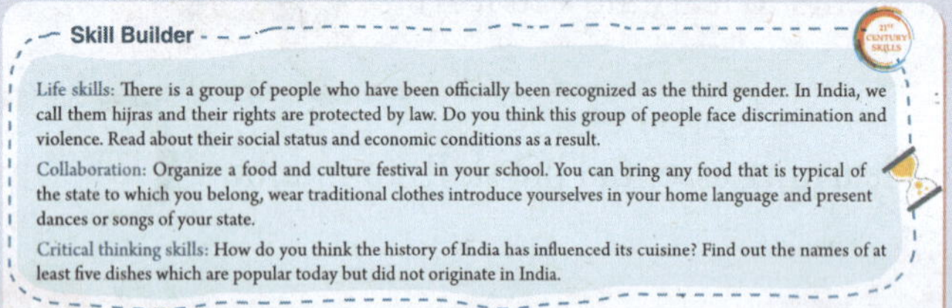

Skill builder has 21st century skills necessary in the age of information

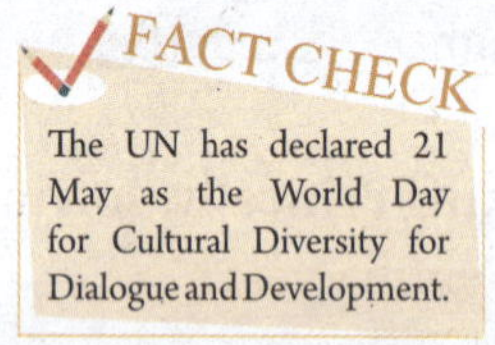

Fact check provides interesting titbits of information

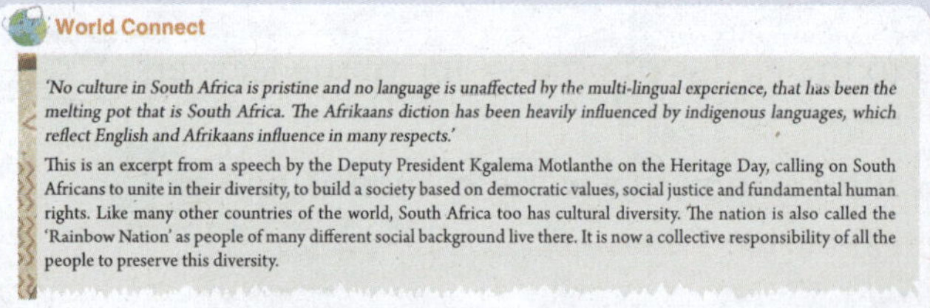

World Connect highlights stories and events from around the world related to the chapter.

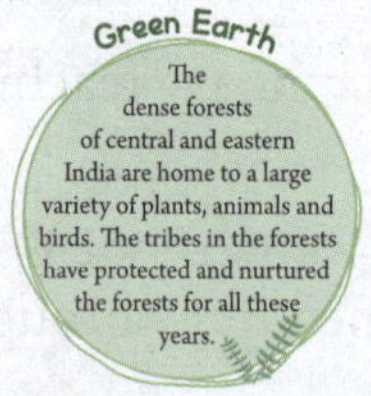

Green Earth sensitizes learners towards conservation of the environment.

Constructivist learning

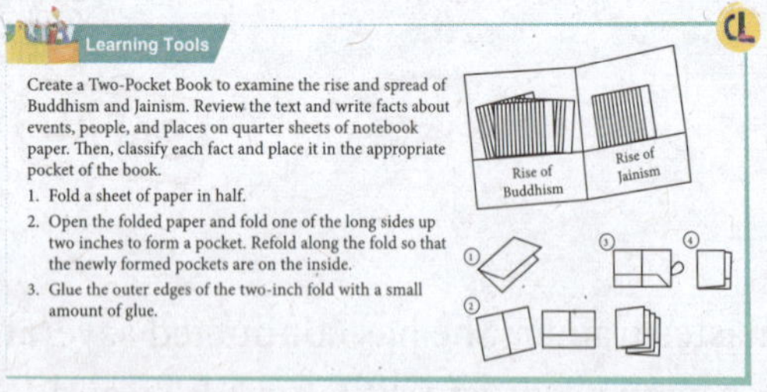

Learning Tools are student-made study guides to organize and arrange data encouraging self learning

Creativity and happiness

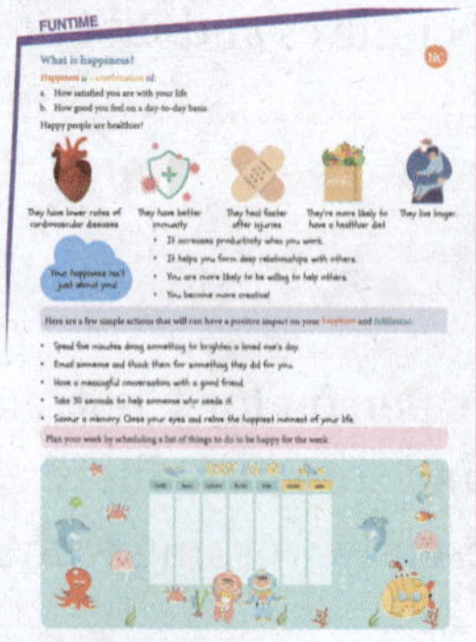

Fun Time addresses wellbeing and happiness of the students through creative and fun tasks

SDG Posters encourage sustainable living

Cross-curricular learning

What's in the picture?

How does this advertisement influence people? Find out ways in which you can recycle water at home.

SAFAL

What's in the picture? provides exercises for inferential learning

Geography skills

On a political map of India highlight all the different states to which your classmates belong. Also highlight the states of India that you have visited. Then, hold a discussion on the special dishes and places of interest in these states.

SAFAL

Geography skills build map skills and improve world overview of learners

Think Big

Integrate with Science

A. Listed below are some of the many ways that we can try to save the endangered animals. Make a chart with the given points and display it in class.

1. Learn more about wildlife by reading books, watching television programmes about nature, visiting zoos and nature preserves.
2. Try to volunteer for a wildlife organisation.
3. Do not pet wild animals.
4. Do not buy products that have been tested on animals.
5. Try to create awareness about endangered species by writing articles and drawing posters.
6. Do not disturb the habitats of wild animals.

B. Discuss the ways in which you can help prevent animal extinction in your country.

Think Big provides varied activities for multidisciplinary learning

Observation and application

Apply it!

'Efforts must be made by all the people, to uphold the dignity of labour in our country. All professions must be treated with respect, because all jobs are important for the smooth functioning of society.'

Write a comprehension on what you understand from these lines.

Apply it! provides application-based activities for experiential learning

Case Study

Discrimination on the Basis of Physical Disability

Nine year old Gabi Shull was just like any other girl of her age very active, and had hobbies, like dancing, singing, reading and playing. She was a talented ballet dancer but her hopes of becoming a dancer came crashing down when she was diagnosed with bone cancer at the age of nine. Her condition required the lower part of her leg, knee down to be amputated. She now had to get an artificial leg. Her road to recovery was very tough but she never gave up hope. She is now back to dancing on her toes as is the requirement of ballet and she is a competition level dancer.

Read about some other famous personalities who have overcome similar challenges.

Gabi Shull

Case Study re-counts in-depth investigations of a single person, group, event or community.

SAFAL

Assessment and practice

Exercises

A. Fill in the blanks.

1. .... is a vast country with diverse geography and cultures.
2. Each period of .... had a distinct influence on the lives of people.
3. The UN has declared 21 May as ....
4. Religion, languages, food, festivals and rituals form ....
5. The Constitution of India promotes and supports .... and national integration in which all people from different races, religions, cultures, castes and backgrounds are treated equally.

ASSESSMENT 1

D. Read the following passage and answer the questions. 3

The Indus Valley Civilization also known as the Indus Civilization, was a Bronze Age civilization in the northwestern regions of South Asia, lasting from 3300 BCE to 1300 BCE. It flourished in the basins of the Indus River, which flows through the length of Pakistan. The civilization's cities were noted for their urban planning, baked brick houses, elaborate drainage systems, water supply systems etc. The large cities of Mohenjo-daro and Harappa very likely grew to contain between 30,000 and 60,000 individuals. The Harappan language is not directly attested, and its affiliation is uncertain as the Indus script has remained undeciphered.

The Indus civilization is also known as the Harappan Civilization, after its type site, Harappa, the first of its sites to be excavated early in the 20th century. The discovery of Harappa and soon afterwards Mohenjo-daro was the culmination of work beginning in 1861 with the finding of the Archaeological Survey of India during the British Raj. By 2002, over 1,000 Mature Harappan cities and settlements had been reported, of which just under a hundred had been excavated. However, there are only five major urban sites: Harappa, Mohenjo-daro (UNESCO World Heritage Site. Dholavira, Ganeriwala, and Rakhigarhi. The early Harappan cultures were preceded by local Neolithic agricultural villages, from which the river plains were populated.

1. The Indus Valley Civilization flourished near the .... river.
2. Name any two Harappan sites.
3. "The Harappan towns were well-planned". Explain the statement.

E. On the outline map of India locate and name the following. $3 \times 1 = 3$

1. The strongest Mahajanapada.
2. The capital of Vajji.
3. Avanti in present-day Madhya Pradesh.

SAFAL

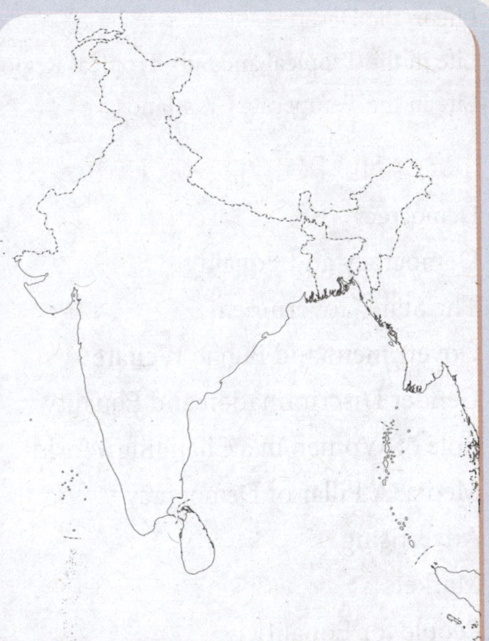

Exercises, **Assessments** and **Outline Maps** for assessment

CONTENTS

1. The Medieval Period

Warm up

Raghav had learnt to draw a treasure hunt map and a map of his classroom in his geography class. He found the activity quite interesting. First, he prepared the old parchment look for the map by ripping the edges, crumpling the paper, pouring coffee on it, blow-drying it and then finally drawing the map on it. He included the cardinal directions, along with various landmarks, throughout the map. He also created many rivers, mountains and houses on the map. Raghav wondered how travellers from different parts of the world set out on explorations with some rough sketches indicating places and directions. His geography teacher had told the class that this development of map making is called cartography.

In India, the medieval period stretched from the 8th century to the 18th century CE. This period witnessed the development of modern Hinduism, the decline of Buddhism in India and the establishment of Islam in the subcontinent. Associated with these changes in the religious make-up of Indian society were important developments in art, architecture and literature.

Diverse Terminology

The Republic of India has been known by many different names. Early Sanskrit texts mention 'Aryavarta' as the land of the Aryans and 'Bharatvarsha' in the *Puranas*. The name 'India' originates from the word *Indus*, which originates from the Persian word *Sindh*. The Indus River was also called Sindhu in Sanskrit. As we read the Constitution of India, 'India' and 'Bharat' have been used interchangeably to describe the country. The historical term 'Hindustan' signifies either the entire Indian subcontinent or its north and north western regions. Each of these names has been used differently at different periods as interpreted by different rulers. When Minhaj-i-Siraj, a Persian historian, used the term 'Hindustan', he used it to describe the areas of Punjab, Haryana and the lands between the rivers Ganga and Yamuna. The Mughals used this term to describe the geography of the place. Subsequent rulers used the term 'Hindustan' to refer to their respective realms. Amir Khusrau used the word 'Hind' in a geographical and cultural aspect. However, he did not attribute any political or national meaning to it.

Sources of History

Literary sources of the medieval period were greater in number than those available on ancient India. Paper, by this time, had become cheap and people started recording events.

Chronicles: Information on the period is gathered from the writings of contemporary **chroniclers**. The famous scholar Al-Biruni wrote the chronicle called *Tārīkh al-Hind* in which he explored different aspects of Indian life during and after the invasion of Mahmud of Ghazni. Another important work, called *Tabaqut-i-Nasiri,* was written by Minhaj-ud-din Siraj and it narrates the history of Muslim dynasties that originated in Iran and Central Asia. Ziauddin Barauni's *Tarik-i-Firoj-Shahi* narrates the events from the reign of Balban to that of Firoz Shah Tughlug. Other contemporary chronicles include the works of Amir Khashru, *Fatuah-i-Firoz Shahi* by the Sultan himself and *Fatuah-us-Salatin* by Isami. The *Ain-i-Akbari* by Abdul Fazal and the *Akbarnama* are remarkable works that give insights into the Mughal empire.

FACT CHECK

Sometimes, deciphering ancient texts is a difficult task for historians as some of these texts were written in ancient languages known only by a few today. Also, the quality of these manuscripts has deteriorated so much over the centuries that they are hardly legible. Sometimes, scribes would miss a word or misrepresent an idea, changing its meaning. Sometimes, even chroniclers would revise their work and leave historians with two different copies of the same book.

Autobiographies and biographies: Autobiographies and biographies also form an important part of literary sources. Some popular examples of autobiographies are Babur's *Baburnama*, which gives information about the geographical features of the Indian subcontinent, *Tuzuk-i-Jahangiri*, which throws light on Jahangir's personal life and the administrative affairs of his kingdom, and *Prithviraj Raso* by Chand Bardai.

An ancient manuscript

Accounts of foreign travellers: These accounts throw light on various aspects of the period such as administration, culture, economy and developments. The earliest African traveller who visited Muslim India was Ibn Battuta. His *Rihla* is a travelogue that details various aspects of the Muslim world. Travellers William Hawkins, Thomas Roe, François Bernier and Jean-Baptiste Tavernier also give us valuable information about medieval India.

Coins and inscriptions: The discovery of coins made of gold, silver and copper helps us reconstruct our past and highlights the development of scientific technology. Coins also shed light on the socioeconomic conditions of the period. The discovery of similar coins in distant places tells us about the extent of trade that took place during that period. They also help us understand the names and titles of the kings who issued them. Inscriptions are writings engraved on metals, rocks and stones. King Ashoka had many inscriptions propagating his *dhamma*. Many inscriptions belonging to the Rajputs and the Cholas have been found, meant to be either royal proclamations or religious instructions.

Buildings and monuments: The medieval period witnessed the construction of innumerable monuments and buildings that help us reconstruct the time period in which they were built. Buildings and monuments help us understand the architectural styles and the different materials used for construction during this period. Monuments also exhibit the economic conditions of the time along with an understanding of the cultural and religious beliefs of the people. The Qutub Minar, the Red Fort, the Taj Mahal and the Jama Masjid are some famous monuments constructed during the medieval period.

chronicler: a person who writes accounts of important or historical events

Paintings and sculptures: A lot of Arabic and Persian influence can be seen in the art and architecture of the medieval period. These paintings generally portray mythological scenes, court scenes and religious scenes. A classic example of painting during the Mughal period is the 'miniature painting' in which natural colours were used. The sculptures were usually made of bronze, wood and stone. The dancing Shiva or Nataraja is a famous sculpture of the medieval period.

Nataraja, the King of Dance

Major Developments During the Medieval Period

Society: During the medieval period, the society came to be divided into sub-castes called *jatis*. These sub-castes were based on professions. People belonging to the same profession belonged to the same sub-caste. The group of scribes who maintained records became very important. They were called *kayasthas*. These jatis framed their own rules and regulations but respected the norms of the villages and the towns that they belonged to.

What's in the picture?

This is a Mughal miniature painting of Timur, Babur and Humayun. What are the elements of grandeur that you see in the painting?

Food and beverages: The Turks brought fruits, like peaches, apricots and melons, to the Indian subcontinent. Apart from these, potatoes, corn and chillies were introduced. Under Mughal rule, Mughlai cuisine was introduced in India, which brought about the use of condiments like saffron and dry fruits like nuts in their dishes. Jainism and Buddhism also heavily influenced the food of the people during this period. Due to the beliefs of both these religions, people started adopting vegetarian diets. Tea was introduced in India by the silk caravans that travelled from China to Europe during this period.

Technology: The Persian wheel in irrigation and the spinning wheel were two important technologies invented during this period. In warfare, gunpowder and gunpowder weapons came to be used during the rule of the Delhi Sultanate at the time of the Mongol invasions of India.

Apply it!

Analyze an archaeological source of history and write a report on it. Choose a monument and note the materials used, the style in architecture and other elements.

Skill Builder

21ST CENTURY SKILLS

Critical thinking skills: Why should we keep historical records?

Life skills: Early medieval period witnessed wars among regional kingdoms from the north to the south of India, whereas the late medieval period saw a number of Muslim invasions by Mughals, Afghans and Turks. Can we say that battles played an important role in expansion during this period?

Communication skills: 'Newspaper reports are a reliable source of history'. Conduct a debate about this in the class.

World Connect

In Europe, the Middle Ages began with the fall of the Roman Empire and ended with the Renaissance—the revival of art and culture in the 14th century. After the fall of the Roman Empire, no single state ruled over Europe. The supremacy of the church was made universal, and kings gained power from their alliance with the church. The supreme authority of the church was the Pope. At times, the church even controlled the armies and the affairs of the state. In 800 CE, Pope Leo III declared the Frankish king, Charlemagne, as the 'Holy Roman Emperor'. During the 12th century, a cultural and economic revival took place. In agriculture, the cultivation of beans helped in providing a balanced diet to all the social classes. The Renaissance witnessed a growth in population, trade and commerce along with the development of Gothic art and architecture.

Wind up

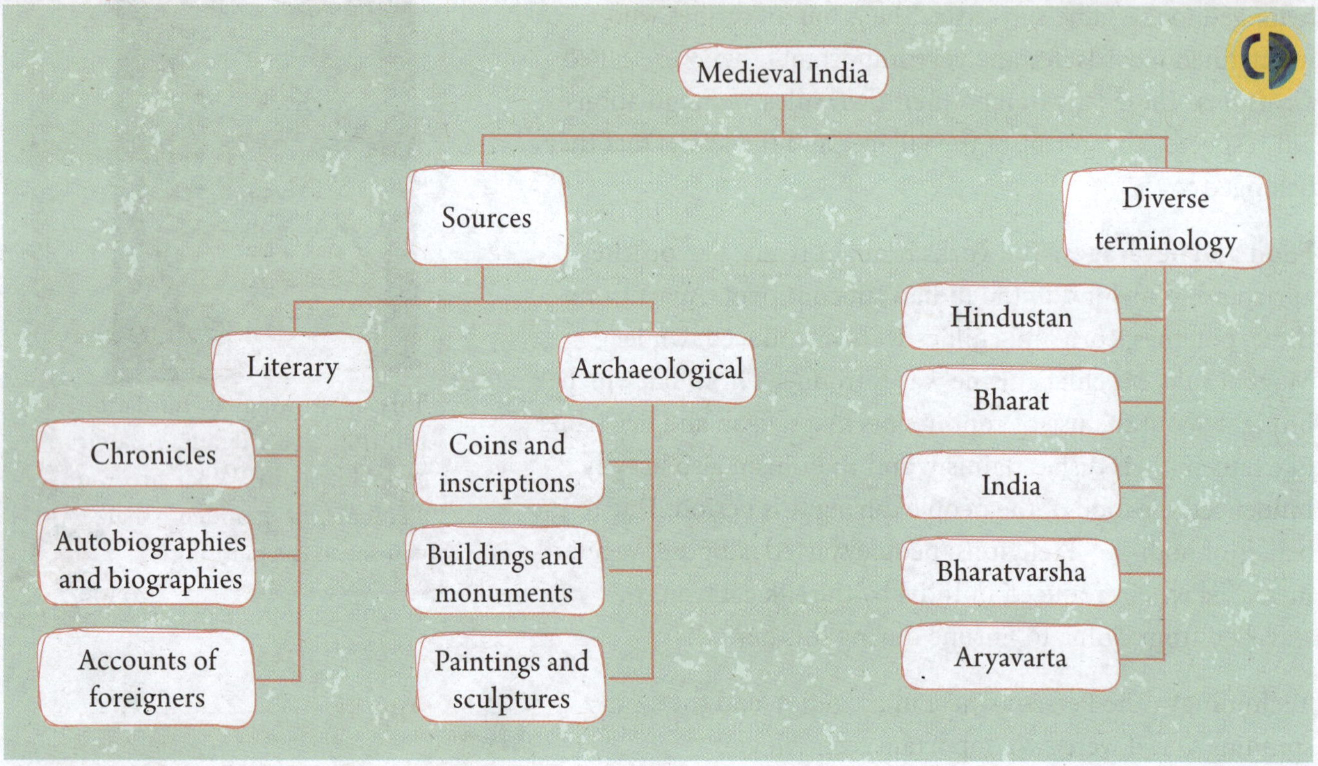

Exercises

A. Choose the correct answers.

1. Al-Biruni wrote the chronicle called
   a. *India in the Medieval Period* b. *India As I See It*
   c. *Learning from India* d. *Tārīkh al-Hind*
2. Examples of archaeological sources are
   a. monuments and coins b. biographies and autobiographies
   c. books and travelogues d. letters
3. Jatis were sub-castes based on
   a. caste b. profession c. religion d. wealth
4. During Mughal rule, the Turks brought this to the Indian subcontinent:
   a. apricots b. peaches c. melons d. all of these

5. The art of map-making is called
   a. calligraphy   b. history   c. archaeology   d. cartography

B. Fill in the blanks.

1. A .... is a person who writes accounts of important or historical events.
2. The famous scholar .... wrote the chronicle called *Tārīkh al-Hind* in which he explored different aspects of Indian life during and after the invasion of Mahmud of Ghazni.
3. The paintings of the medieval period generally portray .... scenes, court scenes and themes of religion.
4. The earliest African traveller who visited medieval India was ....
5. The time from the .... to the 18th century is known as the medieval period.

C. Answer these questions in brief.

1. Give three examples of archaeological sources.
2. Name three literacy sources of medieval India.
3. How did coins and inscriptions serve as a source of medieval history?
4. What new technologies appeared during this period?
5. Who were the *kayasthas*?

D. Answer these questions in detail.

1. Categorize the sources of information on medieval India. Give one example from each category.
2. According to you, which source is the most important to learn about the medieval period? Give reasons to support your answer.
3. In your own words, explain the developments that took place in the medieval period.
4. The medieval period in India was a time for innovation and social changes. Justify this.
5. Write a note on medieval paintings.

E. Read the passage and answer the questions.

Early Sanskrit texts mention 'Aryavarta' as the land of the Aryans and 'Bharatvarsha' in the Puranas. The name India originates from the word Indus, which originates from the Persian word Sindhi. The Indus River was also called Sindhu in Sanskrit. As we read the Constitution of India, 'India' and 'Bharat' have been used interchangeably to describe the country. The historical term 'Hindustan' signifies either the entire Indian subcontinent or its north and north western regions. Each of these names has been used differently at different periods as interpreted by different rulers.

1. Name the various names India has been known by.
2. What names have been used to describe the country in the Constitution of India?
3. What is the Sanskrit name for the Indus river?

Think Big

Integrating with language

Write your own autobiography. Present it with pictures, facts of important milestones and incidences. Details should include information about your birth, parents, family, hobbies and other things of interest.

Learning Tools

Analyze the main differences between ancient India and medieval India by completing the chart below:

	Ancient India	Medieval India
Time frame		
Sources		
Society		
Food		
Technology		

Web links:

https://www.historydiscussion.net/history-of-india/chief-sources-of-medieval-indian-history/2630

Last accessed on 31 August 2021

2. The Age of New Kingdoms

Warm up

At a time when kings fought wars to conquer territories, there was a king of Scotland named Robert the Bruce. He fought many battles and expanded his kingdom. He was defeated in one battle and, dejected, he ran away from the battlefield to hide in a cave. There, he saw a spider trying to reach the roof of the cave, but it kept failing after every try. King Robert noticed that it did not lose heart. The spider reached its web in the seventh attempt. This taught King Robert a good lesson. It filled him with new hope and courage. He left the cave and gathered his forces. This time he fought bravely and was successful in setting his country free.

Regional Conflicts in the North

Before the coming of the Mughals, India and its political order was in a state of turmoil. There were constant struggles for power amongst various powerful kingdoms like the Cholas, the Rajputs, the Pratiharas, the Palas and many others for seven hundred years between the fall of the Gupta Empire and the establishment of the Delhi Sultanate in 1206. Dynasties fought each other for the areas that were strategically located and had fertile lands, important trade routes and indented coastlines that would promote trade and agriculture. All this led to instability in the Indian subcontinent, laying the groundwork for the Islamic rule that followed.

In the north, there were mainly three powers who were in constant struggle for the prized area of Kannauj, as it was strategically located in the Ganga Valley. It was a highway for commerce and communication, making it a convenient location, especially for river traffic in the upper Doab area. This implied that whoever controlled Kannauj would control trade and agriculture in and around this region. Kannauj was very **prosperous** during the 9th and 10th centuries when a large number of Hindu temples and Buddhist monasteries were built.

From the 9th to the 13th century, three powers—the Gurjara Pratiharas of western India, the Palas of Bengal and the Rashtrakutas of the north western Deccan–fought for the control of Kannauj. This has been called the **Tripartite Struggle**.

prosperous: successful in material terms; flourishing financially

Medieval India

Geography skills

Work from this map and locate Kannauj and the regions occupied by the Gurjara Pratiharas, the Palas and the Rashtrakutas on an outline map of India.

The Gurjara Pratiharas

The Gurjara Pratiharas ruled in the region around western India, which included parts of Rajasthan and Gujarat. This dynasty had powerful rulers like Nagabhata I and Mihira Bhoja. Nagabhata I was the founder of the dynasty. Mihira Bhoja built a very large and prosperous empire with Kannauj as its capital. Mihira Bhoja was a devotee of Vishnu. Silver coins issued by him are engraved with the symbol of Vishnu. Mahendrapala, Mihira Bhoja's son, followed and expanded his empire further. Many temples were also built during his reign. A series of weak successors followed him, paving the way for foreign invasion. Soon, Mahmud Ghazni defeated the reigning Pratihara ruler.

FACT CHECK

During the classical period, Kannauj was known as Kanyakubja, which meant 'the city of hunchbacked maidens'. Another name that was given to it during the reign of Mihira Bhoja was Mahodaya.

The Rashtrakutas

The Rashtrakutas ruled in the Deccan, in the area between the rivers Narmada and Krishna. They were the subordinates or *samantas* of the Chalukyas. This kingdom became powerful under Dantidurga, who overthrew his Chalukya overlord. The Rashtrakutas were in conflict with the Palas in the east and with the Pallavas, the Pandyas and the Cholas in the south. The Rashtrakuta rulers encouraged the growth of languages and literature. They also contributed to architecture in a big way. The Kailasa temple at Ellora is an example of architecture during the reign of the Rashtrakutas.

Apply it!

Are inscriptions a good source of history? Support your answer with reasons.

What's in the picture?

This is a scene from a well-known story in Indian traditions. You will find it at the Kailasa Temple in Ellora. Observe the image and try to list some of the incidences or characters you recognize and name the story depicted.

The Palas

The Palas ruled over the region of Bengal, Bihar, parts of Orissa (present-day Odisha) and Nepal. The kingdom was founded by Gopala around 750 CE. The Pala dynasty grew under Dharmapala and his son Devapala. They contributed extensively towards the growth of literature and education in the region. The Vikramashila University was founded by the Pala rulers. They were great patrons of Buddhism. Ramapala was the last known king of the Pala dynasty. The dynasty came to an end with the invasions of the Khaljis.

Administration of New Kingdoms

The king was the head of the state. He was assisted by a council of ministers who advised him on the matters of the state. Many taxes were imposed on the people during this time. Mostly, it was the peasants, cattle keepers and artisans, who often had to part with a portion of their produce. Revenue was also collected from traders. These taxes were used to help build the empire, to maintain armies and fund wars.

Foreign Invasions

The Ghaznavids

The mountain passes in the north west have always been a route through which many invaders have entered India. Mahmud of Ghazni was one of the first invaders who stormed the mountain passes of the north to set up a kingdom in India. Mahmud was a very ambitious ruler who wanted to make Ghazni the most powerful kingdom in Central Asia. To do this, he needed plenty of wealth. Therefore, he not only attacked places like Punjab, Peshwar, Multan, Kannauj and the Somnath temple but also took skilled craftsmen to Ghazni. It is said that Mahmud attacked India seventeen times between 1000 and 1027 CE. He was an excellent general and planned his invasions very well. He took all the wealth back and beautified his home town, Ghazni. *Tarikh-Al-Hind*, composed by Al Biruni, Mahmud Ghazni's court astrologer, details the interaction between Hindus and Muslims at that time. Mahmud set up many universities to encourage the study of subjects such as mathematics, religion and medicine. His empire covered Iran, Turkmenistan, Afghanistan, Uzbekistan, present-day Pakistan and northwest India. However, the empire disintegrated by 1040 CE.

The Ghorids

Ghor was a small kingdom in present-day Afghanistan and was under the control of the Ghaznavid Empire. Muhammad Ghori was an ambitious ruler whose main objective was not only to amass wealth but also to build a great empire. In 1173 CE, he brought an end to the Ghaznavid Empire and began the new era of the Ghorid Empire. Muhammad was successful in his campaign in Multan in 1175 CE and conquered it. However, he was not successful in his invasion of Gujarat. He was intelligent enough to realize that a firm foundation was of utmost importance for future conquests in India. Therefore, he conquered Punjab and established a base in India.

Prithviraj Chauhan, the Rajput ruler of Delhi and Ajmer, was prepared to challenge Muhammad Ghori, and they clashed at Tarain in 1191 CE, where Muhammad Ghori was defeated. He once again prepared himself for a war, and Prithviraj, who obtained the support of all the kings, except for Raja Jaichand of Kannauj, could not match the effectiveness of the Turkish cavalry. Prithivaraj was defeated in the second Battle of Tarain in 1192 CE, and Muhammad took over control of Delhi, the Ganga–Yamuna doab, Bihar and Bengal. He even defeated Jaichand in 1194 CE. He entrusted further conquests to his general Qutubuddin Aibak.

South India

In the Deccan, there were many kingdoms that flourished, like the Yadavas of Devagiri, the Chalukyas of Kalyani and the Kakatiyas and the Hoysalas of Warangal. South India saw the rise of many powerful kingdoms, like the Pallavas of Kanchi, who built many temples as well as the Pandyas of Madurai. The Cholas emerged as the most powerful among them.

Who were the Cholas?

In the 9th century CE, a chieftain of the Pallavas, Vijayalaya, ruled a small territory near Thanjavur. Vijayalaya conquered Thanjavur and made it his capital. He founded the imperial Chola Empire in the medieval period.

Rajaraja Chola (985–1016 CE) was a powerful ruler who developed a powerful navy and sent an expedition to the Maldives to conquer it. He also captured the northern part of Sri Lanka.

He is believed to have defeated the Chalukyas of the Deccan. The city of Thanjavur was magnificent, with elaborate gardens and palaces. The Brihadishvara

Brihadishvara Temple

Temple, built by Rajaraja Chola, is a great example of Chola architecture. He was succeeded by his son, Rajendra Chola. Rajendra Chola I was considered one of the greatest rulers and military generals of India. He was called Gangaikonda Chola because he defeated the ruler of Bengal after crossing the river Ganga. Rajendra built the city of Gangaikonda Cholapuram, which he made the capital of the Chola Empire.

Administration: The king was the central figure and headed the administration. He was instrumental in issuing orders, which were recorded in manuscripts and later inscribed on the temple walls. The king was assisted in the affairs of the administration by officials. The loyal officials were given titles like *araiyar* and *muvendavelan.*

Revenue system: Land revenue was the chief source of income. A proper survey of lands was carried out and lands were classified as taxable and non-taxable. Taxes were also imposed on trade and other professions. The revenue was collected by the local authorities or by royal servants. Besides land revenue, the Chola kings imposed many kinds of taxes. Taxes were levied against potters, goldsmiths, weavers and brokers, amongst many more. The transport of rice, textiles and pepper was also taxable. Tax was also levied on trade, and this became an important source of income for the state.

Military developments: The Cholas had an efficient military system. This has been mentioned in numerous Chola inscriptions. Rajaraja Chola I had created a strong and efficient army, which was further strengthened by his son and successor, Rajendra Chola I. Their army comprised elephants, cavalry and infantry. In fact, Arabian horses of superior quality were imported by them. The Cholas were amongst the first rulers to maintain a navy. This helped them defeat the Cheras and enabled them to control the Coromandel and the Malabar coasts.

Agriculture and irrigation: The Cholas encouraged agriculture all over the kingdom, especially in the Cauvery basin. Many committees, such as the irrigation committee and garden committee, were set up to oversee the distribution of water. Many canals and tanks were also built for irrigating the vast agricultural lands. The Cholas also erected **embankments** to prevent flooding of these lands.

Other contribution: The Chola government stood out for its distinctive qualities. They were extremely unique and innovative and were the first rulers to bring all of south India under their control. They took an active interest in the development of temple centres and also established educational institutions and hospitals around these temples. Rajaraja Chola also encouraged the Sailendra ruler of Sri Vijaya to build a Buddhist vihara at Nagapatinam.

Case Study

The years c. 650–893 CE are best represented by the monuments of the Pallava dynasty at Mahabalipuram. Several monolithic temples, carved out of rocks, stand till today. The Shore Temple, with its elegant complex of shrines, lays testament to the greatness and supremacy of the Pallavas. The Talapurisvara temple at Panamalai is another excellent example. Kanchipuram, its capital city, also boasts of fine temples, the Kailasanatha being one of the most well-known among them. Another splendid temple at Kanchipuram is the Vaikuntha Perumal, which has an interesting arrangement of three sanctums, one above the other, encased within the body of the superstructure.

Q. Describe some of the temples found at Mahabalipuram.

embankment: a wall or bank of earth or stone built to prevent a river flooding an area

Skill Builder

21ST CENTURY SKILLS

Life skills: Do you think Indian rulers would have been able to defend their kingdom from the Turkish rulers if they were united?

Critical thinking skills: Temples are places of worship and important places for making offerings to the deity. The temples of north and south India were distinguished on the basis of some specific features like *sikhara* and gateways. In the north Indian temples, the *sikhara* remained the most prominent component, while the gateway was generally unassuming. The most prominent features of south Indian temples were enclosures around the temples and the *gopurams* (huge gateways). The *gopurams* led the devotees into the sacred courtyard. Can you think of some common features in the Northern and the Southern styles?

Information literacy: Write a report on Kannauj. Find out its location and history and collect pictures of it. Paste them on a chart and present it to the class.

Wind up

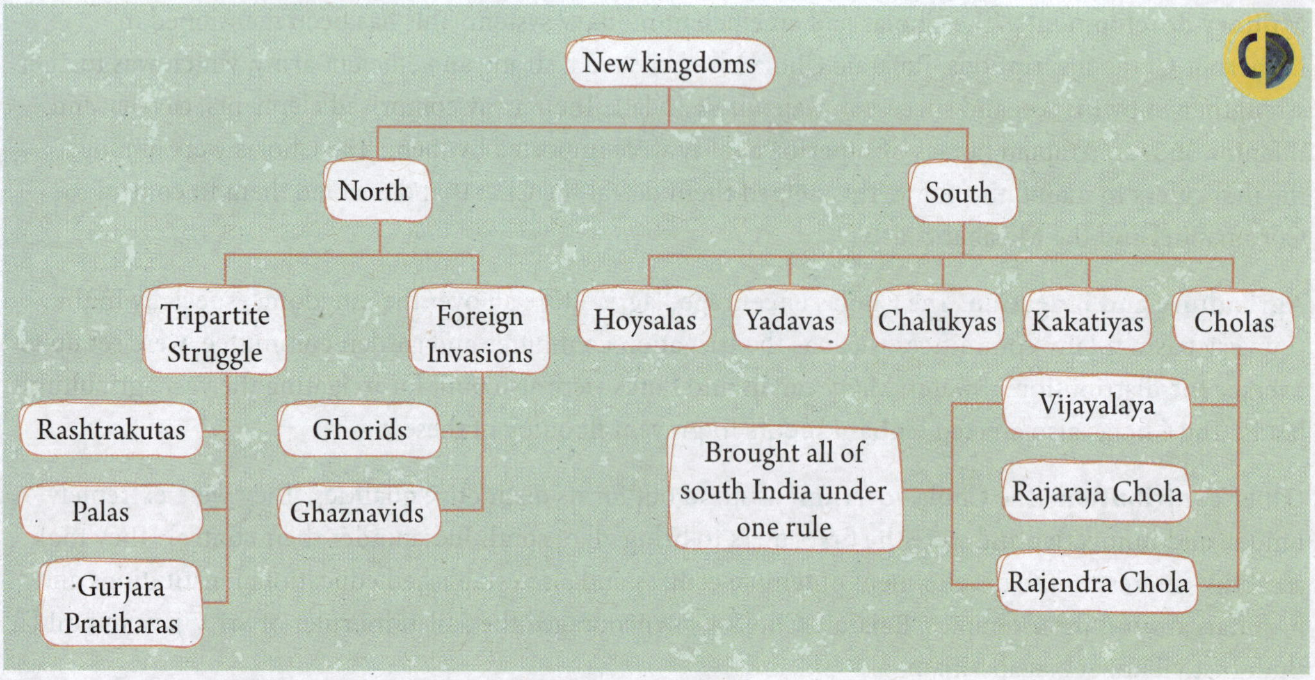

World Connect

After the fall of the Han empire in 220 CE, China experienced more than 350 years of discord. In northern China, this period was marked by the establishment of cruel dynasties, merciless invasions and disruptions. South China, on the other hand, experienced peace, although there were periods of instability caused by the rulers' weakness and inefficiency. Ultimately, in 589, a Chinese general unified the whole of China under his rule, establishing the Sui dynasty. He is known to Chinese history as the emperor Wendi. His governance was firm and he followed polices that improved the lives of the people.

Exercises

A. Fill in the blanks.

1. The Rashtrakuta rulers encouraged the growth of languages and ....
2. Many invaders came to India through the .... in the north-west.
3. The Palas ruled around the region of Bengal, Bihar, parts of Orissa (present-day Odisha) and ....
4. Prithviraj Chauhan challenged Muhammad Ghori at Tarain in .... CE
5. .... were used to help build the empire, to maintain armies and to fund wars.

B. Choose the correct answers.

1. The last known king of the Pala dynasty.
   a. Devpala
   b. Gopala
   c. Dharmapala
   d. Ramapala
2. The Vikramashila University was founded by these rulers.
   a. Rajputs
   b. Palas
   c. Gurjara Pratiharas
   d. Rashtrakutas
3. Ghor was a small kingdom in present-day
   a. Afghanistan
   b. Persia
   c. Iraq
   d. Pakistan
4. Mahmud of Ghazni attacked places like this to accumulate wealth and power.
   a. Punjab
   b. Kannauj
   c. Somnath Temple
   d. all of these

C. Write T for true and F for false.

1. The Cholas erected embankments to prevent flooding of the agricultural lands. ☐
2. It is said that Mahmud attacked India thirteen times between 1000 and 1027 CE. ☐
3. *Tarikh-Al-Hind* was composed by Mahmud of Ghazni. ☐
4. The Cholas had an efficient military system. ☐
5. The Pala dynasty grew under Dharmapala and his son Ramapala. ☐

D. Answer these questions in brief.

1. Who founded the Pala dynasty?
2. Who were the Gujara-Pratiharas?
3. Describe the city of Thanjavur.
4. Who were the Rashtrakutas?
5. Name some kingdoms that flourished in the Deccan.

E. Answer these questions in detail.

1. Compare the intentions and motives of Mahmud of Ghazni and Muhammad Ghori in invading India.
2. Write a note on the irrigation committee set up under the Cholas.
3. State the main developments that made the Chola kingdom outstanding and unique.
4. Explain the outcome of the second battle of Tarain.

Think Big

Integrate with civics

An inscription in the Sri Ambalavana Swamy temple at Manur tells the story of a resolution prescribing qualifications for judges. Judges were elected, records were kept of the fines they collected and they should work towards the people's welfare. If any of them gave wrong rulings, they were fined heavily. The judges were also tested on their knowledge of one Veda and a *Dharmashastra*. Imagine our MPs being tested on their knowledge of the constitution. State your thoughts on this idea.

Learning Tools

Comparing and Contrasting

Make a three-pocket book and record notes about the people, places and events that happened in the north, south and foreign invasions.

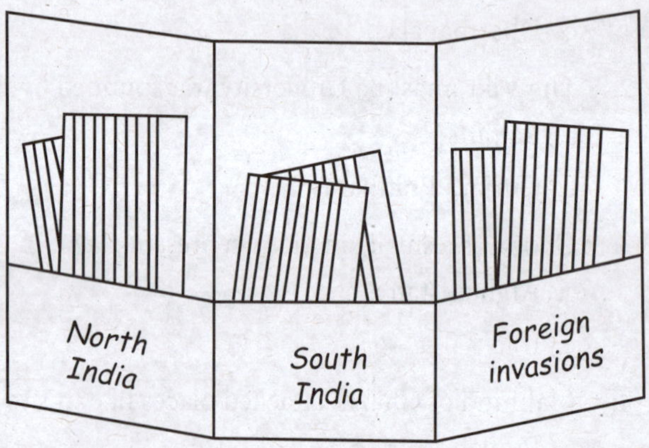

Web links:

https://knowindia.gov.in/culture-and-heritage/medieval-history.php

Last accessed on 31 August 2021

3. The Delhi Sultanate

Warm up

Qutubuddin Aibak started off as a slave of the chief Qazi of Nishapur. He was treated like a son by the qazi, receiving a good education and training in the field of archery and horsemanship. However, when his master died, the qazi's sons sold him to a slave merchant out of jealousy. Fortune once again favoured him and Muhammad Ghori bought him. Out of Ghori's thousand slaves, Aibak became one of his master's favourite and steadily rose through the ranks, eventually becoming an able General. After the victory in the Second Battle of Tarain in 1192 CE, Muhammad Ghori made Aibak in charge of his Indian territories.

The Delhi Sultanate timeline is 320 years long, starting in 1206 and ending in 1526. During these years, five dynasties of the Sultanate ruled.

- The Slave dynasty (84 years)
- The Khalji dynasty (30 years)
- The Tughlaq dynasty (94 years)
- The Sayyid dynasty (37 years)
- The Lodi dynasty (75 years)

1206 CE The Sultanate period begins; Slave dynasty is established

1321 CE Khalji dynasty ends; Tughlaq dynasty comes to power

1451 CE Sayyid dynasty ends; Lodi dynasty comes to power

1290 CE Slave dynasty ends; Khalji dynasty comes to power

1414 CE Tughlaq dynasty ends; Sayyid dynasty comes to power

1526 CE Decline of the Delhi Sultanate

Sources to Study the Delhi Sultanate

The important sources of information available about the Delhi Sultanate are inscriptions and monuments. Inscriptions are found on old coins, historical monuments, milestones and tombstones. The Sultans of Delhi built many monuments that reveal not only the cultural traditions of that period but also the living conditions, faiths and beliefs and the socio cultural outlook of the rulers. One such monument is the Qutub Minar.

The Slave Dynasty

By the early 12th century, Delhi started becoming an important kingdom. The reign of the Tomaras and the Chauhans had already established Delhi as an important commercial city. As we have read in the previous chapter, Muhammad Ghori defeated Prithviraj Chauhan, a Chauhan ruler, during the second battle of Tarain. By 1202 CE, Muhammad Ghori had annexed Bengal and established his supremacy in India. After strengthening his position, he left the Indian territory to his trusted slave and competent general, Qutbuddin Aibak. After the death of Muhammad Ghori in 1206, Qutbuddin Aibak took on the title of Sultan and laid the foundation of the Slave dynasty, which lasted for nearly a century. He made Delhi his capital. The Slave dynasty, or the Mamluk dynasty, was the first of the five unrelated dynasties that together are called the Delhi Sultanate. The Mamluk dynasty was followed by the Khalji and the Tughlaq Dynasty. Both Khaljis and Tughlaqs were of Turkish origin. The later dynasties, the Sayyid and the Lodi Dynasty, were of Afghan origin.

Qutbuddin Aibak (1206–1210 CE)

After Qutbuddin Aibak took over the Indian territories, he quickly gained power and supremacy over all the northern states. The kingdom established by him marked the beginning of the Delhi Sultanate in India. Qutbuddin Aibak was known to be a generous ruler. He was known as *lakh baksh* or the giver of lakhs. He built the Quwwat-ul-Islam mosque, or the Qutub mosque, the oldest mosque in Delhi and started building the Qutub Minar.

Iltutmish (1211–1236 CE)

In 1211, Qutubuddin's son-in-law, Iltutmish, became the ruler of the Slave dynasty. However, his reign was very precarious, as it was opposed by many in the kingdom. This led to many wars and executions within the kingdom. He managed to consolidate his power and regained most territories that had broken away during the struggle for power. He suppressed the rebellions and went on to defeat the Rajput rulers of Ujjain and Ranthambhore. He brought Bengal and Bihar under the Sultanate. The court chronicler Minhaj-i-Siraj's accounts give us information about Iltutmish.

Razia Sultan (1236–1240 CE)

Razia, the daughter of Iltutmish, was the only woman ruler to ascend the throne of the Delhi Sultanate. She was chosen to be the ruler as she was more competent than her brothers. She was a great warrior who ruled ably and established law and order in her kingdom. As the society was male-dominated, many nobles did not accept the rule of a woman. Eventually, Razia was killed in a battle with the nobles, who conspired against her. Even Minhaj-i-Siraj, who appreciated Razia's qualities, remarked that a queen's rule went against the tradition and the will of God.

Balban (1246-1266 CE)

Razia's death was followed by a struggle for power. Razia's brother, Nazruddin Mahmud, was inexperienced. Therefore, Balban, the king's personal attendant, took over and declared himself as the Sultan. Balban was known to be ruthless. His first aim was to crush the power of the nobles. He introduced an efficient spy system to ensure the loyalty of the nobles. He introduced the practice of *sijdah* and *paibos* to elevate the status of the rulers, which went against the practices and principles of Islam.

What's in the picture?

This is Razia Sultana's tomb in Delhi. Would you say this tomb is being properly maintained?

Sijdah was the custom of touching the ground with the forehead to give respect to the sultan, and paibos was the custom of kissing the feet of the sultan.

Balban took several measures to strengthen his position. He suppressed the Rajputs and took measures to check Mongol invasions. Balban died in 1287. His rule was followed by several weak rulers. The last Slave ruler was overthrown by Jalaluddin Khalji.

The Khalji Dynasty

Jalaluddin Khalji (1290–1296 CE)

Jalauddin Khalji was the first sultan of the Khalji dynasty. He was a benevolent ruler who did not carry out severe punishments. He was betrayed and killed by his nephew, Alauddin Khalji.

Alauddin Khalji

Alauddin Khalji (1296–1316 CE)

Alauddin Khalji was an ambitious ruler and a brilliant general. He conquered the Deccan with the help of his commander, Malik Kafur. Alauddin built a garrison town in Siri to keep a check on the Mongols. He kept a detailed account of the soldiers or *chehra* and branded the horses in a process called *daag*.

Apply it!

Why do you think the rulers of the Sultanate needed such a strong spy system for their officials?

Economic measures: Alauddin fixed the prices of goods to keep the soldiers happy. A supervisor was appointed to keep a check on the traders and merchants so that they could not increase the price. Weights and measures were checked and people who cheated on prices and weights were severely punished. Land tax was imposed in the Doab region and farmers had to pay one-half of the total produce. The land under cultivation was measured. Alauddin Khalji appreciated art and respected well-read people. The Sufi poet and scholar, Amir Khusrau, wrote in his court. He built many palaces and mosques, including the Alai Darwaza. After the death of Alauddin in 1316 CE, a war of succession broke out, and power passed into the hands of Ghiyasuddin Tughlaq, who founded the Tughlaq dynasty.

The Tughlaq Dynasty

Ghiyasuddin Tughlaq (1321–1325 CE)

Ghiyasuddin Tughlaq, who was the governor in Punjab under the Khaljis, was the founder of the Tughlaq dynasty. He founded the city of Tughlaqabad.

Empire of Muhammad Bin Tughlaq

Muhammad-bin-Tughlaq (1325–1351 CE)

Muhammad-bin-Tughlaq ascended the throne in 1325 CE. He was a scholarly and brilliant ruler who engaged in intelligent debates with religious authorities. He is remembered as a **judicious** and wise ruler,

judicious: having, showing, or done with good judgement or sense who often questioned the learned theologians and the ***ulemas*** on their ideas, thereby facing **antagonism** from them. While he had all these good qualities, his hastiness and impatience often led to opposition. On one hand, he was brilliant and had outstanding ideas, but on the other, he lacked the vision to foresee the practical problems in the implementation of those ideas. These ideas later became so controversial that they made him unpopular.

Taxation in Doab: Muhammad-bin-Tughlaq wanted to expand his territories. To do so, he needed a well-equipped army. To equip his army, he increased the tax in the Ganga–Yamuna Doab region. The region was fertile and farmers could easily pay the increased tax. However, the tax was imposed at a time when there was a famine, and this move caused resentment amongst the peasant community, causing rebellions. Muhammad-bin-Tughlaq realised his fault and tried to rectify it by offering loans, but he was unable to repair the damage as these measures were taken too late.

The shifting of capital: Another controversial move that Muhammad-bin-Tughlaq made was shifting of the capital from Delhi to Daulatabad. As it was difficult to control the Deccan from Delhi, he decided to shift the capital without consulting anyone. According to a court chronicler, Delhi was as prosperous as Cairo and Baghdad. The shift brought about the ruin of Delhi. People were so inconvenienced by this move that many did not have the strength to complete the journey and died on the way. Two years later, the capital had to be shifted back.

Bronze currency: There was a shortage of silver for currency between 1329 and 1330 CE. Therefore, Muhammad thought of issuing copper and bronze coins that had the same value as silver coins. People now started using copper and bronze coins and began hoarding the silver coins. The cheap coins were used in trade and posed a severe challenge.

Token currency

People even started minting coins at home, and it became difficult to differentiate between fake and genuine coins. Later, these coins were withdrawn. All this impacted the state treasury. The last days of Muhammad were spent in suppressing rebellions. This was tough, as the empire was too large and there were difficulties in communication. This resulted in the disintegration of the Tughlaq hold on many regions. Two important kingdoms emerged at this time—one in north Deccan, known as the Bahmani Kingdom, the other in the south Deccan, known as the Vijayanagara Empire.

Firoz Shah Tughlaq (1351–1388 CE)

Firoz Shah Tughlaq was the cousin of Muhammad-bin-Tughlaq. His reign was marked by a period of peace. He kept the ulema happy and worked towards consolidating the kingdom. During his reign, there were not many rebellions as he did not try to regain control over the areas that had broken away. He introduced many reforms in the administration of the kingdom and patronized scholars like Barani. He contributed a lot to the welfare of his subjects. He built many rest houses, gardens and tombs and opened *madrasas* to encourage education. Many hospitals were built to treat the poor. He developed agriculture and irrigation by constructing five canals and bringing a considerable amount of land under cultivation.

ulema: a body of Muslim scholars who are recognized as having in-depth knowledge of the sacred laws and theology of Islam; antagonism: active hostility or opposition

While he was well-liked throughout the kingdom, his easy-going nature weakened his authority, and after his death, many rebellions followed. As the central authority weakened, Timur, a ruler from Samarkand, invaded India in 1398 CE. He plundered the city and its wealth, gravely affecting the lives of the people and the economy. All of northern India was in total **disarray**, reducing the Sultanate considerably.

The Sayyid Dynasty (1414–1451 CE)

The Sayyid dynasty was founded by Timur's viceroy, Khizr Khan, in 1414 CE. However, the last ruler of this dynasty was not competent, and Bahlul Lodi ascended the throne in 1451 CE.

The Lodi Dynasty (1451–1526 CE)

The most prominent amongst the Lodi sultans was Sikander Lodi. He made Agra his capital. He encouraged literature, and his court was visited by scholars from different places. His successor was Ibrahim Lodi. Ibrahim Lodi was insecure because of the power of the Rajput ruler, Rana Sangram Singh of Mewar, and because of his own noble, Daulat Khan Lodi, the governor of Punjab. Rana Sangram, therefore, invited Babur, the ruler of Kabul, who invaded Lahore and stationed his officers there. Babur then conquered the entire Punjab. The First Battle of Panipat was fought between Ibrahim Lodi and Babur in 1526. This was a turning point in the rule of the Sultanate as it culminated in the defeat of the Lodi ruler and the end of the Delhi Sultanate. After the decline of the Delhi Sultanate, Babur established the Mughal Empire in India.

Administration of the Sultanate

The rule of the sultans of Delhi was authoritarian, and the rulers enjoyed absolute power. Their orders were unquestionable. There were officers to help the Sultan in his administration, like the wazir, who looked after the revenue department, and the military officer, known as *mir bakshi.* The office who looked after religious affairs was known as Diwan-i-Risalat. The Sultanate was divided into provinces called *subas,* which were further divided into *shiqs.* The *shiqs* were further divided into *parganas.* A group of villages formed a pargana.

The province was governed by a *subedar* who maintained law and order in the province. The *shiqdar* was the head of a shiq. The affairs of the pargana were looked after by the *amirs.* The village was the principal unit of local administration. The village headman was called the *muquaddam.* The chief officer of the pargana, who was in charge of the villages, had the duty of collecting land revenue. The *kotwal* was in charge of the police department. The sultans maintained strong and large armies. This helped consolidate their power over the kingdom. The army consisted of archers, foot soldiers, horse soldiers, cavalry and elephants.

Revenue Sources

The main source of income during the Delhi Sultanate was land revenue. Different taxes were levied on the people. The *jizya* was a religious tax on non-Muslims. Those who had no source of income were exempted from this tax. *Zakat* was a religious tax, imposed only on rich Muslims, and it was 2.5% per cent of their income. Other taxes included trade tax, horse tax, house tax, grazing tax and mining tax.

disarray: a state of disorganization or untidiness

Causes of the Downfall of the Delhi Sultanate

- The Delhi Sultans came and conquered India by the force of their armies. But, they never tried to win the confidence and love of their subjects.
- Most Sultans were deeply religious. Sultans like Firoz Shah Tughlaq and Sikander Lodi re-imposed jizya, the much-hated tax on the Hindus. Consequently, the Hindus hated them and became their enemies.
- The Muslim nobility was also much to be blamed for the downfall of the Sultans. The armies and the nobles were too powerful and could be kept under control only by powerful rulers like Alauddin Khaliji and Balban. Whenever a weak ruler ascended the throne, they took advantage and rebelled against them.
- The empire was too vast to be controlled in those days when the means of communication were not so developed.
- Timur's invasion gave the final blow to the already disintegrating Sultanate and the end of the Delhi Sultanate came with Babur's invasion.

Case Study

Tughlaqabad

The Tughlaqabad Fort was built by Ghiyasuddin Tughlaq in 1321. The city spanned through an area of nearly 6.5 km and is located along Mehrauli–Badarpur Road, towards the south-eastern edge of Delhi. This city was distinctly divided into three parts: the wider city area, the citadel and the palace. Its ruins show massive stone fortifications surrounding the city and a mausoleum connected by a causeway to the southern outpost of the fortification. South of the city is a large artificial reservoir. Years after its construction, Muhammad-bin Tughlaq built the Fortress of Adilabad that mirrored the bigger fort in style and substance.

Q. Write a short note on the Tughlaqabad Fort in your own words.

Skill Builder

21ST CENTURY SKILLS

Life skills: 'Razia Sultan failed as a ruler as she was a woman'. How much do you agree?

Critical-thinking skills Mohammad Bin Tughlaq was known as a confused genius. His plans and intentions were good but carried out thoughtlessly. Suggest one such project introduced by him which went against him.

Leadership and responsibility: According to you, should a ruler show his might through military strength or diplomacy?

World Connect

The Mongol Empire emerged from the unification of the nomadic tribes in Mongolia, under the leadership of Genghis Khan, in 1206 CE. The empire grew rapidly under his rule, and then under his descendants. The Mongols believed in the continuous policy of expansion and they invaded territories in every direction. Originating from the Steppes of Central Asia, the Mongol Empire stretched from Eastern Europe to the Sea of Japan, northwards into Siberia, eastwards into the Indian subcontinent and westwards as far as Arabia. The empire began to split due to wars of succession among the grandchildren of Genghis Khan. Kublai Khan, one of the grandsons of Genghis Khan, conquered China, founding the Yuan dynasty in the country.

Wind up

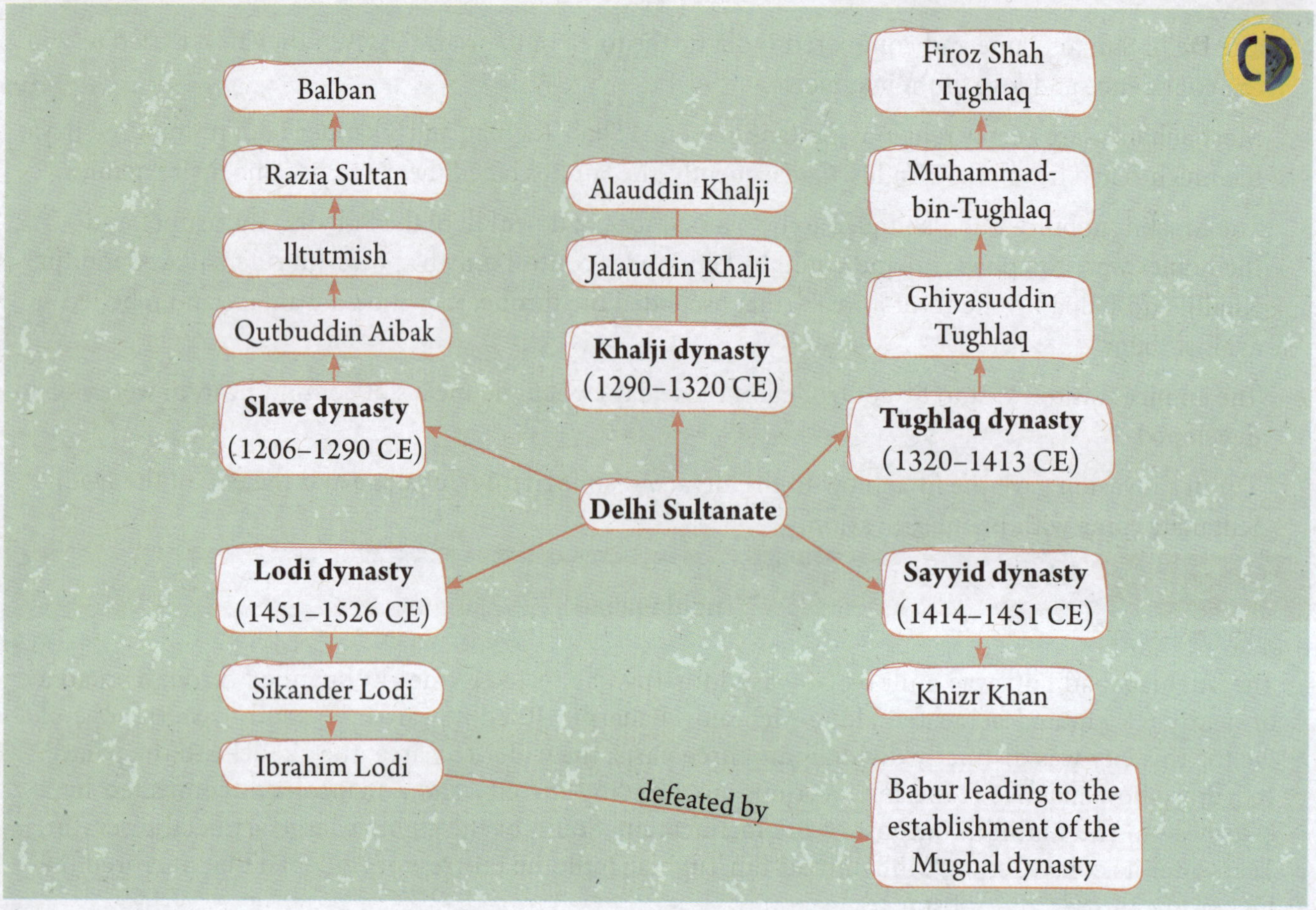

Exercises

A. Choose the correct answers.

1. Malik Kafur was a commander to
   a. Iltutmish   b. Sikander Lodi   c. Balban   d. Alauddin Khalji
2. The practice of *sijdah* was introduced in the court of
   a. Iltutmish   b. Balban   c. Qutbuddin   d. none of these
3. He was Qutubuddin's son-in-law.
   a. Iltutmish   b. Firoz Shah Tughlaq   c. Alauddin   d. Ibrahim Lodi
4. Illtutmish made Razia Sultan sit on the throne, even though she had brothers because
   a. she was a woman   b. she was more interested in royal pleasures
   c. Razia was skilled and intelligent   d. all of these
5. The dynasty established by Qutbuddin Aibak is known as the
   a. Slave dynasty   b. Khalji dynasty   c. Tughlaq dynasty   d. Lodi dynasty

B. Fill in the blanks.

1. The rule of the sultans of Delhi was ...., and they enjoyed absolute power.
2. Alauddin was the nephew of ....
3. The Delhi Sultanate timeline is .... years long.
4. .... invasion brought the end of the Delhi Sultanate.
5. The Muslim .... was also much to be blamed for the downfall of the Sultans.

C. Answer these questions in brief.

1. Name the five dynasties of the Delhi Sultanate.
2. Who was Muhammad Ghori?
3. Who was Timur?
4. Who were the Lodis?
5. What was zakat?

D. Answer these questions in detail.

1. Write a note on Razia Sultan.
2. Why was Alauddin praised for his administrative measures?
3. Evaluate the major policies undertaken by Muhammad-bin-Tughlaq and analyze the drawbacks of these policies.
4. Discuss the main contributions of Firoz Shah Tughlaq.
5. Give three reasons that led to the downfall of Delhi Sultanate.

Think Big

Integrate with language

There is always excitement in leaning new vocabulary and key terminology in history. So here are some new words to learn with their meanings.

Illuminated manuscript: a manuscript in which the text is supplemented by the addition of decoration.

Paleography: the study of old handwriting

Working class: the lower levels of society, whose members must work to survive

Intelligentsia: people who develop ideas, theories and policies in a society

Economic: people, institutions and activities that produce society's wants and need

Research and find out five more new words that are associated with history.

Learning Tools

Create this five-tab book to describe the characteristics and important points of each dynasty of the Delhi Sultanate:

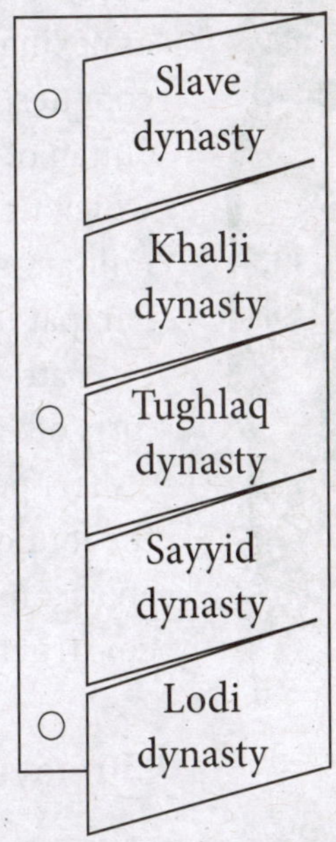

Web links:

https://www.jagranjosh.com/general-knowledge/timeline-of-delhi-sultanate-1491285979-1

Last accessed on 31 August 2021

4. The Mughals in India

Warm up

Akbar was known to be a great hunter. At the age of 19, Akbar came across a tigress and three cubs in a forest and killed the tigress with nothing but a sword. He hunted frequently during peace time in his empire. His hunts included cheetahs, lions, tigers, black buck and even elephants. It is said that, in one of the hunts, Akbar was wounded and recovered miraculously, but many still believe it could have been a major reason for Akbar's mysterious death at the age of 63.

When we read about India in the medieval period, we cannot ignore the diverse heritage of the Mughals. Also known as the 'gun powder' empire, in territorial terms, it controlled almost the whole of the subcontinent. The empire was ruled by several emperors, some of them weak and inefficient, but the six mighty Mughals, Babur, Humayun, Akbar, Jahangir, Shah Jahan and Aurangzeb, left lasting legacies, many of which are visible even today.

Babur

Babur was an ambitious ruler born in a small place called Farghana in Central Asia. He became a ruler at the age of eleven, after the death of his father. He was successful in annexing Samarkand, but lost it soon, along with Farghana. However, he was successful in conquering Kabul in 1504 CE. He was invited by Daulat Khan Lodi to oust the unpopular Sultan of Delhi, Ibrahim Lodi. Babur conquered Punjab and made plans to annex Delhi, which turned Daulat Khan Lodi against him. Babur was a great leader and an even greater military strategist. This made him victorious over Ibrahim Lodhi in the First Battle of Panipat in 1526 CE leading to the establishment of the Mughal Empire. He also won the Battle of Khanua, where he defeated Rana Sanga of Mewar. He also conquered the forts of Gwalior, Mewar and Dholpur and further strengthened his position in India. In a short period of four years, Babur managed to annex many territories in India and laid the foundation of a new empire that reached its peak during the reign of Akbar. He was an accomplished musician and loved music and poetry. He was in love with nature and constructed many gardens.

Humayun

Humayun, Babur's eldest son, succeeded him to the throne in 1530. In 1540, the Pashtun ruler, Sher Shah Suri, defeated Humayun twice, first at the Battle of Chausa in 1539 and second at the Battle of Kannauj in 1540, thereby deposing him. Humayun fled to Kabul after his defeat and between Rajasthan, Sind and Persia till 1545. He only regained his throne with aid from Persia in 1555 but met an unfortunate end a year later, when he slipped down the library steps and died.

Although Humayun was a capable soldier, a learned ruler, trusting and loving towards his brothers, he lacked the vision and the skills to deal with problems. We get details of his life from *Humayun-Nama*, a biography written by Humayun's sister, Gulbadan Begum.

Akbar (1556–1605 CE)

Akbar was born in 1542 when his father, Humayun, was in exile. At the age of 13, Akbar was appointed the governor of Punjab. Humayun died when Akbar was only 14 years old. Bairam Khan became Akbar's regent. As Akbar was young, Bairam Khan handled all the administrative affairs. Bairam Khan was unpopular and created enemies because of his arrogant behaviour. Akbar then decided to take on the affairs of the kingdom himself.

Akbar the Great

Akbar's Campaigns

Akbar's objective was to bring all of India under his control. His army conquered central India and parts of Malwa in 1560. The important forts of Chittore and Ranthambhore were captured as well. Rana Pratap was defeated at Haldighati by Akbar in 1576. Apart from this, Akbar conquered Gujarat, Bengal, Orissa (present-day Odisha) and parts of northern Deccan, including Ahmednagar.

Akbar's Policy Towards Rajputs

From the beginning, Akbar recognized that the Rajputs were skilled warriors whose loyalty and fidelity could be relied upon. He sought their cooperation in expanding his kingdom by awarding them with high posts. He was very friendly and gained support from several powerful Rajput chiefs, who he came to realize were loyal and serviceable. Akbar also welcomed marriage alliances between the Mughals and the Rajputs. Some of his allies included Raja Todarmal, Raja Bhagwan Das and his son Man Singh. Rulers who resisted him, like the Rajputs of Mewar, ultimately surrendered to him and were treated with utmost respect and allowed to rule their territories.

Akbar had a very liberal policy towards all religions. He celebrated all festivals and respected the saints belonging to different religions. Guru Ramdas was granted land at Amritsar, where the shrine of Harmindar Sahib is situated. Akbar held discussions with religious scholars of different faiths in the Ibadat Khana, a house of worship at Fatehpur Sikri. He took the best from all religions and combined them under one religion, called the *Din-i-ilahi* or divine faith, and the idea of *sulh-i-kul*, or universal peace, was a part of this. We get to know about Akbar from the biography called *Akbarnama*, written by Abul Fazl.

Administration

The *Ain-i-Akbari* gives us information about Akbar's administration. Akbar's administration can be divided into central administration, provincial administration and local administration.

Central administration: The king was the central figure. He was assisted by a council of ministers. The *diwan* was in charge of the revenue department, the *bakshi* was in charge of military affairs, the *sadr* was in charge of the religious affairs and the *qazi* was in charge of the judicial department. The *Diwan-i-Khas* was reserved for distinguished guests. The *Diwan-i-Aam* was an assembly of officials and was converted into a house of justice on certain days when the Emperor gave his judgement.

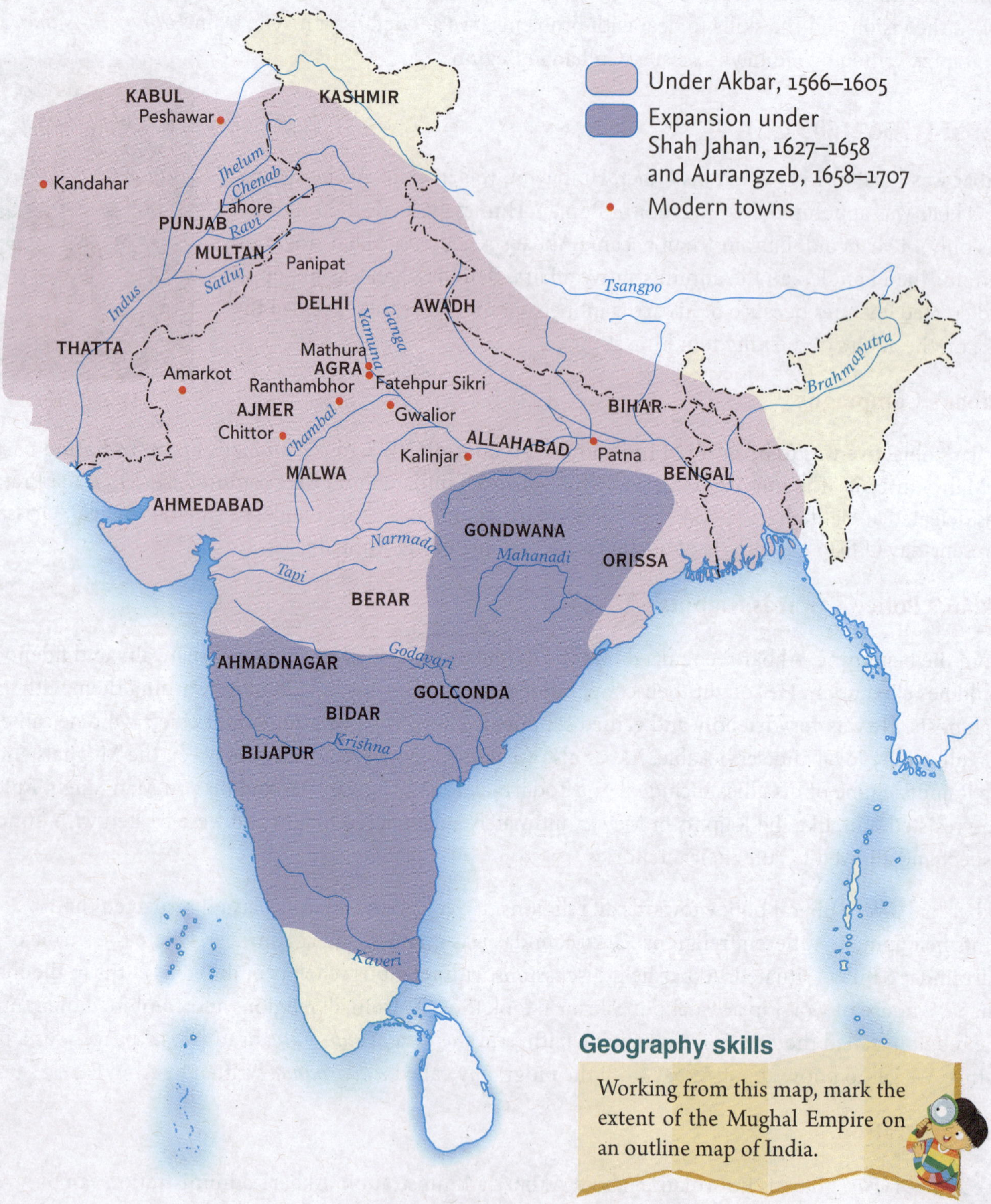

Geography skills

Working from this map, mark the extent of the Mughal Empire on an outline map of India.

The Mughal Empire at its peak

Provincial administration: The empire was divided into fifteen provinces called *subas*, which were governed by subedars (governors) assisted by a diwan. The provinces were further divided into *paraganas*, which were further divided into villages. Panchayats looked into the affairs of the villages.

Local administration: Law and order was looked after by the kotwal. He also checked cheating and malpractices. Weights and measures were also standardized. Officials were paid in cash and granted *jagirs*. The most important official in the village was the headman, also known as *muqaddam* or Chaudhari.

Akbar introduced the *mansabdari* system. The term *mansab* meant 'rank'. The person who held such a rank was known as the mansabdar. While joining, the mansabdar had a low rank but could rise to a higher rank, depending on his loyalty and service to the emperor. The mansabdari ranking depended on two factors—*zat* and *sawar*. The *zat* rank decided the mansabdar's personal status and salary, while the *sawar* rank fixed the number of *sawars* or men a mansabdar had to maintain. The mansabdar's responsibility was to get the horses inspected and the sawars registered and reviewed. The system of *daag* and *chehra* continued. Some mansabdars were paid in cash, but generally, they were paid in *jagirs*. These jagirs had to be carefully assessed as the revenue from them should have been equivalent to the cash salary of the mansabdars. The jagirs were allotted only for a period of four years. In due course, the mansabdari system became hereditary, and during Aurangzeb's time, the number of jagirdars increased, causing a shortage of jagirs. This resulted in the jagirdars trying to extract as much money as possible from their jagir. This left a huge economic contrast between the jagirdars, the emperor and the peasantry, leaving the peasantry in a distressing state.

Revenue System: Akbar's revenue system was designed by Raja Todar Mal. It was based on Sher Shah's revenue system. Land was measured and the yield assessed. Data regarding the area, local produce and the price of each crop was calculated for a period of ten years. This system was known as *zabt*. Revenue could be collected in cash or in kind. This system was applicable in the provinces between Lahore and Allahabad as well as Malwa and Gujarat. Provinces were divided into revenue circles and each circle had separate revenue rates. Akbar was undoubtedly one of the greatest Mughal Emperors. He died in 1605, nominating Salim, also known as Jahangir, as his successor.

Jahangir (1605–1627 CE)

Jahangir inherited a prosperous and strong empire, and his reign was pretty smooth, except for the revolt by his son Khusrau, which was suppressed. Jahangir was married to a talented woman named Nur Jahan. He issued coins in her name and made land grants. She had a tremendous influence over Jahangir's life and her family members enjoyed high posts in the royal administration.

It was during the time of Jahangir that two ambassadors from the English East India Company, Captain William Hawkins and Sir Thomas Roe, arrived. Jahangir gave them trading concessions to carry out trade in Surat. Jahangir was known to be a very just ruler. He loved painting and patronized the art of painting.

Shah Jahan (1628–1658 CE)

Prince Khurram was known as Shah Jahan, which means 'king of the world' in Persian. During his rule, he subjugated the Deccan states of Golconda, Bijapur and Ahmednagar. He also crushed the revolt of the Bundela Rajputs. We get detailed accounts of Shah Jahan's reign from the *Padshahnama*, written by his court chronicler Abdul Hamid Lahori.

Shah Jahan with his wife Mumtaz Mahal

Shah Jahan was married to Mumtaz Mahal, Nur Jahan's niece. Art and architecture flourished during this period. Shah Jahan was a great builder and constructed one of the greatest wonders of medieval India—the Taj Mahal, in memory of his wife,

Mumtaz Mahal. Shah Jahan was a very competent ruler and was said to have been an excellent administrator. He took care of each and every detail of his administration, though he was lavish in his lifestyle. Shah Jahan's reign has rightly been considered the golden age of the Mughal era. There were a lot of differences and conflicts between his four sons, Dara, Shuja, Murad and Aurangzeb, even before his death. This led to a war of succession ultimately leading to the succession of Aurangzeb to the throne.

Green Earth

India's white-marble Taj Mahal is turning yellow and green as the 17th century mausoleum weathers filthy air in the world's eighth-most polluted city. One of the Seven Wonders of the World, the Taj Mahal flanks a garbage-strewn river and is often enveloped by dust and smog from the belching smokestacks and vehicles.

Aurangzeb (1658–1707 CE)

Aurangzeb, as history tells us, was a strict disciplinarian, an **orthodox** god-fearing Muslim or a *zinda pir* as he led a simple life. He did not practise or follow the liberal policy followed by the rulers before him. Although he had mastered Persian and Arabic and spoke Hindi fluently too, his qualities were overshadowed by his biased attitude. He re-imposed the *jizya* tax and forbade celebrations of festivals in his court. All these measures made him very unpopular.

Significant Developments

During Aurangzeb's reign, there were many rebellions. There was the struggle with the Ahoms of the northeast, peasant rebellions in the Jat community in the Agra–Delhi region and conflicts with the Satnamis, which had to be suppressed. He also antagonized the Sikhs by executing their ninth Guru, Guru Tegh Bahadur. Under the leadership of the tenth Sikh guru, Guru Gobind Singh, the institution of Khalsa was set up to fight against the Mughals. His policy of interfering with the Rajputs caused disturbances in the west. His longest campaign was in the Deccan region. Although successful in annexing Bijapur and Golconda, the Marathas under Shivaji became a tough challenge for him. His expeditions in the Deccan forced him to neglect the northern region of his Empire. Meanwhile, the Marathas emerged as an independent state. North India faced the threat of invasions by Nadir Shah and Ahmed Shah Abdali. All this led to the **fragmentation** and disintegration of the Mughal Empire and to the emergence of many independent and partly independent kingdoms.

What's in the picture?

This is a painting of the last Mughal emperor, Aurangzeb. What does this painting tell you about the ruler?

orthodox: following or conforming to the traditional or generally accepted rules or beliefs of a religion, philosophy, or practice; fragmentation: the process or state of breaking or being broken into fragments

- 1526 CE Babur founded the Mughal Empire; defeated Ibrahim Lodi at the First Battle of Panipat
- 1530-1540 CE, 1555-1556 CE: Reign of Humayun
- 1556-1605 CE: Reign of Akbar the Great
- 1605-1627 CE: Reign of Jahangir
- 1628–1658 CE: Reign of Shah Jahan
- 1658–1707 CE: Reign of Aurangzeb

Wind up

Mughal Empire

- **Babur founded the Mughal empire**
- **Humayun, his son, ascended the throne**
  - Deposed by Sher Shah Suri for 15 years; came back to power in 1555 but died shortly after
- **Akbar ascended the throne at the age of 14**
  - Expanded the kingdom through his campaigns
  - Tolerant; formed alliances with the Rajputs
  - Mansabdari system
  - Revenue system
- **Jahangir ascended**
  - Married to Nur Jahan
  - Ambassadors from the East India Company came during his reign
- **Shah Jahan ascended**
  - Married to Mumtaz Mahal
  - Built the Taj Mahal
  - Art and architecture flourished
- **Aurangzeb ascended**
  - Strict disciplinarian and orthodox Muslim
  - Re-imposed jizya
  - Many rebellions during his reign
  - Marathas were a tough challenge for him
  - Antagonized the Sikhs
  - Many independent kingdoms arose

Case Study

Sher Shah Suri

Farid Khan, also known as Sher Khan, was the son of a *jagirdar* of Jaunpur. He was proficient in Arabic and Persian and tutored Jalal Khan, the son of the ruler of Bihar. It is said that he killed a tiger during this time, which gave him the title of Sher Khan. He emerged as a strong ruler of Bihar and took over the throne of Delhi by defeating the Mughal emperor, Humayun, in 1540. Sher khan is remembered for his contribution in administration. He improved his administration and took care of the smallest details. He maintained a large standing army and continued with the system of branding the horses. He gave special instructions to his soldiers not to trample or damage the enemies' crops. Several measures were undertaken to look after travellers. Caravanserais were built and fruit trees were planted. To ensure the safety of the travellers on the highways and roads, special rules and regulations were made to protect them from thieves and robbers. The introduction of new weights and measures helped in the progress of trade and commerce.

His greatest contribution was his revenue system. Land was surveyed carefully and categorized according to its fertility. One-third of the total produce was paid in cash, or in kind, as tax. He also introduced the *rupiya*. The postal service was introduced by him, and horses were used for communicating messages. He also built a network of roads. The Grand Trunk Road, which connects Sonargaon in Bengal to Peshwar, was the longest road built by him. Thus, during the five years of his rule, he laid the foundations for what would become one of the strongest empires in Indian history.

Q. Why was Sher Shah Suri given the name 'Sher'?

Skill Builder

21ST CENTURY SKILLS

Life skills: Mughal women were well educated not only in the religious texts but also in arts, sciences and warfare. Suggest examples.

Critical thinking skills: Popularly known as Jodha Bai, a Hindu Princess was married to Muslim king Akbar. What can you understand about Akbar's liberal policy on this account?

Communication skill: During its conquests throughout the centuries, the military of the Mughal Empire used a variety of weapons, including swords, bows and arrows, horses, camels, elephants, some of the world's largest cannons, muskets and flintlock blunderbusses. Write a report on this and present it in class.

World Connect

The Elizabethan era was a great period in English history. English drama flourished under William Shakespeare and overseas adventure gained momentum under various explorers, like Sir Francis Drake. Her reign gave great stability to the kingdom and Britain acquired a national identity. During that period, the kingdom was threatened by grave internal divisions; yet, Elizabeth's blend of shrewdness, courage and majestic self-display inspired ardent expressions of loyalty and helped unify the nation against foreign powers. The admiration bestowed upon her, both in her lifetime and in the ensuing centuries, was not altogether spontaneous. It was the result of a carefully crafted, brilliantly executed campaign, in which the queen fashioned herself as the glittering symbol of the nation's destiny. This political symbolism, common to monarchies, had more substance than usual, for the queen was by no means a mere figurehead. While she did not wield the absolute power of which Renaissance rulers dreamed, she upheld her authority to make critical decisions and to set certain key policies of both the state and the church. The latter half of the 16th century in England is justly called the Elizabethan Age: rarely has the collective life of a whole era been given so distinctively personal a stamp.

Exercises

A. Choose the correct answers.

1. The First Battle of Panipat was fought in the year
   a. 1565 b. 1526 c. 1545 d. 1525
2. Gulbadan Begum wrote the
   a. *Akbarnama* b. *Ain-i-Akbari* c. *Padshahnama* d. *Humayun-Nama*
3. Akbar's revenue system was designed by
   a. Raja Todar Mal b. Sher Shah c. Aurangzeb d. the council of ministers
4. Babur won the Battle of Khanua, where he defeated
   a. Ibrahim Lodi b. Daulat Khan Lodi c. Sher Shah d. Rana Sanga of Mewar
5. The Marathas under .... became a tough challenge for Aurangzeb.
   a. Rana Sanga b. Guru Gobind Singh c. Shivaji d. None of these

B. Fill in the blanks.

1. Mughal rule began in the .... century.
2. Akbar's regent was ....
3. Babur wrote the book ....
4. Under Sher Shah Suris administration, ... were built and fruit trees were planted.
5. Prince Khurram was known as ...., which means 'king of the world' in Persian.

C. Answer these questions in brief.

1. Who was the founder of the Mughal dynasty?
2. What is the meaning of *Din-i-Ilahi*?
3. Name the Sikh Guru who formed the institution of Khalsa.
4. What measures were introduced by Aurangzeb that made him unpopular?
5. Who was Mumtaz Mahal?

D. Answer these questions in detail.

1. What were the challenges faced by Humayun as an emperor?
2. Discuss Akbar's religious policy in detail.
3. Explain the mansabdari system. What do you think was its drawback?
4. Describe Akbar's revenue policy as designed by Raja Todar Mal.
5. Give a short sketch of Akbar's conquests.

E. Read the passage and answer the questions.

Shah Jahan was a very competent ruler and was said to have been an excellent administrator. He took care of each and every detail of his administration, though he was lavish in his lifestyle. Shah Jahan's reign has rightly been considered the golden age of the Mughal era. There were a lot of differences and conflicts between his four sons, Dara, Shuja, Murad and Aurangzeb, even before his death. This led to a war of succession ultimately leading to the succession of Aurangzeb to the throne.

1. Why was Shah Jahan's reign called the golden age of the Mughal era?
2. What kind of ruler was he?

Think Big

Integrate with art

When you think about India, what are the things that immediately come to mind? Spicy food might be one, lots of people might be another. What about the Taj Mahal? It is as famous as the Eiffel Tower or the Statue of Liberty, but the Taj Mahal is much older than these two icons. The Taj Mahal was built some 400 years ago, during the reign of the Mughal Empire Shah Jahan. Here's an easy way to draw India's most famous monument. Try it in your drawing book.

Learning Tools

After reading the chapter, use the major headings of this section to create an outline of the chapter:

Babur	Humayun	Akbar
....	....	....
....	....	....
....	....	....
....	....	....

Jahangir	Shah Jahan	Aurangzeb
....	....	....
....	....	....
....	....	....
....	....	....

Web links:

https://www.indiatoday.in/education-today/gk-current-affairs/story/from-babur-to-aurangzeb-facts-on-the-six-major-mughal-emperors-of-india-1580020-2019-08-12

Last accessed on 31 August 2021

5. Architecture in Medieval India

Warm up

Two brothers, Dilip and Aditya, went on a trip to the Red Fort in Delhi with their parents. A guide was hired and he was giving them a narration that described the historic monument. 'This monument gets its name from the red-coloured sandstone used for construction by the Mughals. Constructed in the 17th century, this monument is an attraction by itself. The fort covers 254 acres of land covering 2.4 km. The fort is octagonal in shape and many regions of the fort are decorated with marble work. The Kohinoor diamond is said to be a part of the decoration', the guide informed the family. Just then, Dilip noticed that one part of the monument was damaged with ugly scribbling and scratches. The guide explained that historical monuments of any country reflect the history of the country and that is why the governments of different countries try their best to preserve their monuments. Internationally too, there are certain organizations, like UNESCO, who do their best to save all the historical monuments in the world.

His father then added 'The government cannot do much if the public is reckless and destructive towards national historical property. People should work together towards the preservation of historical monuments in the country'. Aditya went on to say, 'The monuments belong to our country, and it is our responsibility to save them.'

The medieval period has seen some great developments in the field of architecture. With every new power crossing the Himalayas to reach India, a new culture and tradition in architecture emerged. A mix of Persian, Arabic, Hindu and Buddhist influences led to the enrichment of the heritage of India, with the construction of some of the most remarkable structures the world has ever seen. Buildings and monuments were built for different reasons—to **commemorate** the dead, to **epitomize** the power and supremacy of the rulers or as tokens of love and faithfulness. Great rulers patronized sculptors, artists and craftsmen, giving us a deep insight into the lives and times of the people in the past.

Islamic Architecture

The Delhi Sultans built palaces, forts, tombs, gardens, **baolis** and minars. Their structures included features like domes, arches and minarets. Many Hindu motifs, such as the swastika, the bell and the lotus, have also been found in their buildings. The use of calligraphy was an important element in Islamic architecture and has been regarded as one of the most important art forms of Islam.

Limestone was extensively used as it was probably a commonly available material and could be cut and polished easily. The use of limestone made construction work easier and faster. Gems, gold and silver were also used to give the buildings a grand look. Mosaic work was also applied in many buildings.

commemorate: recall and show respect for (someone or something); epitomize: be a perfect example of; baoli: a reservoir in which water can be stored

Taj Mahal

The most beautiful monument constructed during the reign of Shah Jahan is the Taj Mahal, a tribute to his wife Mumtaz Mahal. A mixture of Islamic, Indian and Persian styles, it was constructed with materials brought from many parts of the world. Constructed mainly of white marble, the structure is inlaid with precious and semi-precious gems, lapis lazuli and decorated with inlay work called pietra dura. The doorways are bordered with beautiful motifs of flowers and verses from the *Quran*. The perfect symmetry of the structure can be seen in its huge dome and the four minarets on the four sides. The gardens that surround the Taj are said to have been designed following the description of heaven in the *Quran*. The Taj has been declared a World Heritage Site by UNESCO.

Humayun's Tomb

Humayun's tomb is the tomb of the Mughal emperor, Humayun, in Delhi. It was built by his widow Haji Begum in 1558 CE. It stands in the centre of a garden and was the first of its kind in the Indian subcontinent. Built on a high platform terrace, the double-storeyed structure has an octagonal plan with four long sides, topped with a white marble dome. The mausoleum is decorated with elegant arches, arched **alcoves** and corridors. The central chamber houses the graves of the family members, while the grave of the emperor lies on the basement floor.

What's in the picture?

In your own words, briefly describe Humayun's tomb.

Agra Fort

The Agra Fort was initially built by Akbar, but many of its features were later added by his grandson, Shah Jahan. It is a massive structure made of solid red sandstone. Two gateways lead to the fort's entrance, Delhi Gate being the main entrance, and Hathi Pol or elephant Gate being the other. The Delhi Gate entrance archway is bordered by two double-storeyed octagonal bastions topped with octagonal domes. The gateway is decorated with beautiful panels of coloured tiles and marble inlay work. A deep moat surrounds the fort. Some of the important buildings inside the fort are the Jahangiri Mahal, the Moti Masjid and Mina Bazaars.

Agra Fort

Buland Darwaza

When Emperor Akbar conquered Gujarat, he built a magnificent gateway to commemorate his conquest. It is the main entrance to the Jama Masjid at Fatehpur Sikri. Built with red sandstone and marble and

---

alcove: a recess in the wall of a room or garden

decorated with white and black marble, it is said to be the 'most perfect architectural achievement in India'. A flight of steps leads to the gateway, which is about 53 metres in height and 39 metres in width. The entrance is through a huge arched domed recess. A broad rectangular strip bordering the archway has calligraphic inscriptions on it. An inscription on the gateway, that elucidates the advice of Jesus Christ to his followers, testifies to Akbar's religious toleration.

Apply it!

The Mughal gardens were built by the Mughals in the Persian style of architecture. This style was heavily influenced by the Persian gardens, particularly the Charbagh structure, which intended to create a representation of an earthly utopia where humans co-exist in perfect harmony with all the elements of nature. Can you name some of the famous Mughal Gardens in India?

Hindu Architecture

Indian art developed over a period of two thousand years and almost all Indian art was religious. Temples were places of worship as well as symbols of power and wealth of the ruler who commissioned their construction. A temple symbolized the love of the ruler towards his personal deity, mostly either Lord Vishnu or Lord Shiva. Sometimes, the temples were referred to by both the name of the deity and the patron. For example, the Brihadishvara Temple is also known as the Rajarajeshwara Temple as it was built by Rajaraja Chola I. The deity was endowed with certain qualities and the rulers always liked to follow them. Throughout history, temples have been targeted by invaders. Large temples were built to demonstrate power and resources. Invaders like Mahmud of Ghazni attacked and looted such temples and with the amassed wealth, he built a beautiful city in Ghazni.

FACT CHECK

Uttar Pradesh has the maximum monuments in India, which has a total number of 3,685 monuments. The state is known as the 'heartland of India' due to its cultural heritage and historical relevance.

Style and Features of the Temples

At the beginning, temples were built in strict accordance with the conservatism of the age. Influences emerging from geographical, climatic, ethnic, racial, historical and religious diversity brought about the unique styles exhibited in different temples located in different regions. Temple architecture had two distinct styles—the Nagara or the Northern style and the Dravida or the Southern style.

In the north, the Nagara style was followed for temple construction, whereas, in the south, the Dravidian style of temple construction was followed. Both the styles had stone pillars to support the roof. In the early medieval period, the Nagara style included the garbhagriha, which was a shrine inside a temple complex where the main deity was installed. It has been compared by many to a **sanctum sanctorum**. The *pradakshana patha* was a passage around the temple that the devotees could use to walk around. The *shikhara*, was a peak-like, beehive-shaped structure, placed above the shrine and was the most visible feature of the temple.

sanctum sanctorium: holy of the holies / a private place

A well-known example of temples built in this style is the Kandariya Mahadeva Temple, built by the Chandelas at Khajuraho in Madhya Pradesh. This temple has Lord Shiva as the main deity and a high shikhra along with many smaller ones. The temple has magnificent sculptures too. Some other north Indian temples include the Jagannath temple at Puri, the Sun Temple at Konark and the Dilwara Temple at Mount Abu. The Dravadian style of architecture is reflected in the temples of south India. The Pallavas and the Cholas have been associated with building some of the most magnificent temples. An example of the Dravidian style is projected in the rock-cut temples of the Pallavas. The Brihadishvara Temple of Tanjore is another example of the Dravidian style. This temple, dedicated to Lord Shiva, has very large courtyards. It has a tower like a pyramid. The top of the temple is made from a single block of rock. The corridors have some very fine sculptures, and the *garbhagriha* can be reached through a corridor. The tower above the *garbhagriha* is known as the *vimana*. The courtyard is enclosed with gateways called gopurams.

Sun Temple at Konark

Some other examples of temples belonging to the early medieval period of south India include the Kailashnath Temples built by the rulers of the Vijayanagar Empire, the Shore Temple at Mahabalipuram and the Meenakshi Temple at Madurai.

Difference between Hindu and Muslim Architecture

For a proper understanding of the Indo-Islamic architecture, which evolved as a result of the synthesis of the Hindu and Islamic architecture, it is desirable to have an idea about these two systems of architecture. The Hindu art was decorative, while Islamic art was characterised by its simplicity.

Rows of pillars and long beams to span the spaces to bridge spaces are common in Hindu architecture, while arches and graceful domes were erected in Muslim architecture.

Hindu architecture possessed infinite richness and variety of sculpture. They conveyed meaning through the carved figures on the buildings. Usually, their monuments were enriched with rich idols of divinities. Muslim buildings, on the other hand, were simple and spacious, their walls were plain and smooth faced. As Muslims did not believe in idol worship, they did not represent any figures on the walls. They only used colours and other ingenious geometric patterns.

Sikh Temples

In 1579, Guru Ramdas, the fourth Guru of the Sikhs, founded the city of Amritsar in Punjab. He first constructed a pool and named it Amrit Sar, or 'Pool of Nectar', on a stretch of land gifted to him by Akbar. His successor, Guru Arjun Dev, built a temple in the middle of the pool to enshrine the *Guru Granth Sahib*, the sacred book of the Sikhs. In 1803, Maharaja Ranjit Singh, the Ruler of Punjab, improved the temple. The lower half of the temple was covered with marble and the upper half with copper, over which a pure gold leaf of 400 kgs was covered. Since then, this 'Hari Mandir' is called the 'Golden Temple'.

Golden Temple

It has four entrances in the four cardinal directions. A marble causeway across the water connects the entrance gateway to the main shrine. Floral patterns of coloured semi-precious stone inlay work, glass work and beautiful fresco paintings decorate the inner walls and ceiling of the temple. The architecture is a combination of Hindu and Muslim styles and emphasizes upon calmness and serenity. A marble-paved square construction, adjacent to the Golden Temple, is the Akal Takht or Immortal Throne—the seat of the Sikh religion. The weapons used by the Sikh Gurus are also kept here. The temple with its beautiful domes, throwing its reflection in the pool, is a piece of grace and beauty. Other important places of worship in Punjab for the Sikhs are the Gurudwara at Tarn Taran Sahib, designed in Mughal style, the Fatehgarh Sahib at Sirhind, where the young sons of Guru Gobind Singh were buried alive by Aurangzeb and the Gurudwara at Anandpur Sahib, where Guru Gobind Singh initiated the Khalsa.

Decline in Architecture

Architectural creation and art declined during the reign of the Mughal Emperor Aurangzeb. Brick and rubble began to replace stone and marble, and attention to detail and precision, which was highly prevalent in earlier Mughal architecture, took a back seat. The buildings that were made during Aurangzeb's reign were replicas and imitations of the architectural structures made in the past. The Safdarjung Tomb, which was completed in 1753, bore a stark resemblance to Humayun's tomb, built by Humayun's widow in Delhi.

Case Study

Konark Sun Temple Architecture

The word Konark means corner (kona) and sun (ark) and is dedicated to the sun god. It was built at the mouth of the Chandrabhaga River. The entire temple has been conceived as a chariot of the sun god, with 24 wheels, each about 10 feet in diameter, with a set of spokes and elaborate carvings. Seven horses drag the temple and two lions guard the entry, crushing the elephants.

It was built in a way so that the first ray of the sun would fall on the gigantic sun idol kept inside the main temple complex, and even today, you can tell the time by the rays of the sun falling on the wheels, acting as sundials. One of the most fascinating things of this temple was that the sun idol was suspended in the air as there were magnets used in the construction. So, when you entered the main temple, you would see a tall idol suspended mid-air. For years, it was a mystery as to how this happened. People did not realise it was the magnetic field from all four sides that made this happen. But, this also led to the removal of the idol. It is believed that this magnetic field affected the compass navigation for sailors and when they were invading India, they ordered the magnets to be removed. Thus, the idol could no longer be suspended in the air.

Skill Builder 21ST CENTURY SKILLS

Critical thinking skills: Why did the medieval rulers build spectacular and grand structures?

Life skills: Write an essay on 'Monuments are our historical heritage'. You may include why we need to preserve the monuments, what we need to do to protect the historical sites and how we can help in the conservation and preservation of our national heritage.

Communication skills: *'As it was the proud statement of Augustus that he found Rome built of bricks and left it of marble, similarly Shah Jahan had found the Mughal cities of stones, he left them of marble'.*

—Percy Brown (art critic)

Discuss this in class.

World Connect

Gothic architecture

Gothic architecture flourished in the late medieval period. It originated in 12th century France from Romanesque architecture and was succeeded by Renaissance architecture. The building skills were limited and large blocks of stone were used in Romanesque architecture. The stone castles of earlier times were dark, cold and damp. The stones were chiseled and shaped in the Gothic style. Gothic architecture was characterized by tall spires and pointed arches, stained windows and flying buttresses. This style of architecture, especially the flying butresses, allowed architects to spread the weight to different points of the building. The walls were thinner with wider window openings. Gothic buildings appeared grand with spires on top of tall towers. The pointed arch was an innovation of the Gothic style. The arches had practical utility and were decorative in their appearance. Gothic architecture was used in the construction of churches, abbeys and castles. Florence Cathedral in Italy, Basilica of St Denis in Paris and Cologne cathedral in Germany are a few examples of Gothic architecture. One peculiar feature of Gothic architecture is the gargoyle. A gargoyle is a decorative monster-like creature carved out of stone and perched on the roofs and ledges of Gothic buildings. A gargoyle had a practical purpose. The sculpture had a spout from which rainwater could drain off from the building. The evil-looking stone image was also intended to strike fear into the hearts of peasants and force them to seek shelter inside the church.

Wind up

Medieval India Architecture

- Islamic architecture
  - Features: domes, arches, minarets, red sandstone, limestone, mosaic
- Hindu architecture
  - Features: *garbhagriha*, *pradakshana patha*, *shikhara*
- Sikh temples
  - Features: a combination of Hindu and Muslim styles and lays stress on calmness and serenity

Exercises

A. Choose the correct answers.

1. This monumemt is believed to be the most perfect architectural achievement in the whole of India.
   a. Gol Gumbaz b. Moti Masjid c. Jama Masjid d. Buland Darwaza
2. Guru Ramdas, the fourth Guru of the Sikhs constucted the
   a. Moonlight Pool b. Pool of Nectar c. Classical Water d. none of the above
3. The Buland Darwaza was built to commemorate Akbar's victory in
   a. Ahmed Nagar b. Hyderabad c. Gujarat d. Bijapur

4. The Taj Mahal was made of
   a. black marble b. white marble c. red marble d. brown marble
5. The Kandariya Mahadeva Temple built by the Chandelas at Khajuraho in Madhya Pradesh has this god as the main deity
   a. Krishna b. Shiva c. Ram d. Vishnu

B. Fill in the blanks.

1. With the coming of the Mughals, Indian architecture was greatly influenced by .... styles.
2. Guru Gobind Singh initiated the Khalsa in the gurudwara at ....
3. The Meenakshi Temple at Madurai is an example of .... architecture.
4. The Brihadishvara Temple of Tanjore is an example of the .... style of architecture.
5. Architectural creation and art declined during the reign of the Mughal Emperor ....

C. Answer these questions in brief.

1. Why was limestone extensively used for construction?
2. What were the main characteristic features of Mughal architecture?
3. Who built the Agra Fort?
4. What is placed at the Golden Temple in the Akal Takht?
5. What is a *garbhagriha*?

D. Answer these questions in detail.

1. Discuss the differences between the two styles of temple architecture of India.
2. Explain the significance of south Indian temples.
3. Architecture was used a symbol of power by the Mughal rulers. Discuss.
4. Write a note on the Golden Temple.
5. What is the difference between Hindu and Muslim architecture?
6. List the features of the two styles of temple architecture.

Think Big

Integrate with geometry

How is geometry used in architecture? Each elevation of a building is distinctive and geometrical, depending on the approach. Geometry is the fundamental science of forms and their order. Geometric figures, forms and transformations build the material of architectural design.

In the history of architecture, geometric rules are based on the ideas of proportions. Symmetries form fixed tools for architectural design. Firstly, they use geometry because it defines the spatial form of a building. Secondly, they use mathematics to design the forms considered beautiful or harmonious. The geometric designs in Islamic art are often built on the combinations of repeated squares and circles, which may be overlapped and interlaced, as can arabesques (with which they are often combined), to form intricate and complex patterns, including a wide variety of tessellations. These may constitute the entire decoration, may form a framework for floral or calligraphic embellishments or may retreat into the background around other motifs.

Learning Tools

Taking notes

Create sheets like the one below for each of the monuments you have learnt about in this chapter:

Name of the monument	Ruler who built it	Distinctive features
....	....	....
....	....	....
Location	**Type of monument**	....
....	....	....
....	....	....

Web links:

https://www.historydiscussion.net/history-of-india/medieval-age/architecture-and-sculpture-in-medieval-india/62240

Last accessed on 31 August 2021

6. Towns, Traders and Craftsmen

Warm up

Vivan always enjoyed listening to stories about their ancestral village from his grandfather. Their ancestral village is in the state of Assam in the Goalpara district. Once, when he accompanied his grandfather for a family reunion, he noticed that it was free from the hustle and bustle of city life. The village was full of greenery; the air was clean. Most people were farmers, others worked as potters, carpenters and blacksmiths. One day, Vivan visited the village fair. He saw that the rural craftsman and artisans exhibited local handmade goods. Handmade goods, such as toys, whistles, combs, hairpins, cheap ornaments, cosmetics, looking glasses, balloons and dolls, were sold there. There were magic shows, traditional games and merry-go-rounds and were most enjoyed by the children. Vivan compared the village fair with modern bazaars and supermarkets. He found the real soul of India in the village.

We have already learnt that during the rule of the Delhi Sultanate, there was centralization of power within the country. Due to the political and economic stability within the country, an urban revolution was initiated. Large villages eventually grew into towns and cities where trade flourished. The Delhi Sultans, who were till then using the silver currency tanka, introduced a second currency, the copper jital. This revitalized trade in north India, which led to the emergence of urban centres and started the development of marketplaces in both towns and villages. These cities received royal patronage and witnessed a growth in cultural activities, such as music and literature.

Temple Towns

During the medieval period, towns usually grew around temples. People belonging to different occupations settled down near them. These included priests, garland makers, musicians and sculptors. Some famous temple towns are Tanjore, Kanchipuram, Somnath and Madurai.

Tanjore became a flourishing town only because of its temples. Amritsar is yet another significant place, around which the town of Ramdaspur developed. Ajmer is very popular as it is the home to the dargah of the popular sufi saint Khwaja Chisti. The famous Pushkar Lake is also located nearby.

Tanjore

Craft Centres

When merchants, travellers and craftsmen, following a particular trade and profession, settled down in one place, it led to the growth of craft centres. These craftsmen were specialized in making specific crafts. Some craft centres were Bidar, famous for its bidri work, Hyderabad for gem-cutting and Tanjore for bronze sculptures. Special workshops, known as *karkhanas*, were set up, from where these craftspeople worked. Other crafts that they specialized in were weaving and leather work, amongst other things.

Green Earth

Although the Mughal rulers built many parks and gardens, there was no restriction on cutting of trees or hunting. Forest wealth shrank considerably during the medieval period.

Commercial Trading Towns

Trade developed with a surplus production of goods and the development of transportation. Most trading and commercial towns emerged in areas with access to trade routes and ports, where products were easily available. Sometimes, commercial and trading centres came up near the places where there was a **mandi**. From spices to cattle, various items were traded in mandis. Fairs were organized in towns where buyers and sellers could meet for trade. Some such towns were Ahmedabad, Masulipatnam and Surat.

Port Towns

India had good trade relations with other countries so port towns developed in places like Bharuch, Khambhat, Cochin and Masulipatnam. The French, the English and the Dutch traded from Masulipatnam or Machilipatnam. It was also famous for its dyed cotton cloth, known as chintz. Machilipatnam, as the name signifies, is a fish port town on the banks of the river Krishna. It came up in the 14th century in Golconda. The port engaged in active trade with different regions of India too. For example, it exported tobacco and cotton textiles to Bengal.

What's in the picture?

What type of town would you say this picture depicts?

Impact of the Emergence of Towns

Money Transactions

Money exchange became convenient with the emergence of **hundis** and banking houses. The money earned through internal and foreign trade was deposited with the shroff or the money changers. The use of hundis made long-distance travel convenient as people would receive money by producing these hundis when they reached their destination.

mandi: marketplace; hundi: used as a form of remittance instrument to transfer money from place to place, as a form of credit instrument or IOU to borrow money and as a bill of exchange in trade transactions

Apply it!

Each town centre had different occupations and their significance varied from town to town. Today, there are many people without jobs and without the means for living decent lives. Follow these steps to understand the situation:

8 DECENT WORK AND ECONOMIC GROWTH

- Place yourselves in a circle which symbolizes the job market. One person has to be inside the circle to symbolize a job. One person has to be outside the circle to symbolize a job hunter.
- Now, work together and keep the person outside the circle from entering and catching the person inside the circle.
- You can change roles when the 'job' person has been caught or touched by the job hunter.

How does it feel to be outside the circle?

Formation of Guilds

People who traded in the same products formed associations. These associations were known as guilds. These guilds functioned through certain guidelines and norms that were very strict and the members had to adhere to these rules. These guilds also looked after the marketing of products and the needs of the members. Some examples of guilds in south India are Manigramam and Nanadesi.

Trade Links with Foreign Countries

India established trade relations with West Asia, Africa, Arabia and Syria. Merchant communities, like the Baniyas and the Bohras, were actively involved in trade. Maritime trade developed with South East Asia and China.

Specialists in Crafts

As the cities and towns grew, there was a greater demand for items like silk, ornaments, weapons and even decorative items. Most of these items required skilled artisans to keep up with the increasing demand of such goods. Special communities of craftsmen and artisans like the Saliya community began to grow. There were separate communities of stone workers, metalworkers and goldsmiths.

Case Study

Kanchipuram, also known as the 'City of Thousand Temples', is one of India's seven sacred cities and is famous globally for its exquisite temples. Apart from Hindu temples, Kanchipuram is also home to few Jain temples, Buddhist monasteries and mosques. The city is divided into two sectors – Vishnu Kanchi and Shiva Kanchi. While Lord Vishnu resides in the former division, Lord Shiva and Goddess Parvati can be found in the latter. The Ekambareswarar, Kailasanathar, Thirumarugal, Varadharaja Perumal, Kamakshi Amman and Devarajaswami temples are amongst the prominent ones.

Dedicated to Lord Shiva, the Ekambareswarar Temple has been spoken about by Tamil poets of the second century. The temple is enormous and the doors are nearly 40 feet tall. The temple has a mango tree, which is 3,500 years old. Goddess Shakti is worshiped in three major cities, out of which Kanchipuram ranks first in importance.

The gold-plated main tower and the golden chariot are the special features of the Kamakshi Amman Temple. This temple is constructed on five acres of land. It houses a gallery that presents the life history of Adisankaracharya.

Belonging to the eighth century, Kailasanathar Temple is amongst the oldest structures of the city and is dedicated to Lord Shiva. The construction was commenced by Rajasimha Pallava, while his son Mahendra Varma Pallava completed it. The Devarajaswami Temple is dedicated to Lord Vishnu and was constructed by the Vijayanagar kings. A 10-metre tall statue of Lord Vishnu lies immersed in a large tank, which is drained once every 40 years. It is that time when the statue can be viewed.

Q. Dedicated to Lord Shiva, describe the Ekambareswarar Temple in your own words.

Skill Builder

21ST CENTURY SKILLS

Critical thinking skills: Indian exports far exceeded its imports, both in the number of items and its value. Do you think this was the reason India was known far and wide? Could this also be the reason foreign invaders became attracted to the region?

Life skills: The accounts of foreign travellers contain descriptions of a wide range of exquisite goods sold in the Indian markets. This gave new impetus to trade and commerce. Can you name some of these goods?

Creativity: Imagine you are a foreigner visiting Masulipatnam in the 16th century. Write a diary entry describing your first day in this port town.

World Connect

Vasco da Gama

Vasco da Gama was a Portuguese explorer who was appointed by King Manuel of Portugal to find a sea route to the East in 1497. Spice trade with India existed in Europe, but it was through land routes, which were expensive and took a long time to reach. By this time, Portugal had become one of the most powerful maritime countries in Europe. King Manuel wanted to find a direct trade route to India.

In 1487, Bartolomeu Dias had discovered the Cape of Good Hope at the southern tip of Africa. This was significant as it proved for the first time that the Atlantic Ocean and the Indian Ocean were connected. It was thought that there was a way round the Cape of Good Hope, northwards to India. King Manuel gave a fleet of ships to Vasco da Gama and asked him to find a trade route around Africa to India. He was also told to find any other trading opportunities along the way. Vasco da Gama left on his first voyage from Lisbon, Portugal on 8 July, 1497. He sailed with 170 men in four ships. His discovery of the sea route to India was significant as it led to the establishment of the Portuguese colonial empire in the Indian subcontinent. Nearly a century later, other European powers, such as England, France and Denmark were finally able to challenge and break Portugal's monopoly over the sea route via the Cape of Good Hope to the East.

Wind up

Many towns emerged as a result of political and economic growth → Some towns developed because of their religious significance → Port cities like Surat and Masulipatnam grew in importance for international trade → Karkhanas and guilds came into existence → Banking houses developed as a result of trade

Exercises

A. Choose the correct answers.

1. The French, the English and the Dutch traded from
   a. Cochin   b. Masulipatnam   c. Khambhat   d. Bharuch
2. A port town
   a. Ahmedabad   b. Hyderabad   c. Masulipatnam   d. Ajmer
3. Located on the banks of the river Krishna
   a. Hampi   b. Agra   c. Surat   d. Masulipatnam
4. Hyderabad was famous for
   a. bronze work   b. stone work   c. pottery   d. gem-cutting
5. They looked after the marketing of products and the needs of the members
   a. markets   b. temple towns
   c. commercial centres   d. guilds

B. Fill in the blanks.

1. Tanjore was famous for ....
2. Two examples of merchant communities are .... and ....
3. A special workshop from where these crafts people worked was called a ....
4. .... were organized in towns where buyers and sellers could meet for trade.
5. Commercial and trading centres came up near the places where there was a ....

C. Answer these questions in brief.

1. Name two craft centres.
2. What are temple towns?
3. What is a mandi?
4. How did money exchange become convenient?
5. How did trade develop?

D. Answer these questions in detail.

1. What was the impact of emergence of towns?
2. On a table list three towns of each—temple, craft, commercial and port town.
3. What were the factors that encouraged the growth of commercial trading centres?
4. Compare and contrast between a temple town and a commercial trading town.

E. Read the passage and answer the questions.

During the medieval period, towns usually grew around temples. People belonging to different occupations settled down near them. These included priests, garland makers, musicians and sculptors. Some famous temple towns are Tanjore, Kanchipuram, Somnath and Madurai. Tanjore became a flourishing town only because of its temples. Amritsar is yet another significant place, around which the town of Ramdaspur developed.

1. People from which occupations were found in temple towns?
2. Name some examples of temple towns.

Think Big

Integrate with art

Explore some traditional villages or towns that specialize in a particular craft with your classmates and teacher. Prepare a project on what you have experienced and present it in the class.

Learning Tools

Make your own study guide by following these steps.

MAIN POINTS

(Note down the important headings and the main ideas)

→ ....

→ ....

→ ....

→ ....

→ ....

→ ....

→ ....

Keywords

- ....
- ....
- ....
- ....
- ....
- ....

Web links:

https://www.clearias.com/medieval-india-towns-traders-and-craftpersons/

Last accessed on 31 August 2021

7. Tribal Communities

Warm up

Birsa Munda was an Indian tribal freedom fighter, religious leader and folk hero, belonging to the Munda tribe of the Chhotanagpur Plateau area. In the 19th century, Birsa Munda started a tribal religious Millenarian Movement in the Bengal Presidency (present-day Jharkhand). Imagine a 25-year-old individual who took on an empire, left an indelible mark on tribal rights across the country and was seen as a mystic and folk hero by hundreds of thousands of people. Few would have achieved so much in so short a time, and it is not surprising that Birsa Munda's portrait hangs proudly in India's parliament.

What is a Tribe?

A tribe may be defined as a group of families who are associated due to common social, economic or blood ties, follow a common culture and led by a tribal chief or leader. They were criminalized for a long time till they received legal recognition and limited autonomy, previously by Brahmins, who were at the top of the social order, and later, by the national states. They communicate through a common dialect. A tribe is further divided into smaller tribes, where each small tribe has its own leader. Both men and women enjoy equal status in a tribe.

These tribes practise hunting, gathering and in most cases, engage in very primitive forms of cultivation. Some tribes are linked to specific regions. For instance, some live in the hills, while others live in the deserts. Initially, most tribes were pastoral or forest tribes, but as the society expanded, they were absorbed into the mainstream society and acquired a status. When these powerful tribal chiefs became a part of the main society, they were recognized as Kshatriyas. Most tribes, however, did not want to be assimilated within the folds of the main society. They resisted and eventually were defeated in war.

Apply it!

E

Adivasis have been included in forest-protection activities by state governments. The Kokrebellur village of Karnataka, the state government defined roles for the local community to ensure reduction in bird poaching and encourage recreational activities to make the Kokrebellur bird sanctuary a tourist spot. Compare this to the current situation of deforestation, global warming and animal extinction. Do you agree that tribes teach us the need to be in harmony with nature?

Tribal Societies

Tribes of the Nilgiris

The Nilgiri Mountains have many tribes like the Todas, the Irulas, the Badagas, the Kotas and the Kurumbas, who have lived there for generations together. The Toda and Kota tribes are confined to the Nilgiris, and they live in cluster settlements at the peak, whereas the Kurumbas and the Irulas live mainly on the lower slopes. Each tribe is identified by its distinctive language, social hierarchies, rules, lifestyles and languages. People of one tribe would never live in another tribe's village. The Todas are a pastoral community. Their villages and hamlets are called *mundi*. The women weave shawls called *puthukulis*. The Kotas are dancers, musicians, blacksmiths, carpenters, rope makers and potters.

What's in the picture?

This photograph of a Toda home was taken in 1902. In your own words, describe the home in the picture.

Banjaras

The Banjara people, also known as the Lambadis, are the tribal people that live in parts of Rajasthan, Karnataka, Andhra Pradesh, Maharashtra and Telangana. They moved from Rajasthan to the Deccan. It is believed that they moved to this region in search of food. Another theory is that these tribes were trying to escape the advancing army of Aurangzeb, the last of the great Mughal Emperors. The Lambadis were involved in cattle herding. These people did not believe in owning lands. Their settlements were called *tandas*, which are hamlets. It is believed that some of them were salt hawkers and moved from one place to another.

A Banjara woman in traditional dress

The most important and integral part of the Banjara society is the celebration of festivals. Weddings, birth of a child and festivals are all accompanied by music and dance. A typical Banjara wedding used to be celebrated for one month, but now the celebrations are limited to only three days.

The Bodos of Assam

The Bodos are one of the most important tribes of Assam and belong to the Bodo-Kachari clan. The Bodos originate from the Brahmaputra valley and are amongst the most progressive tribes in India. Bodos' native language is Deodahi, but they also know Tibeto-Burmese and Devnagari.

Bodos primarily undertake tea plantation activities. They work in tea estates in Assam, which is a major source of income for them. Sericulture is another occupation they pursue. They practise silk rearing and also undertake pig and poultry farming.

A Bhil woman in traditional dress

The Bhils of Rajasthan

The Bhils of Rajasthan belong to the Mewar region of the state. Bhil means bow, signifying that the Bhil tribes are archers by profession. A primary occupation of the Bhil tribes in ancient times was safeguarding the royal families and acting as huntsmen. Bhils also reside in Gujarat, Madhya Pradesh, Maharashtra and Tripura as well as in Bangladesh. The Bhils have a traditional dance form known as the ghoomar.

Bhils depend on agriculture for all their economic needs. They undertake the slash-and-burn cultivation, whereby they burn forests to clear the land for cultivation. They also gather forest produce and undertake fishing and hunting of wild beasts. They always lived in temporary settlements. While some Bhils have moved to brick and mortar houses, a lot of them still live in huts, vacating them only if a disaster strikes. The Bhil men wear turbans and waistcoats, whereas women wear saris. They are also known for their practice of adopting children.

Ahoms

In the region of northeast, a tribe that belonged to the Shan tribe of China and South East Asia settled down in Assam, which was then known as Kamarupa. They were the Ahoms. They came to Assam in the 13th century. They gradually expanded their territories and conquered the tribal kingdom of Sutiya and some kingdoms of local rulers. Sukaphaa was the first Ahom king who ruled for as long as forty years. He made friends with the local tribes.

FACT CHECK

Ahoms built well-known cities like Garhgaon and Rangpur. Rang Ghar is the oldest amphitheatre in Asia and was built by them.

The rulers of Bengal and the Ahoms were in conflict as both wanted to control the Brahmaputra valley. Ultimately, the western part of the valley was taken over by the Turkish rulers, and the Ahoms retained control over the eastern parts. During the 17th century, the Ahoms tried to resist the Mughals, and they were in conflict with Aurangzeb. However in the 19th century, they were ousted by the British.

Society: The Ahoms had a very powerful village community. Rice was cultivated. The people lived in houses made of bamboo. Tribal gods were worshipped by the people. There was a group of people called *paiks* who were forced to work for the state in both peace and war. They would multi-task and build important public utility services like dams and roads. They cultivated land by utilizing forests and marshy land. Everyone who was not a part of the nobility or the royal household had to contribute towards public work. There were two major classes of paiks. The kanri paiks were archers and they functioned as soldiers as well. The other group of paiks had a greater social standing and were known as the *chamua paiks*. They did non-manual work. The kanri paiks gradually progressed to become chamua paiks.

Case Study

Munda Tribe in India

The Munda tribe mainly inhabit the region of Jharkhand, although they are well spread in the states of West Bengal, Chhattisgarh, Orissa and Bihar. Munda generally means the headman of the village. The language they speak is Mundari. Although Christianity is the main religion, the Mundas also have their own religion known as Sarna. Sarna stresses on the belief of one God, a Supreme Being known as the Singbonga, which means the Sun God. Some Mundas also worship Lord Shiva.

Mundas were traditionally hunters and while some still continue hunting, many have settled as agriculturists. Most of them do not have land of their own. They are largely dependent on the labour work from the fields to earn their livelihood. Their staple food is rice, and they eat various pulses, vegetables and meat. Munda men usually wear pant and shirts, while Munda women usually wear cotton saris with cholis or blouse. Mage, Phagu, Karam, Sarhul and Sohrai are a few festivals celebrated among the Munda tribe.

Q. Write briefly about the religion of the Mundas.

Skill Builder

Critical thinking skills: In India, Chhatisgarh is a popular destination for tourists to see the lifestyle and the culture of various tribes that go back several thousands of years without much change. Name some of India's oldest tribes from this region.

Life skills: Many tribal schools are plagued by high dropout rates. Children attend for the first three to four years of primary school only to lapse into illiteracy later. Few who enter continue up to the tenth grade, and among those who do, few manage to finish high school. Therefore, very few are eligible to attend institutions of higher education, where the high rate of attrition continues. What steps can you suggest for improving this dropout rate in tribal schools?

Communication skills: 9 August is celebrated as the International Day of the World's Indigenous Peoples or World Tribal Day. Another important event happened at the All India Congress committee session on 9 August. Can you identify the day?

World Connect

Along the banks of the Maici river in Brazil lives a hunter–gatherer tribe called the Pirahã. These people are known for their survival skill, which is solely to live off the land, rejecting everything that modern civilization could offer. The people speak a unique language that does not appear to use numbers. It does not have a word to express the concept of "one" or any other specific number. They share all their belongings, thereby highlighting the fact that they felt no need to keep track of their belongings. They follow no social hierarchy and have no leaders. They fish for food along the river and build simple huts for shelter. It was not until 2012 that a school, a clinic, electricity and television were installed in the area, without any opposition from the people.

Wind up

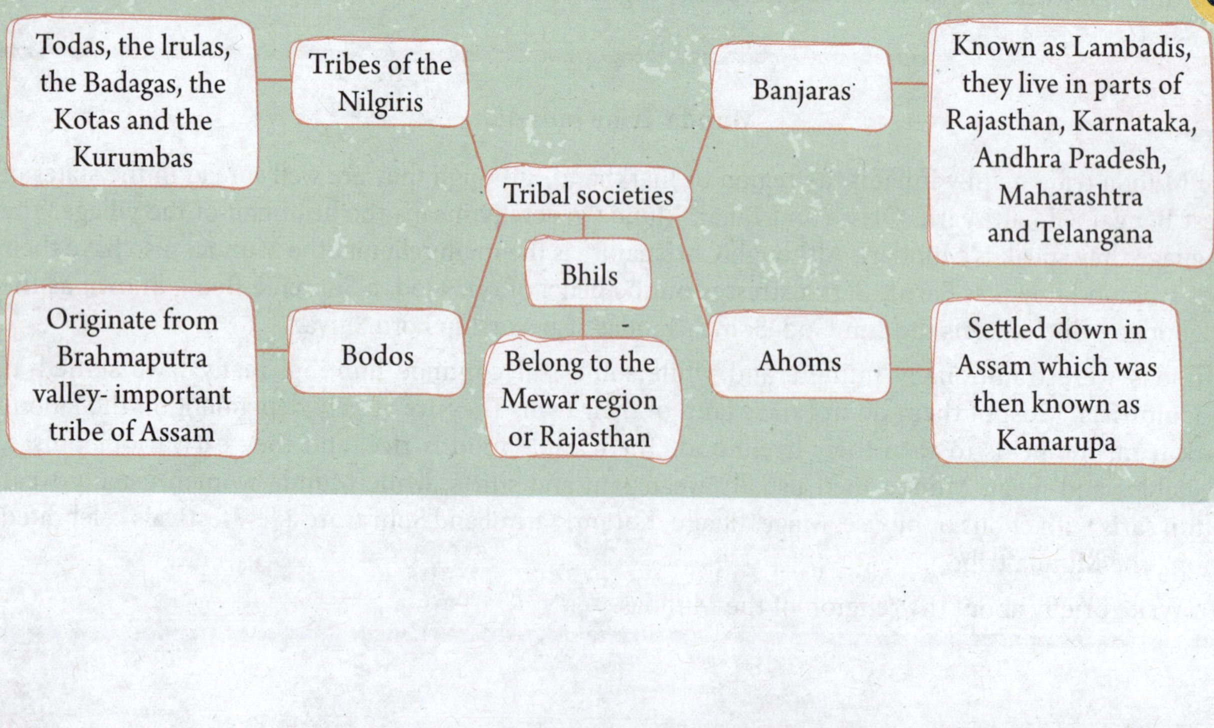

Exercises

A. Choose the correct answers.

1. The Ahoms originally belonged to the
   a. Rajasthan b. Nepal c. Shan tribe d. Nilgiris
2. Which of the following is not a tribal practice by nature?
   a. They live in close community b. They live close to nature
   c. The position of the leader is hereditary c. They live an easy life in the forest
3. Bhil means bow, signifying that by profession the Bhil tribes are
   a. carpenters b. archers c. potters d. blacksmiths
4. The Banjara people are tribes that live in parts of
   a. Rajasthan b. Karnataka c. Andhra Pradesh d. All of them

B. Fill in the blanks.

1. The tribal people also practise .... and ....
2. .... was the first Ahom king who ruled for as long as forty years.
3. The Bhils have a traditional dance form known as ....
4. The Kota tribe mainly inhabit in the region of ....
5. Bodos primarily undertake .... plantation activities.

C. Answer these questions in brief.

1. What is a tribe?
2. Name some Nilgiri tribes.
3. Who are paiks?
4. Mention the parts of India where the Cheros built their forts.
5. Which is the most prominent tribe of Assam?

D. Answer these questions in detail.

1. Write a note on the Banjaras.
2. What are the common characteristics of most tribal communities?
3. Explain the position of the *paiks* in society.
4. Describe the social customs and rituals followed by most tribal people.
5. Write a note on the Ahoms.

Think Big — Integrate with art

This is a warli painting, a form of tribal art, mostly made up of geometric patterns. Make an imitation of this painting in your drawing book.

Learning Tools

Create your own study guides by compiling the necessary information for swift recap

Main ideas	Why it matters	Important terms and names
....	....	....
....	....	....
....	....	....
....	....	....
....	....	....
....	....	....
....	....	....
....	....	....
....	....	....
....	....	....
....	....	....

Web links:

https://www.clearias.com/medieval-india-tribes-nomads-settled-communities/

Last accessed on 31 August 2021

8. Religion and Philosophy in Medieval India

Warm up

Meera always enjoys her mornings at her grandmother's place. Every morning, she would get up and help clean up the house, especially the temple area, pick flowers from the garden; chants would be heard around the house. Daily prayers were a family affair, and Meera relished the prasad distributed at the end of it. She always demanded a larger share for herself. She noticed many gods and goddesses in the marble temple in the house. She asked her grandmother one day, 'Why are there so many gods in the temple'? Her grandmother told her that they bless the home and bring peace. 'Even your name was taken from the mystic saint from the middle ages', said her grandmother. 'Meera Bai was a staunch devotee of Lord Krishna, so we named you Meera after the saintly woman.' Hearing this, Meera felt very proud that her name has a beautiful story.

In the previous chapters, we read about the different cultures that thrived in medieval India. This was mainly due to the many rulers who came to the Indian subcontinent, not only to loot and plunder but also to conquer. Some even came with the objective of developing trade relations, while some came as religious preachers with the aim of spreading their ideas and philosophy.

India, as you have read earlier, was a caste-based society. However, not only were many tribal communities recognized by Brahmins, their deities were also linked to the main gods and goddesses, like Shiva, Vishnu, Parvati and Lakshmi. In a caste-based society, a person's profession and status was decided on the basis of the caste he or she belonged to. People belonging to the lower caste were not allowed to enter the temples or perform religious rituals. Many people felt that this was unjust and were ready to break away from the caste system. These conditions favoured change and India was set to go through a period of transition, yet again.

The rigidity of the caste system made it unpopular and people became followers of Buddhism and Jainism, the main tenets of which were based on equality.

Trade and commerce flourished during this period. This brought in new opportunities for work and people began to change their professions. New ideas and thoughts also came about. The Bhakti and Sufi movements were the most prominent of these.

The Bhakti Movement

The *Bhakti* movement saw its birth between the 7th and 12th centuries, when some religious leaders decided to reinforce the ideas described in the ancient scriptures, with modifications made to certain beliefs and practices. These thinkers stressed on devotion towards god rather than complicated rituals. These saints looked upon religion as a bond between the devotees and god.

Teachings of the Bhakti Saints

The Bhakti saints **postulated** that to reach out to God, one does not need to perform elaborate rituals. They stressed on the importance of having a pure heart and mind. Equality was one of the key concepts of this movement, as it urged equality of all human beings, despite caste, gender or economic background. It was believed that God did not create the differences that divide people into different social and economic groups; hence, real devotion should transcend them all. The Bhakti saints emphasized humanism; qualities like empathy and the willingness to share were highly valued. Some Bhakti saints even preached selfless devotion to a personal deity. Knowledge became an important component of the devotees of Bhakti. One of the most valuable contributions made by the Bhakti saints to India was the dismantling of the barriers that existed within Hinduism.

Apply it! E

What was the advantage of preaching in the local language?

Saints of South India

The Bhakti movement in south India gathered momentum because of the Alwars, who were saints devoted to Lord Vishnu, and the Nayanars who were the devotees of Lord Shiva. Both the Alwars and the Nayanars composed several hymns in praise of their god. The hymns composed by the Alwars were known as *Divyaprabandham*, and those of the Nayanars were known as the Devaram. Some popular religious preachers of this period in south India were Ramanuja and Shankaracharya. Virashaivism became a popular movement.

Ramanuja: He was a Vaishnava saint who believed that Bhakti, or devotion to God, was more important than knowledge. His philosophy is called Visishtadvaita. He believed that one should completely surrender oneself to god. Good deeds would help save the soul of a person. He believed that the soul, the God and the universe are all a part of a particular reality, yet each one of them maintains a certain uniqueness with respect to others.

Ramanuja

Shankaracharya: He was an eighth-century saint of south India. He believed that knowledge was the only way to reach God, and the only way to gain knowledge was to unite with the supreme soul, known as the Brahma. Shankarachraya established the four mathas, namely Badrinath, Puri, Dwarka and Shringeri. These mathas became important centres of pilgrimage. His philosophy is called Advaita.

Virashaivas: This movement began in Karnataka under the leadership of Basava. He was also known as Basavanna. This was a Shaivite movement that rejected the caste system and meaningless rituals. The Virashaivas gave women equal importance as men. Akkamahadevi, who was the daughter of an affluent merchant, was a Virashaiva saint.

Saints of Maharashtra

Maharashtra was famous for a great number of poets like Tukaram, Namdev and Jnaneshwar, who worshipped Lord Vittala, whose temple is at Pandharpur. The devotional songs composed by them were known as *Abhang*, composed in Marathi. They led a family life and rejected unnecessary rituals.

postulated: suggest or assume the existence, fact, or truth of (something) as a basis for reasoning, discussion, or belief

The Nathpanthis, Siddhacharas and Yogis: They stressed on yoga and meditation to attain oneness with God, in order to train the mind and body. They stressed on the **renunciation** of the world and focused on devotional religion instead of conventional religion. People from low castes, like fisherfolk, cobblers, washermen, followed this way of life.

Saints of North India

Tulsidas: He was a great poet and a devotee. He stressed on aspects like knowledge, devotion, worship and meditation and believed that the existing beliefs and practices should be accessible to all.

Surdas: He was a devotee of Krishna. He preached love and devotion to a personal God.

Shankaradeva: Shankaradeva of Assam was a devotee of Vishnu. He set up houses of worship or prayer called *namghars,* which still exist today.

Kabir: He was a well-known poet and saint whose teachings inspired both Hindus and Muslims. His teachings were simple and guided people from all walks of life. He stressed on the belief that there is 'one True God', and different people addressed him in different ways. His teachings aimed at brotherhood and unity amongst people. He rejected discrimination based on caste, religion and economic and social background. *Adi Granth*, the first rendition of the *Guru Granth Sahib*, the holy book of Sikhism, contained Kabir's verses.

What's in the picture?

This is a painting of Kabir. In not more than 100 words, explain what you see in the painting.

Mira Bai: Mira Bai was a queen in Rajasthan, who is known for her devotion towards Lord Krishna. She was born in 1498 CE and was married at the age of 13. From an early age, she showed more interest in religious devotions than towards her worldly responsibilities. It is said that she neglected her marital responsibilities. When queried about it, she said that it was impossible for her to be married to a king when she was already married to Lord Krishna. A major change in her life occurred at the time of the death of her husband. It was customary in those days for a wife to commit sati (burning oneself on the funeral pyre of her husband). She refused to comply, whereupon her in-laws began harassing her. She then left the palace and began wandering throughout Rajasthan, preaching and gaining followers. She dedicated her entire life to Krishna and endured all the entailing difficulties that came with it. Mira is known for her bhajans, sung in praise of Krishna. These bhajans are held in great esteem for their high literary value.

The Sufi Movement and the Teachings of Islam

In the eighth century, Islam was introduced to India by Arab traders. As a religion, it had elaborate rituals and a strict code of conduct. A group of Muslim mystics, called sufis, rejected these practices and seeked to find the truth of divine love and knowledge through direct personal experience of God.

renunciation: the formal rejection of something, typically a belief, claim, or course of action

Teachings of the Sufi Saints

Sufi teachings were based on divine spirituality, cosmic harmony, love and humanity. They believed in helping the poor through the practice of *zakat*. They were deeply spiritual and followed the teachings of the *Quran,* the holy book of the Muslims. Although the Sufi movement was Islamic in philosophy, it was deeply influenced by Hindu, Greek and Buddhist religious ideas and provided solace to many Hindu communities of that period. The Sufis also instilled a new liberal outlook within Islam.

The word 'sufi' originated from the word *suf*, meaning 'wool'. Their followers would wear rough clothes, led simple lives and were against any kind of extravagant life. They insisted on self-discipline, and like the Bhakti saints, believed that love and devotion were the only ways to reach god. The Sufis lived in *khanqahs*, where people gathered to sing songs, seek advice and receive spiritual guidance.

The Sufi teacher was known as the *pir* and under his guidance, a disciple would be trained in practices like *zikr*, which was the name chanting, and *sama*, which was a form of devotional music. The Sufi saints were organized into religious orders, which were known as *silsilahs*.

The *qawwalis* sung by the Sufi saints became very popular. The grave of a *pir* is known as a *dargah*. There were fourteen *silsilahs*. The most prominent of them were the Chishti, Suhrawardi, Firdawsi, Qadiri and Naqshbandi *silsilahs*.

The Chishti Silsilah

Some of the most well-known Sufi saints include Khwaja Muinuddin Chisti, Qutbuddin Baktiyar Kaki, Baba Farid and Shaikh Nizamuddin Auliya.

Khwaja Muinuddin Chishti: He was a Sufi saint who came to India in around 1192 and founded the Chishti silsilah. He believed that serving mankind was the noblest form of devotion. Due to this belief, he worked towards uplifting the oppressed and poverty-stricken population. Ajmer was the main centre for his teachings. Qutubuddin Bakhtiyar Kaki was one of his most devoted disciples and his spiritual successor as the head of the Chishti order.

Qutubuddin Bakhtiyar Kaki: He was a Muslim Sufi, saint and scholar of the Chishti order. It was during his time that the Chishti order was firmly established in Delhi. Like his predecessor, Qutubuddin Bakhtiyar Kaki continued to develop the traditional ideas of brotherhood and charity within the order. Till today, his khanqah continues to be visited from people from all walks of life.

Baba Farid: He was a Sufi saint who wrote many verses propagating Sufism and the Chishti order. Some of his poems have been quoted in the *Adi Granth*. His verses brought solace to both the Hindu and Muslim communities.

Shaikh Nizamuddin Auliya: He was Baba Farid's most famous disciple. During his tenure as the leader of the Chishti silsilah, he made Delhi an important centre, from which his teachings could be heard. He carried on the tradition of charity of the Chishti order and worked towards the welfare of the poor and downtrodden.

Major differences between the Sufis and Orthodox Muslims

Sufis	Orthodox Muslims
Sufis highlighted inner purity.	They focused on the external conduct in the society along with other laws.
They consider love and devotion to be the only means of attaining salvation.	They believed in the observance of rituals which they thought would help individuals transform.

Sikhism

Guru Nanak

Sikhism is a very popular religion that originated in the Punjab region during the 15th century. It is now the world's ninth-largest religion. However, like all other religions, it had its humble beginnings. It is based on the teachings of Guru Nanak and the ten Sikh Gurus who followed him. The devotees of Guru Nanak spread his messages and those of his successors and met at *dharamshalas*. These *dharamshalas* later became gurdwaras. The gurdwara also has a community kitchen, known as *langar,* where free meals are provided to all, irrespective of their caste or class. *Kirtan* and group singing were a part of Sikhism. It was the tenth guru, Govind Singh, who founded the Khalsa Panth.

The Teachings of Guru Nanak

Guru Nanak stressed on the belief of one god and emphasized that a person's character and conduct should be clean and pure. He rejected the caste system and emphasized the need of a guru for guidance. Guru Nanak advocated the ***nirguna*** way of worship, and his teachings became popular amongst the farmers, artisans and craftsmen. Guru Nanak preached that his followers should be householders and should be engaged in useful occupation to earn their living through hard work.

Principles of Sikhism

Sikhism is based on three principles: *Naam Japo*, which means meditating in the name of god, *Kirt Karo*, which means to earn a living through hard work and honest means, and *Vand Chhako*, which means to help the needy by sharing one's earning. The fundamental beliefs of the Sikhs include faith, meditation, unity, equality and honesty.

Case Study

Women Saints of India

Periyalvar was an Alwar saint from South India. The Alwars were ardent devotees of Vishnu and every day, Periyalvar would make a garland for Lord Vishnu. Once, in the temple premises, he found a baby girl below a Tulsi plant. He named her Andal, and under his guidance, the child soon became a devotee of Lord Krishna, an incarnation of Vishnu. Every day, she would offer the garland worn by her to Lord Krishna. One day, when her father noticed this, he got very angry and admonished her. However, Lord Krishna appeared in her father's dream and told him to only offer the garlands worn by Andal during prayer. Andal is said to have composed great works like Thiruppavai and Nachiyar Thirumozhi.

nirguna: worship of the divine as formless

Skill Builder

Critical thinking skills: Langar was started in 1481, when Guru Nanak Dev decided to commit himself to feed everyone. The temple serves a hot meal to everyone who comes to the door, irrespective of their religion and faith. Describe any other religious practice of the Sikhs.

Life skills: The teachings of the Bhakti saints had a profound influence on the society. It challenged the caste system and the treatment of people from lower castes. How were the Brahmins affected by this movement?

Communication skill: Kabir was a mystic poet, a musician, an important saint of Hinduism and was considered as a Sufi by Muslims. He was never formally educated and was almost completely illiterate. Can you recollect a popular doha written by him? Recite it in class.

World Connect

All Saints' Day is a day commemorating all the saints in Christianity. It is celebrated on 1 November in Western churches, whereas the Eastern churches celebrate it on the first Sunday after Pentecost. People commemorate this day with the belief that there is a connection between those in heaven and those on Earth. People give thanks to God for the lives and deaths of saints. It is a national holiday in various Catholic countries and people are required to attend the Mass on this day.

Wind up

Religion and philosophy

- **Bhakti movement**
  - Criticized elaborate rituals
  - Stressed on having a pure heart and mind
  - Focused on equality, humanism, empathy, sharing, selfless devotion to a personal deity
  - Dismantled the barriers of Hinduism

  Communities: Alwars, Nayanars, Nathpanthis, Siddhacharas, Yogis
  Saints: Ramanuja, Meera Bai, Shankaracharya, Virashaivas, Tukaram, Namdev, Jnaneshwar, Tulsidas, Surdas, Shankaradev, Kabir

- **Sufi movement**
  - Sufism was an offshoot of Islam
  - Did not believe in elaborate rituals and the strict code of conduct of Islam
  - Encouraged simple living and helping the poor

  Saints: Muinuddin Chishti, Qutubuddin Bakhtiyar Kaki, Shaikh Nizanuddin Auliya, Baba Farid

- **Sikhism**
  - Guru Nanak - Founder of Sikhism
  - Believer of the Bhakti movement
  - Wanted to bridge the gap between the Hindus and the Muslims
  - Rejected social classes, elaborate rituals and ceremonies
  - Believed in universal brotherhood and serving the poor

  Naam Japo, Kirt Karo, Vand Chhako

Exercises

A. Choose the correct answers.

1. The word 'sufi' originated from the word suf, which means ________.
   a. cotton b. skin c. wool d. jute
2. He believed that knowledge was the only way to reach God.
   a. Shankaracharya b. Alvars c. Tulsidas d. Surdas
3. The Sufi teacher was known as the
   a. pir b. saint c. guru d. none of these
4. Kabir's verses can be found in the book.
   a. *Guru Granth Sahib* b. *Sursagar* c. *Quran* d. *Kabir Bijak*
5. The practice of having a common kitchen which was started by Guru Nanak and known as
   a. karkhanas b. ibadat khana c. khanquahs d. langar

B. Fill in the blanks.

1. The Bhakti movement was started by the Alwars, who were .... saints and the Nayanars, who were .... saints.
2. Surdas was a devotee of ....
3. The fundamental beliefs of the Sikhs include faith, meditation, unity .... and ....
4. .... was famous for a great number of poets, like Tukaram, Namdev and Jnaneshwar.
5. The only woman Alwar saint of India was ....

C. Answer these questions in brief.

1. Explain the term 'bhakti'.
2. Who was Ramanuja?
3. Name any three Bhakti saints of the medieval period.
4. What is a dargah?
5. Where did the Sufi saints live?

D. Answer these questions in detail.

1. Draw a comparison between the main principles of the Bhakti and the Sufi movements.
2. What were the basic principles that all the Bhakti saints emphasized?
3. Sikhism is a very practical religion. Explain this.
4. Explain the teachings of Guru Nanak.
5. Who were the Nathpanthis, Siddhacharas and Yogis? What did they stress upon?

E. Read the passage and answer the questions.

Guru Nanak stressed on the belief of one god and emphasized that a person's character and conduct should be clean and pure. He rejected the caste system and emphasized the need of a guru for guidance. Guru Nanak advocated the nirguna way of worship, and his teachings became popular amongst the farmers, artisans and craftsmen. Guru Nanak preached that his followers should be householders and should be engaged in useful occupation to earn their living through hard work.

1. In your own words, explain the teachings of Guru Nanak.
2. What was Guru Nanak's stance on the caste system?

Think Big

Integrate with music

MS Subbulakshmi, a very famous Carnatic musician, played the role of Meera in a historical fiction made in 1945. Find out about the movie and listen to the popular bhajans sung by her.

Learning Tools

Create your own study guides by compiling the necessary information for swift recap:

Bhakti movement	Similarities	Sufi movement
Important facts	....	Important facts
	....	
	....	
	....	
	....	
	....	
	....	
	....	
	....	

Sikhism	
Important facts	Questions I have ...

Web links:

https://www.historydiscussion.net/history-of-india/sufi-and-bhakti-movement-in-india/3052

Last accessed on 31 August 2021

9. The Arrival of Regional Cultures

Warm up

Sanskrit has captured the imagination of the world. Former Indian President APJ Abdul Kalam visited Greece in April 2007. It was a pleasant surprise for him when his Greek counterpart Karolos Papoulias greeted him in Sanskrit at the banquet ceremony hosted in honour of the visiting dignitary. 'Rashtrapatm Mahabhaga, Sur Swagatam Yavana dishe (President, welcome to you)', thus began the Greek President his speech at the banquet hosted at the Presidential palace, much to the delight of the Indian delegation. Papoulias had studied Sanskrit in Germany and the reason why he studied the Indian classical language was to understand India better. 'I wanted to welcome you in Sanskrit, the ancient Indian language that is related to ancient Greek, and which I had the opportunity to learn and love during my time as a student in Germany,' the Greek President said.

India is known for its diverse languages, festivals, music, dance, customs and traditions, all of which have shaped its rich culture.

Malayalam Literature

In the 9th century, the Cheras established their kingdom in Mahodayapuram, located in the present-day state of Kerala. They decided to make Malayalam their official language. This was the first time that a regional language was used in official documents. It is well-known that the language of the West Coast, Kodum Tamil, grew and developed into Malayalam. There are references about this language in the *Ramayana*, *Bharatam*, *Harivamsam* and several other books. This language was greatly influenced by Sanskrit. Another text, named *Lilatilakam*, which deals with grammar and poetics, also refers to both Malayalam and Sanskrit and calls them 'diamonds and corals'. Many sources like inscriptions, place names, literary style and literary works, folk songs, riddles, proverbs and coins help in understanding the history of the language. This helps us understand how languages change and evolve over hundreds of years.

The Religious Traditions of Odisha

Lord Shiva was a very popular god in Orissa and was worshipped till the Ganga dynasty came to power. During the 11th century, Anantavarman became a very important ruler. He built many Vishnu temples and in the 12th century, Anantavarman began building a temple for Lord Jagannath (Lord of the World) at Puri. Anagabhima completed the temple and proclaimed himself as the subordinate of Lord Jagannath.

FACT CHECK

The Rath Yatra festival is celebrated every year in the month of June or July.

To date, the local tribal people make the wooden deity, which suggests that the deity was originally a local god, who was later identified with Vishnu. In the Jagannath temple, his brother Balaram and sister Subhadra are worshipped too. Every twelve years, new idols of the deities are made.

Development of Language

Delhi Sultanate: Apart from Braj and Awadhi, regional languages like Punjabi, Odia, and Assamese also developed. The Bhakti saints encouraged the use of regional languages. Persian became the language of the administration during the medieval period. The fusion of Hindi and Persian gave rise to a new language called Urdu, which means 'camp'. This new language originated in the camps of the soldiers and was understood by all. Many literary works came up during this period and a lot of them were translated.

Mughal Period: Since Persian was the language of the court, all records were written in Persian. Urdu was used in many literary works and poetry. It is believed that Akbar got the *Ramayana* and the *Mahabharata* translated to Persian. Writers and poets were encouraged and patronized, leading to progressive growth in the field of literature.

Dance

A classical dance form associated with north India is Kathak. Kathak originated from the tradition of storytelling. The kathakars were a community of storytellers. The stories enacted by them were mostly mythological. They picked up themes from the *Ramayana*, the *Mahabharata*, the *Puranas* and other ancient stories. The most popular theme enacted by the Kathak dancers was the Rasa Leela, which were stories about Radha-Krishna. These dances combined folk culture with the basic movements and gestures of Kathak. It was performed in the temples.

Kathak

The Kathak dance form underwent a major transformation when it reached the Mughal courts. It has now developed a distinctive style. Further, it developed into two *gharanas*, namely the Jaipur and Lucknow gharanas. Wajid Ali Shah, the Nawab of Awadh, patronized this dance form. A great deal of importance was laid on intricate foot work, facial expressions, gestures and elaborate costumes. This dance slowly reached other regions like Haryana, Jammu and Kashmir, Bihar and Madhya Pradesh. It was of course viewed unfavourably by British administrators. After independence, it was recognized as one of the six classical dance forms of India.

What's in the picture?

Study the painting and create a story based on it.

Painting

During the medieval period, 'miniatures' became very popular. Many rulers and wealthy people were instrumental in promoting these paintings. These paintings were made on materials like paper, cloth, wood, leather and even ivory. Natural paints, like vegetable dyes, were used, and gold and silver paints were added too. These paintings depicted scenes from the royal courts, portraits, wildlife and hunting and battle scenes. Akbar had special places or workshops for making these paintings. These were known as *karkhanas*. Here, painters belonging to different places would work together.

The Mughal style of painting influenced the regional styles. Examples of such paintings can be seen in the region of Rajasthan, where court scenes, festivals, hunting scenes and portraits have been illustrated. This was because after the decline of the Mughal Empire, Mughal court painters moved to other regions and influenced their style of painting. There were three main centres of art—Mewar, Bundi and Kishangarh. Miniature paintings were adopted in the region of Himachal Pradesh. They were pronounced and intense and developed in the Kangra region. They were called *basholi*. The most popular subject to be painted in this region was Bhanudatta's *Rasmanjari*. Shah Jahan also appreciated paintings. Painters were richly rewarded, and paintings were widely exchanged as royal gifts.

Green Earth

The paintings produced at the time of Akbar and Jahangir give numerous examples of figures of animals and birds in different actions, and these paintings have a strong sympathy towards naturalistic representation. Pictures of elephants and horses in different poses were very common in the paintings from the Mughal period.

Music

Music and dance were very popular with the medieval rulers. Both the Rajputs and the Cholas encouraged them. Dances were performed in temples. Temple panels during this time projected music and dance performance. Music became very popular and musicians were richly rewarded for their performance. Classical music based on the *ragas* became very popular. In the north, classical music was known as Hindustani music, and in south India, it was called Carnatic music.

Developments in Bengal

Bengal came under the influence of the Sanskrit culture only after it was conquered by the Mauryas. It was very different before this. When commercial ties developed between Bengal and Magadha, Sanskrit started influencing the language spoken by the people of Bengal. During the reign of the Mauryas, Bengal was influenced by Buddhism too. Bengal was under the rule of Magadha till the reign of the Guptas. The Palas showed a lot of appreciation for language and literature. Therefore, languages like Bengali, Odia and Assamese developed. Some Sanskrit *prashastis* of the Pala kings have been found. When the spirit of Bhakti became popular, Krishna worship spread throughout Bengal and was reflected in their literature. The Vaishnavite teachers of Bengal preached in the regional language. The influence of Chaitanya Deva of Bengal spread over this region. Several literary works have been written about this saint. Krishnadas Kaviraj wrote a biography of Chaitanya, called the *Chaitanya Charitamrita*. Epics like the *Ramayana* and *Mahabharata* were translated from Sanskrit into Bengali.

Architecture and occupation: The temple architecture of Bengal is very unique. It reflects a tribal style and shows the influence of tribal traditions. The deities were worshipped in *chala* (thatched) shrines. Later on, the temples had a sloping roof, made of two pieces of thatch, known as *dochala*, or *chauchala*, a roof made of four pieces of thatch. Some of the temples have beautiful terracotta bricks and panels on the walls. Many areas around Bengal are delta regions. Therefore, fishing was not only an important occupation, but it was also an important part of the diet of Bengal. Fish was considered auspicious and used in important rituals, like marriages. Fish was depicted even in art forms, like paintings and sculptures. The *Brihad Dharma Purana* in Sanskrit, which is written in the Bengali script, mentions a rule that allows Brahmins to eat only certain types of fish.

Rajput Traditions

The Rajputs were known for their bravery. They belonged to the Kshatriya caste and became very important in the north–west region of India. Stories about the Rajputs always revolve around qualities like loyalty, chivalry, friendship and love. They fought to protect the women and to guard their honour. They opted for death in the battlefield rather than escaping the challenges of war. The women committed *jauhar* (suicide) when faced with defeat in the hands of the enemies.

Skill Builder

21ST CENTURY SKILLS

Critical thinking skills: What do you think would be the impact if rulers did not appreciate different kinds of art, like music, dance and painting?

Life skills: You have visited an art gallery and found a very fascinating painting. Study that painting and create a story based on it.

Information literacy: Form groups and find out about these artists and their work.

- Leonardo da Vinci
- Michelangelo
- Raphael
- Raja Ravi Verma

World Connect

Europe's Search for Stability

In the 16th century, Europe witnessed one of the greatest revolutions, known as the Reformation. This religious, political and cultural upheaval separated the European Christians into two segments - Protestants and Catholics. The Reformation ushered in the Modern Age in Europe. Once religious unity was destroyed, people began to think in terms of their own regional interests. With the diversity of interests arose new political, social and economic beliefs. Reformers like Martin Luther of Germany and John Calvin challenged the Catholic church's Papal authority. Historians usually date the beginning of the Reformation with the publication of Martin Luther's *The Ninety-five Theses* in 1517. The key ideas of the Reformation—a call to purify the church and a belief that the Bible, not tradition, should be the sole source of spiritual authority—were not novel. However, Luther and the other reformers became the first to skilfully use the power of the printing press to give their ideas a wide audience. The printing press was invented in the 15th century and soon became popular in Europe. By the time the Reformation took place in 1517, there were printing centres in more than 200 European cities.

Wind up

- The Malayalam language was influenced by Sanskrit.
- The famous Jagannath Temple was built by Anatavarman.
- The classical dance form of Kathak originated from the art of ancient story tellers called Kathakars
- The Rajputs were known for their loyalty and heroism .
- Different styles of miniature painting developed in different regions.
- Bengal was influenced by Sanskrit culture.

Exercises

A. Choose the correct answers.

1. The Malayalam language was influenced by
   a. Tamil　b. Marathi　c. Sanskrit　d. Telugu
2. Carnatic music was associated with
   a. south India　b. north India　c. central India　d. western India
3. Kathak originated from the tradition of
   a. storytelling　b. hunting　c. farming　d. puppetry
4. Miniature paintings were made on materials like
   a. paper　b. cloth　c. ivory　d. all of these
5. It was considered auspicious and depicted in art forms, like paintings and sculptures in Bengal.
   a. parrot　b. elephant　c. fish　d. bird

B. Fill in the blanks.

1. In the north, classical music was known as .... music.
2. Miniature paintings that developed in the Kangra region were known as ....
3. An example of an art centre in Rajasthan was .... in the medieval period.
4. Akbar got the *Ramayana* and the *Mahabharata* translated to ....

C. Answer these questions in brief.

1. Who wrote the *Chaitanya Charitamrita*?
2. In which form were the stories enacted by the Kathak ali?
3. Whom do the idols at the Jagannath temple represent, and what are these idols made of?
4. During the reign of the Mauryas, Bengal was influenced by which religion?

D. Answer these questions in detail.

1. Discuss the developments in music during the medieval period.
2. What changes did Kathak undergo during the medieval period?
3. Write a note on medieval Bengali architecture in your own words.
4. Give a description of the religious traditions of Odisha.

Think Big

Integrate with art

Let us learn how to study a work of art.

Describe it: Notice the kind of things you see in the painting. Does it tell a story? Imagine describing the painting to someone who cannot see it.

Relate to it: Think of what the painting reminds you of and how it is different from real life.

Analyze it: Identify whether the painting is realistic, abstract, impressionism, etc. Analyze what the most important part of the painting is.

Interpret it: Draw up reasons why you think the artist made this painting, and what could have been his or her inspiration.

Now, in your own words, study the painting on the right and describe it.

Learning Tools

Summarising information

Complete a chart like the one below describing the cultural heritage of India.

	Names	Features
Literature and language		
Dance		
Painting		
Music		

Web links:

https://www.toppr.com/guides/history/making-regional-cultures/regional-cultures/

Last accessed on 31 August 2021

10. The Decline of the Mughal Empire

Warm up

Ruling Indian subcontinent was a difficult task in medieval period. The Mughals came closest to ruling this vast territory that makes up today's India for nearly 300 years, a feat which seemed impossible for that period. The empire was ruled by several emperors; some of them were weak and inefficient, but the six mighty Mughals — Babur, Humayun, Akbar, Jahangir, Shah Jahan and Aurangzeb — left lasting legacies.

The decline of the Mughal Empire led to many developments. Mughal rule, which began with Babur, saw immense disturbances during Aurangzeb's reign. His long-drawn war in the Deccan and his absence from his capital gave ambitious nobles and officials an opportunity to amass power. Thus, many independent kingdoms emerged during this time.

Causes of the Decline of the Mughal Empire

- **No law of succession:** In the Mughal tradition of succession, the inheritance was divided amongst all the sons. However, in many instances of Mughal rule, one of the sons revolted against his father to gain complete control over the empire or would wage war against his brothers after the death of his father. This weakened the Mughal Empire, especially after Aurangzeb, and increased the power of the nobles as they sided with one contender, and then the next.
- **Aurangzeb's policies:** Aurangzeb gave little consideration for the willing support of the people and lost the support of the Rajputs, the Sikhs, the Marathas and the Jats through his policies, turning them into bitter foes. Aurangzeb's long wars in the south depleted the treasury.
- **The later Mughals:** The later Mughals ruled for about 150 years. The most prominent amongst them were Bahadur Shah I (1707–12), Farrukhsiyar (1713–19) and Muhammad Shah (1719–48). These rulers were neither competent nor efficient, which led to a quick change of rulers, depletion of revenue and corrupt revenue collectors, who took advantage of the chaotic situation, resulting in the weakening of the economic and political situation, paving way for foreign invasion and peasant revolts.
- **Nadir Shah's invasions:** Nadir Shah of Persia invaded India in 1739 and at this time, his invasion proved costly for the Mughals. He defeated the Mughal ruler Muhammad Shah at the battle of Karnal in 1739, captured Delhi and plundered the city, taking all its wealth. He returned to Persia with so much wealth that the Persian citizens were exempted from paying their taxes for three years.

Nadir Shah

- **Challenge from regional powers:** Many independent states arose out of the constant turmoils, and the vast Mughal Empire had become too vast to be properly administered. Inefficient, weak rulers and their policies led to this. Let us learn more about this period.

Emergence of Independent States

When the political scenario changed, many independent states, once a part of the Mughal Empire, emerged. Rajput states, like Amber and Jodhpur, which were *watan jagirs* under the Mughals, now worked as independent states. There were other groups like the Jats, the Marathas and the Sikhs, who revolted against the Mughals and attained independence.

What's in the picture?

1. Which is this famous jewelled throne?
2. Who was the original owner of the throne?
3. What were the special features of the throne?

Bengal

Murshid Quli Khan was the diwan during Aurangzeb's time. As Murshid Quli Khan was very competent, he also served as the deputy governor of Bengal and the governor of Orissa (present-day Odisha). He realized the absence of a strong central authority at an early stage and took advantage of this situation to rule independently. He brought a lot of improvement to the state of Bengal, as he took some stern steps by transferring the Mughal jagirdars to Orissa. He surveyed all the cultivatable land, took an assessment of it and fixed new rates of revenue. Revenue collectors were appointed to collect revenue and make payments on time to the state. These revenue collectors were appointed contractually. These people later became zamindars or landlords. This gave rise to a new group of politically influential people—the rich class of bankers and moneylenders. The most prominent amongst the moneylenders was the banking house of Fateh Chand, also popularly known as Jagath Seth. This group eventually became very powerful and prosperous.

FACT CHECK

Under Murshid Quli Khan, inland and maritime trade became prosperous, and there was active trade of silk textiles.

Awadh

Awadh was located in modern-day Uttar Pradesh. It was situated at a very strategic location. It had fertile land and an important trade route that linked Bengal and north-western India. It had the advantage of being close to Delhi, from where all the administrative affairs of the Mughals took place. In 1722, Saadat Khan was appointed as the Governor of Awadh by Muhammad Shah. During this period, some local chiefs were becoming powerful and Saadat Khan was appointed and given the duty of suppressing these revolts.

He strengthened the region by carrying out reforms in the revenue system. He also held the joint offices of the *subedar* (political), the *faugdar* (military) and the *diwan* (revenue). He promoted trade and developed the region economically. He gave the right of revenue collection to the jagirdars (revenue farmers). Strict deadlines regarding revenue payments forced both the cultivators and the revenue farmers to take loans from bankers and moneylenders. However, he was successful in suppressing the oppressive zamindars and protecting the peasants.

Hyderabad

During the rule of Farrukhsiyar and Muhammad Shah, a loyal noble, Chin Qilich Khan, was given the title of Nizam-ul-Mulk for his loyalty and appointed as the governor of the Deccan. He is regarded as the founder of the independent state of Hyderabad. He ruled without any interference from the Mughals and made decisions about the allocation of jagirs to his faithful officials. He was in conflict with the Telugu chiefs (*nayakas*) and the Marathas. He tried to control the prosperous trade of the Carnatic region. When the governors died, the Nizam took control of that region as well. The death of the Nizam in 1748 led to the war for succession in Hyderabad and the Carnatic region.

The Sikhs

The Sikhs organized themselves under Guru Gobind Singh. After his death, the leadership passed in to the hands of his able disciple, Banda Bahadur, and the Sikhs became a very powerful group under him, fighting the Mughal authority. Unfortunately, he, too, was put to death during the time of Farrukhsiyar. However, Banda Bahadur's death did not dampen the spirit of the Sikh community. They organized themselves into small groups known as *misls*, or bands. They held regular meetings and during Baisakhi, met at Amritsar. The misls were under the Dal Khalsa. The decisions of the Dal Khalsa were known as *gurmat*. Maharaja Ranjit Singh united the Sikhs residing in the west and established the independent state of Punjab. Apart from this, he also conquered Kashmir, Peshawar and Multan.

Guru Gobind Singh

The Rajput States

The Rajput rulers had enjoyed a lot of freedom as *watan jagirs* and they became stronger under the later Mughals. They became so independent that they established their own states and occupied high posts. Examples of such rulers were Maharaja Ajit Singh of Jodhpur, who became the governor of Ajmer and Gujarat, and Maharaja Jai Singh, who became the governor of Malwa and Agra. Raja Jai Singh was also known as Sawai Raja Singh, and he founded the city of Jaipur.

The Maratha Army

Shivaji took the support of the kunbis, peasant pastoralists, to meet the challenges of the Mughals. The Chitpavan Brahmins also served Shivaji as Peshwas or prime ministers. The Maratha army was very well-organized and they raided cities and positioned their army at strategic areas where they felt the supply lines and reinforcements could easily be disrupted. Under the Marathas, trade was encouraged, and many industries, like the brass work industry in Kalyan, the silk, cotton and brocade industry of Aurangabad, the textile industry of Chanderi and Burhanpur and the perfume industry of Pune, flourished. Eventually, the Maratha Empire declined due to the rivalries and conflicts amongst various Maratha chiefs together with a lack of a central authority.

The Jats

In the regions around Delhi, Agra and Mathura, there were a group of farmers known as the Jats. They revolted against the Mughals as they were troubled by the strict revenue collectors. Later, during the 17th century, the state of Bharatpur was established, led by Churaman and Badan Singh. Suraj Mal (1756–63) was the greatest ruler of the Jat community. He built new forts during his rule, like the Deeg Fort. It was under the leadership of Suraj Mal that the Jats targeted Ahmed Shah Abdali.

Case Study

The Marathas

When there is a reference to the Marathas, the first name that comes to one's mind is Shivaji. Shivaji was born in 1627 at Poona. He was the son of Shahaji Bhonsle, who was a chief at the court of Bijapur, and his mother was Jijabai. Shivaji was highly influenced by his mother. He had to meet a lot of challenges, both from the Sultan of Bijapur and the Mughal ruler, Aurangzeb. He finally emerged victorious over both and laid the foundation for a strong Maratha empire, which included Poona, Satara, Nasik and Kohlapur. In 1674, he was crowned as the Chhatrapati, and his capital became Raigad. Shivaji was not only brave but also a master in the art of guerrilla warfare.

Q. Who was Shivaji?

Skill Builder

21ST CENTURY SKILLS

Critical thinking skills: The last Mughal Emperor, Bahadur Shah II, supported the Indian Rebellion of 1857, and as a result, was imprisoned by the British and exiled to Burma. Was this the main reason for the collapse of the Mughal empire?

Life skills: If Aurangzeb had powerful successors, do you think our history would have been different? Give reasons for your answer.

Communication skills: Have a class discussion about which ruler was the best. List each of their qualities and note down which of these are important for a ruler to possess.

World Connect

The Decline of the Ottoman Empire

The Ottoman Empire of Turkey was at its peak during the reign of King Suleiman I. As Suleiman was tired of the lengthy battles and administrative duties, he gave powers to his Prime Minister to run the kingdom on his behalf. This resulted in the weakening of the central command over the Empire. The absence of a clear policy of succession, weak successors and the emergence of strong, centralized monarchies in western Europe, were some factors that led to the decline of the Ottomans in Turkey.

Wind up

- Decline of the Mughal Empire
  - Weak Successors
    - Bahadur Shah I, Farrukhsiyar and Muhammad Shah were the most prominent
  - Nadir Shah's invasion
    - He defeated the Mughal ruler Muhammad Shah at the battle of Karnal, captured Delhi and plundered the city
  - Emergence of independent states
    - The Rajput states
    - Bengal under Murshid Quli Khan
    - The Marathas under Shivaji
    - Awadh under Saadat Khan
    - Hyderabad under Chin Qilich Khan
    - The Sikhs under Guru Gobind Singh
    - The Jats led by Churaman and Badan Singh

Exercises

A. Choose the correct answers.

1. The Jats were farmers in the regions of
   a. Delhi b. Agra c. Mathura d. All of these
2. Under the Marathas, trade was encouraged, and many industries like this developed in Aurangabad.
   a. Cotton industry b. Iron industry c. Steel industry d. All of these
3. Shivaji was born in
   a. Hyderabad b. Poona c. Aurangabad d. West Bengal
4. He was not a Mughal ruler.
   a. Bahadur Shah I b. Nadir Shah c. Farrukhsiyar d. Aurangzeb
5. He united the Sikhs residing in the west and established the independent state of Punjab.
   a. Guru Gobind Singh b. Banda Bahadur c. Ranjit Singh d. Badan Singh

B. Fill in the blanks.

1: .... death marked the end of an era in Indian history.
2. In 1674, Shivaji was crowned as the Chhatrapati, and his capital became ....
3. Chin Qilich Khan was given the title of .... for his loyalty.
4. .... was a Mughal ruler who ruled from 1719 to 1748.
5. The state established by the Jats was called ....

C. Answer these questions in brief.

1. What went wrong with the policies of Aurungzeb?
2. Mention the types of industries developed under the Marathas.
3. Name the leader who took on the leadership after Guru Gobind Singh's death.
4. State the importance of the Dal Khalsa.
5. Who was the founder of the independent state of Hyderabad?

D. Answer these questions in detail.

1. How did Murshid Quli Khan improve the revenue system of Bengal?
2. What was the result of the loyalty shown by Chin Qilich Khan?
3. Discuss the importance of bankers and moneylenders during the medieval period.
4. How did Saadat Khan carry out reforms in the revenue system?
5. State the developments in the Deccan under the Marathas.

E. Read the passage and answer the questions.

When the political scenario changed, many independent states, once a part of the Mughal Empire, emerged. Rajput states, like Amber and Jodhpur, which were watan jagirs under the Mughals, now worked as independent states. There were other groups like the Jats, the Marathas and the Sikhs, who revolted against the Mughals and attained independence.

1. Which states emerged as independent states after the fall of the Mughals?
2. Which groups revolted against the Mughals and formed independent states?

Think Big

Integrate with language

You have read stories about the brave Rajputs, Sikhs and Marathas. Which story was your favourite? Rewrite the story in your own words and read it to your friends.

Learning Tools

Create your own study guides by compiling the necessary information for swift recap:

Main ideas	Why it matters	Important terms and names
....	....	....
....	....	....
....	....	....
....	....	....
....	....	....
....	....	....
....	....	....
....	....	....
....	....	....
....	....	....
....	....	

Web links:

https://www.historydiscussion.net/history-of-india/decline-of-the-mughal-empire-in-india/1529

https://www.clearias.com/india-in-1750/

Last accessed on 31 August 2021

1. The Environment

Warm up

Do you think that planet Earth was always blue since its formation? Do you think it supported soil and life at the beginning? No! The land we inhabit today, the air we breathe, the water we drink, etc. have all been formed through a number of complex processes over billions of years. The air in the earlier years of the planet's formation contained no oxygen but hydrogen and helium. The oceans were formed billions of years ago. With the living organisms performing photosynthesis, the earth and its environment changed further. Let us learn more about the environment we live in.

Everything that we see around us makes up the environment. The term environment refers to all the external conditions in which organisms live. It is derived from the French word *environer*, which means 'to surround'.

On the basis of its origin, an environment can be classified into two types—natural environment and human-made environment.

Natural Environment

The natural environment consists of land, water, air, plants and animals. It has two components—abiotic and biotic. The abiotic environment comprises non-living elements that are a part of the lithosphere, atmosphere and hydrosphere. Water, air, soil, sunlight and minerals are some examples of abiotic components. The biotic environment comprises living organisms. These are a part of the biosphere. Animals, birds, plants and fungi are some examples of biotic components.

Natural environment

What's in the picture?

What elements of the environment can be identified in the picture?

Lithosphere: Realm of the Earth's Surface

The rigid, rocky upper layer of the Earth is called the lithosphere. It consists of the crust and the rigid upper layer of the mantle. The average thickness of the lithosphere is about 100 km. The uppermost part of the lithosphere forms a thin layer of soil. The soil is capable of supporting life on the Earth. The lithosphere consists of mountains, plateaus, plains and valleys, both on the landmasses and the ocean floor. It is an important source of minerals. It provides land for building houses, roads, factories and for agriculture.

Hydrosphere: Realm of Water

When seen from space, the Earth looks blue. This is because two-third of it is covered with water. There are different sources of water on Earth. Much of the water on Earth is salty and found in seas and oceans. Freshwater constitutes only about one per cent of the total water on Earth. Its sources include rivers, lakes, ponds, backwaters, natural springs and underground water.

Water is vital for all organisms. It dissolves and transports nutrients. It is used by plants for making food. Water is also necessary for carrying out the chemical reactions within the body of living organisms.

Atmosphere: Realm of Air

The Earth is enveloped by a thin blanket of gases known as the atmosphere. It also consists of water vapour and dust particles. The atmosphere maintains a constant temperature on the Earth, thereby making it **habitable**. The ozone layer, which is a part of the atmosphere, protects living organisms from the harmful ultraviolet rays of the Sun. The gases present in the air support life. Oxygen helps in respiration, carbon dioxide helps green plants to prepare food through photosynthesis and nitrogen helps in the growth of both plants and animals. The atmosphere is held to Earth by the force of **gravity**.

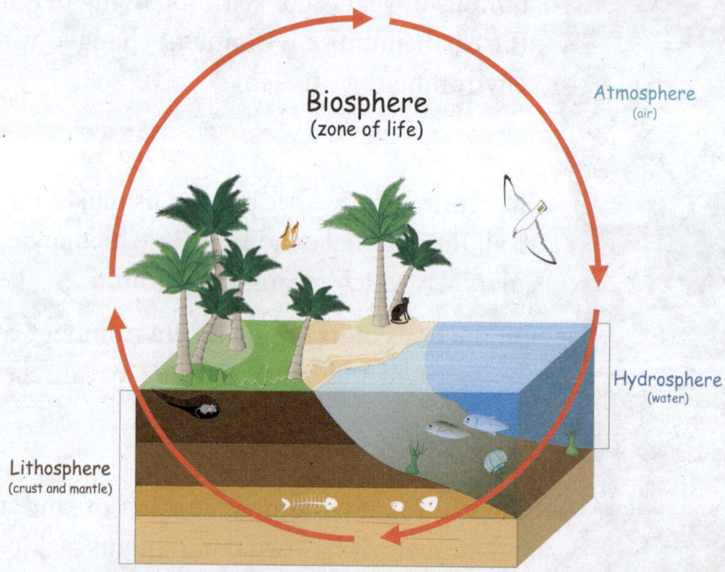

Realms of the Earth

Biosphere

Life exists everywhere, on the ground, underneath the soil, in water bodies as well as in the air. Thus, the biosphere can be defined as the relatively narrow belt of living organisms found a little above and a little below the surface of the Earth. It is referred to as a zone where all the three other realms of environment—atmosphere, lithosphere and hydrosphere—interact.

Life in the biosphere is classified into two major groups—the plant kingdom and the animal kingdom. Within the biosphere, all living organisms, which include the producers, consumers and decomposers are **interdependent.** Producers are also called **autotrophs.** They are the plants that make their own food with chlorophyll, water, carbon dioxide and sunlight. Consumers are also known as **heterotrophs.** These are the living organisms that are directly or indirectly dependent on plants for their food. The three types of consumers are herbivores, carnivores and omnivores. Decomposers are organisms that help in the breakdown and decomposition of dead animals and plants. Energy is transferred from one living thing to another through various food chains. Many food chains together form a food web.

habitable: suitable or good enough to live in; gravity: the force that causes things to drop to the ground; interdependent: dependent on each other; autotrophs: organisms that are able to form nutritional organic substances from simple inorganic substances such as carbon dioxide; heterotrophs: organisms deriving nutritional requirements from complex organic substances

Relationship Between Components of the Environment

The biosphere is made up of distinct zones, each having its own physical and biological environment. The complex system of interactions between the organisms and their physical environment in a particular area is referred to as an ecosystem. The size of an ecosystem varies greatly. It can be as large as the rainforests, grasslands, deserts, lakes and rivers or as small as a pond.

Smoke from factories

Human Environment

In the past, humans fulfilled all their requirements from nature. Their needs were simple and basic. However, with the development of civilization and the growth of nations, we have started modifying our natural environment by using up the Earth's resources and polluting its land, water and soil. Population explosion has led to deforestation due to a rising demand of food and houses. Human requirements increased, which resulted in mass production of various goods and services, leading to the growth of industries. Industries emit smoke into the air, which gradually causes global warming and adversely affects the natural environment.

FACT CHECK

Global warming is the gradual rise in the Earth's average temperature caused by a number of greenhouse gases. Carbon dioxide is the most abundant greenhouse gas responsible for global warming. It is largely released in the environment due to the burning of fossil fuels.

Green Earth

Walk, ride a bike or take public transport to work or school. Inside our cars, the air that we breathe is considered to be close to ten times more polluted than the air outside.

Human–Environment Interaction

Human beings are dependent on the environment for their material needs. Primary activities like farming, fishing, forestry and mining are the providers of raw materials and food—without which further progress and development is impossible. Despite this dependence on the environment, human beings and their activities pose the greatest threat to the environment. A perfect balance is required between the natural and human environment through careful and **judicious** planning in terms of use of resource, waste disposal, land management and population growth. World Environment Day is celebrated on 5th June every year to generate more awareness regarding the importance of conserving our environment.

Apply it! HC E

You will need: Two 2-litre bottles, one bottle cap, duct tape, one piece of heavy cotton string cut about 6 inches long, distilled water, 8–10 cm of planting soil and a couple of small plants with the roots attached.

1. Take one bottle, and cut it in the middle. Take another bottle; cut out the part having the inlet of the bottle. This cut out from the bottle is to be used with the other bottle.
2. Using duct tape, connect the three pieces as shown in the picture.
3. Drill or punch a hole in the bottom lid and place a cotton string through it.
4. Fill the top portion with 8 –10 cm of planting soil.
5. Fill the bottom portion with distilled water so that the cap is just above the water line.
6. Plant two or three small plants in the soil.

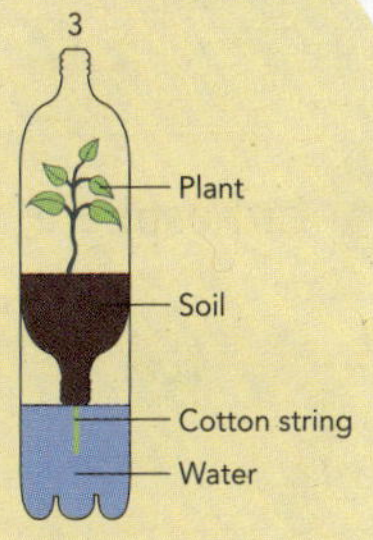

judicious: having, showing or done with good judgement or sense

Skill Builder

Critical thinking skills: Give reasons for the following.

- Earth is a habitable planet.
- Atmosphere is important to us.
- Hydrosphere is important to us.
- Plants and animals depend on each other.

Life skills: This is a list of some old things that can be reused. Write what they can be reused as in the blanks.

1. Toilet paper roll ....
2. Sweater ....
3. Plastic cup ....
4. Can ....
5. A used up notebook ....
6. Milk carton ....

Information literacy: Discuss the importance of water bodies like ocean and seas on the Earth. Find out why oceans are crucial to our existence on Earth.

World Connect

The world's largest coral reef system, the Great Barrier Reef, located off the coast of Queensland in northeastern Australia, has often been regarded as the largest living thing on the Earth. Corals are microscopic organisms in the sea that secrete a substance that forms a hard skeleton around them. This coral reef system is even visible from space. However, new findings show that the Great Barrier Reef is undergoing a complete ecosystem collapse. It has been found that the number of fish has greatly plunged and existing corals have bleached despite winter. Coral bleaching is the process when corals expel algae living in their tissues causing them to turn white during summer months when the water is warm. This is believed to have been caused by climate change.

Wind up

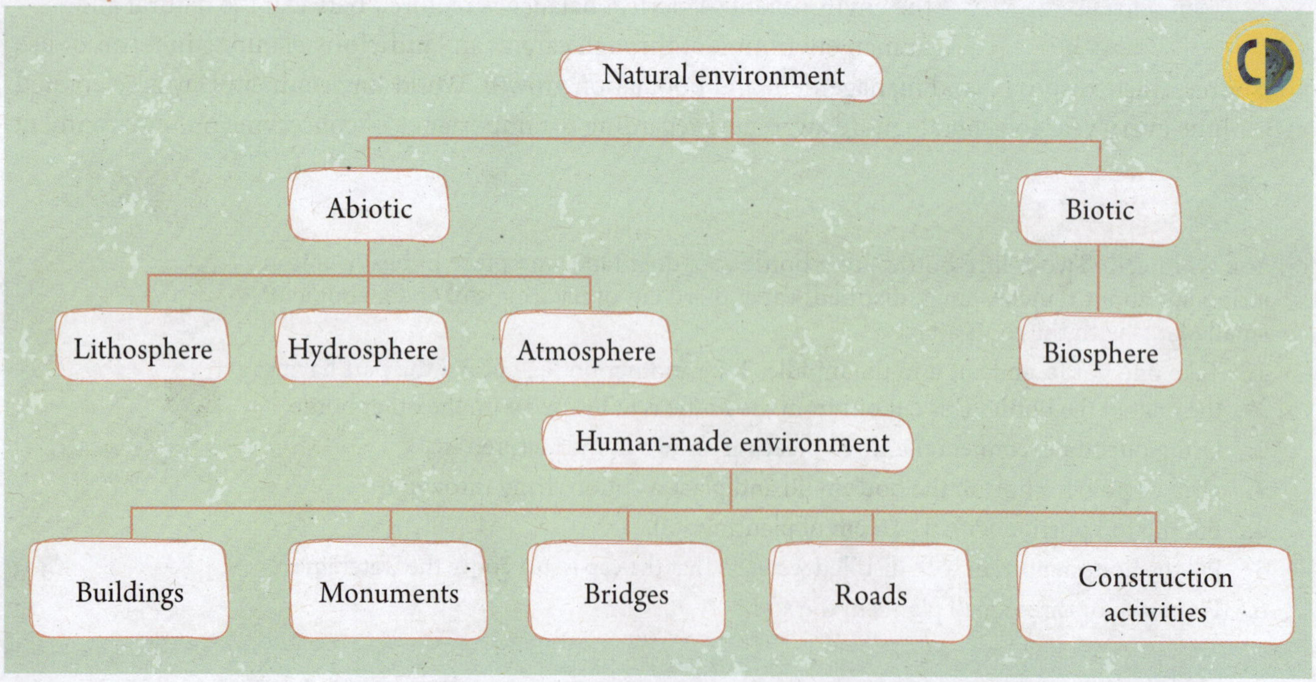

Exercises

A. Choose the correct answers.

1. Which one of the following is created by nature?
   a. Cars, scooters and buses
   b. Mountains, rivers and trees.
   c. Roads, books, pen and copies
   d. All of these
2. The domain of water is referred to as
   a. hydrosphere
   b. lithosphere
   c. atmosphere
   d. biosphere
3. What do the plant and animal kingdom make together?
   a. Biosphere
   b. Hydrosphere
   c. Atmosphere
   d. All of these
4. The ozone layer is a part of the
   a. hydrosphere
   b. atmosphere
   c. lithosphere
   d. biosphere
5. When is World Environment Day celebrated every year?
   a. 25th December
   b. 23rd June
   c. 26th January
   d. 5th June
6. Who interacts with the environment and modifies it according to their needs?
   a. Human beings
   b. Animals
   c. Rivers
   d. Mountains

B. Fill in the blanks.

1. The .... is capable of supporting life on Earth.
2. The average thickness of the lithosphere is about .... km.
3. The greatest danger to the environment is from ....
4. The complex system of interactions between the organisms and their physical environment in a particular area is referred to as an ....

C. Write two examples of each of the following.

1. Abiotic components ....
2. Ecoystems ....
3. Secondary activities ....
4. Biotic components ....
5. Human-made environment ....
6. Biotic components ....

D. Answer these questions in brief.

1. What is the natural environment comprised of?
2. Name three things that constitute the human-made environment.
3. What does the ozone layer do?
4. What is an ecosystem?
5. Why does the Earth look blue when seen from space?

E. Answer these questions in detail.

1. Distinguish between the natural and human-made environment.
2. Discuss the importance of the atmosphere.
3. How have human needs affected the environment that we live in? How can we solve these problems?
4. Why do plants and animals depend on each other?

Think Big

Integrate with Art

The atmosphere is made up of different layers. Each layer has its own importance. Explore their importance. With the help of your geography and art teacher, make a clay model of the layers of the atmosphere. Put a flag in each layer and mention its respective importance.

Learning Tools

Based on what you have studied in the chapter, write your own notes on the following.

Lithosphere

....

....

....

....

....

Atmosphere

....

....

....

....

....

Biosphere

....

....

....

....

....

Hydrosphere

....

....

....

....

....

Human-environment Interaction

....

....

....

....

....

....

Web links:

https://www.britannica.com/science/environment

https://gml.noaa.gov/education/info_activities/pdfs/TBI_earth_spheres.pdf

Last accessed on 31 August 2021

2. Inside the Earth

Warm up

A'mir was completing a school project where he had to build a model of the Earth with clay. While doing so, he wondered, 'What is inside the Earth? Is it covered in soil or rock throughout?' He asked his father this question during dinner and his father told him 'At first glance, it appears to be one big solid rock but it is actually made up of several layers. These layers get denser towards the centre of the Earth. While it is not possible to reach the innermost part of the Earth because the temperature inside increases with the increase in depth, scientists say that the temperature at its centre is as high as 5000° C'. Amir became very interested in the topic and decided to read about it some more.

Much of our knowledge about the Earth's interior comes from the study of **seismic** waves. Seismic waves are created by the movement of the Earth's tectonic plates or during the eruption of volcanoes. These waves travel in different parts of the Earth and at different speeds. These waves deflect when they meet an obstruction and bend when they pass from one medium to another. Scientists learn about the inner parts of the Earth by recording and measuring their strength, path and the materials that they collide with.

Structure of the Earth

The Earth has many layers and each has its own distinct characteristics. The study of seismic waves has revealed three main layers of the Earth's interior. They are the crust, the mantle and the core.

The Crust

It is the outermost and relatively thin layer of rock that envelops the Earth. The thickness of the crust is greater below the continents than under the ocean floor. The average thickness of the continental crust is around 30 km, while that of oceanic crust is around 6 km. The crust is made of soild rocks and the density of these rocks increases with depth. The continental crust is composed of rocks rich in silica and alumina, thus, the layer is known as sial. On the other hand, the oceanic crust is composed of rocks rich in silica and magnesium, thus, this layer is known as sima. Silicon, aluminium and magnesium are the main elements that are present in this layer.

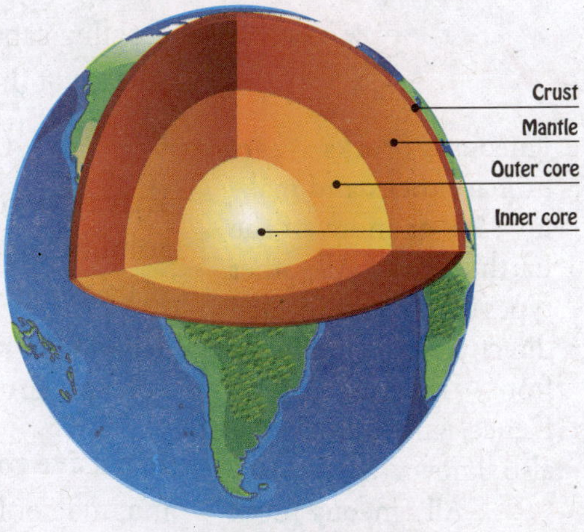

Structure of the Earth

seismic: vibrations caused by either breaking of rocks inside the Earth's surface or by an explosion.

The Mantle

This layer lies below the crust. Its average thickness is 2,900 km. It is made up of dense and heavy rocks comprising iron and magnesium. Magma is found in this part of the Earth's interior. The rocks melt due to the extremely high temperature and form magma. The mantle is divided into two layers—upper mantle and lower mantle.

The Core

The core forms the centre of the Earth. The core is divided into two parts—the inner core and the outer core. The entire core has a diameter of about 7000 km. The outer core is the densest layer of the Earth and is made up of hot, molten rocks comprising mainly iron and nickel. Thus, this layer of the Earth's interior is also known as nife. The pressure in the inner core is so high that it keeps this layer firm and solid despite a temperature as high as 5000° C. The inner core is the hottest part of the Earth. It is very heavy because most of it is made up of metals.

What's in the picture?

Did you know that the inside of the Earth is similar to that of a hard boiled egg? Take a hard boiled egg and cut it in half crosswise. Do you see layers? Now mark which layer is which in the image.

Rocks and Minerals

The outer layer of the Earth—the crust—is composed of rocks. Rocks are solid materials that form the Earth's crust. They are made up of substances known as minerals. Minerals are naturally occurring substances found in the Earth's crust that are formed by geological processes. They have definite physical properties and chemical composition. Rocks are found in a variety of shapes, colours and textures. Based on the way they are formed, rocks are classified into three types—igneous rocks, sedimentary rocks and metamorphic rocks.

Igneous Rocks

The word igneous is derived from the Latin word *ignis*, which means fire. Igneous rocks are formed by the fiery molten material that is formed far below the surface of the Earth. Igneous rocks are formed by the cooling and **solidification** of magma. Cooling can take place on the surface or below the surface of the Earth. Depending on where cooling takes place, two types of igneous rocks are formed.

Basalt is an igneous rock

FACT CHECK

Igneous rocks are primary rocks and make up 85% or more of the Earth's crust. All other types of rocks are formed directly or indirectly from igneous rocks. Hence, igneous rocks are also known as primary rocks. All igneous rocks are crystalline in nature.

Extrusive rocks: These are formed when the lava seeps out from beneath and solidifies upon cooling on the Earth's surface. The cooling of magma takes place rapidly, leading to the formation of small and fine grained crystals. These are also called volcanic rocks as lava comes to the surface during a volcanic eruption. Basalt is an example of extrusive rock.

Intrusive rocks: Below the surface of the Earth, magma cools slowly. When magma cools down slowly, it leads to the formation of large crystals like granite and dolerite. These are called intrusive rocks.

solidification: make or become hard or solid

Sandstone is a sedimentary rock

Sedimentary Rocks

The word sedimentary is derived from the Latin word *sedimentum*, which means settling. About 70 per cent of the rocks on the surface of the Earth is sedimentary rock. Rocks on the surface of the Earth are broken up into bits and pieces of all sizes by various agents like wind, water, glaciers as well as changing temperatures. These smaller pieces of rock, known as sediment, are usually transported and deposited in layers by running water and air at the bottom of lakes, seas and oceans. Thus, rocks formed from the **debris** of other rocks and living matters are called sedimentary rocks. Grains are **compressed** and **cemented** together to form sedimentary rocks. Sandstone is a sedimentary rock. Water between grains of sediment gets squeezed out by the weight of more sediment. In this way, clay becomes mudstone. Sedimentary rock layers hold all reserves of coal, oil and natural gas.

Metamorphic Rocks

Metamorphic rocks are formed when igneous and sedimentary rocks are transformed by the action of intense heat and pressure. The process of formation of the metamorphic rock is known as metamorphism. Metamorphism takes place deep beneath the Earth's surface when rocks are subjected to volcanic activity and movements in the Earth's crust. The rock does not melt, but it is changed underground by intense heat and pressure. In due course of time, shale may change into slate, limestone into marble, sandstone to quartzite and granite to gneiss. Metamorphic rocks are very hard.

Quartzite is a metamorphic rock

Apply it!

Name the rock or mineral used in:

1. Making pottery: ....
2. Making glass: ....
3. Building roads and houses: ....
4. Making jewellery: ....
5. Manufacture of fertilizers: ....

Rock Cycle

The rock cycle is the relationship between the three types of rocks—igneous, sedimentary and metamorphic. Igneous rocks are formed due to the cooling of magma. These igneous rocks are then weathered and eroded to form sediments. Nearly all the sediment produced is eventually transported to deep basins under the sea and areas of great thickness where sediments accumulate. The layers of sediment upon compression harden and form sedimentary rocks. This process of compaction is known as lithification. Sedimentary rocks as well as igneous rocks under extreme pressure and temperature are folded and squeezed, leading to their transformation into metamorphic rocks. These metamorphic rocks, which are still under great heat and pressure, again melt to form molten magma. The cooling of molten

debris: scattered pieces of rubbish or remains; compressed: flattened by pressure; cemented: settle or establish firmly

magma further forms igneous rocks. The energy to power the rock cycle is derived from two sources:

- The heat of the Sun which indirectly breaks down the existing rocks into sediments
- The heat from the Earth's interior which melts the existing material to form igneous rocks

The rock cycle is a continuous process through which old rocks are transformed into new ones. The speed of different parts of the cycle varies. A single layer of sedimentary rock may take thousands of years to build and centuries to wear away. However, when magma comes in contact with a rock, changes can occur in days or even minutes.

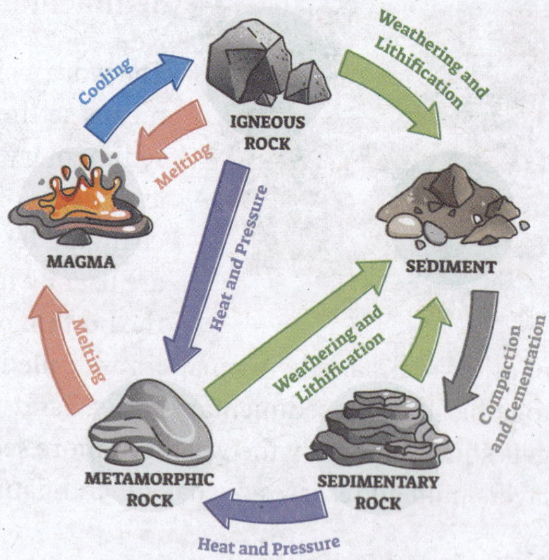

Rock Cycle

Skill Builder

21ST CENTURY SKILLS

Critical-thinking skills: What would have happened if there was only one type of rock found on the Earth?

Life skills: Find out how are rocks useful to us. Also, prepare a list showing the ways in which you make use of rocks in your everyday routine.

World Connect

The Bingham Canyon mine is an open-pit mining operation in Salt Lake City, Utah, USA. This is the largest human-made excavation in the world. It was set up in 1906 and has resulted in the creation of a pit over 970 metres deep. In 1966, this mine was designated a National Historic Landmark under the name Bingham Canyon Open Pit Copper Mine. This mine has, however, adverse effects on the environment. It has been observed that the mining operations have disrupted the habitats of fish and wild animals and have brought about widespread air and water pollution in the region. This has created a number of health hazards for the people living in the region.

Wind up

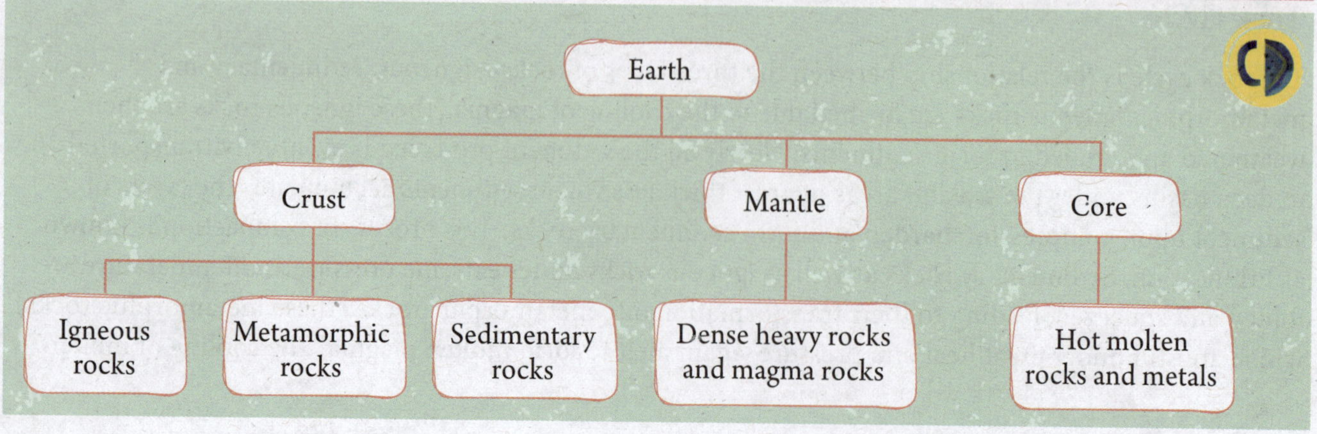

Exercises

A. Fill in the blanks.

1. The Earth is made up of .... layers.
2. The crust is about .... km on the continental mass and .... km on the ocean floor.
3. The mantle extends upto a depth of .... km.
4. The core has a diameter of about .... km.
5. Grains are compressed and cemented together to form .... rocks.

B. Choose the correct answers.

1. Which of the following is not a source of energy that powers the rock cycle?
   a. Heat from the Sun
   b. Heat from Earth's interior
   c. Pressure from wind
   d. None of the above
2. The upper most layer of the Earth is called
   a. the crust b. the crest c. the roads d. the forest
3. The temperature in the inner core can get as high as
   a. 3480 ° C b. 6000 ° C c. 5000 ° C d. 7500 ° C
4. Any solid material that forms the Earth's crust is called a
   a. rock b. road c. sediment d. none of these
5. Which rock is formed by the molten magma below the surface of the Earth?
   a. igneous b. metamorphic c. sedimentary d. none of these

C. Match the columns.

	Column A		Column B
1.	Sial	a.	Extrusive igneous rocks
2.	Sima	b.	Intrusive igneous rocks
3.	Nife	c.	Metamorphic rocks
4.	Basalt	d.	Silica and alumina
5.	Granite	e.	Silica and magnesium
6.	Slate and marble	f.	Nickel and ferrous

D. Answer these questions in brief.

1. What are minerals?
2. Name the three types of rocks.
3. Name the three main layers constituting the Earth's interior.
4. How are extrusive rocks formed?
5. How are metamorphic rocks formed?

E. Answer these questions in detail.

1. Distinguish between extrusive and intrusive rocks.
2. Why are igneous rocks also known as primary rocks?
3. Why do intrusive igneous rocks have large crystals?
4. How are rocks and minerals important to us?
5. With the help of a diagram, explain the rock cycle.

Think Big

Integrate with Art

The rock cycle is a complex yet important phenomenon. Make a poster of the rock cycle to explain how rocks undergo changes.

Learning Tools

Identify each layer, and write a few notes about each of them.

Web links:

https://www.gsi.ie/en-ie/education/our-planet-earth/Pages/The-Earth-structure.aspx

Last accessed on 31 August 2021

3. Our Changing Earth

Warm up

Nepal experienced a powerful earthquake of magnitude 7.8 on the morning of 25 April, 2015. The earthquake triggered an avalanche on Mount Everest that killed 13 mountaineers. Landslides struck a number of villages near Pokhara and destroyed nearly half of the houses in the Lumle village. The number of casualties was reported to be around 8,800 and more than 20,000 people suffered serious injuries. Events like the Nepal earthquake bring with it a number of changes that alter and modify the Earth's surface. Do you know that the Himalayas were not always present on the Earth but were formed some 40 million years ago?

A landform is a formation made up of rock and dirt that occurs naturally on the Earth. It varies in size and stature, taking the shape of a large mountain range, a hill, a large continent or a small valley. The science of studying how landforms are created as well as how they change and interact with one another is called geomorphology. These landforms were formed years ago due to the movement of tectonic plates. The Earth is made up of seventeen major tectonic plates and several minor plates that continuously drift around the surface of the Earth, and they fit together like the pieces of a puzzle.

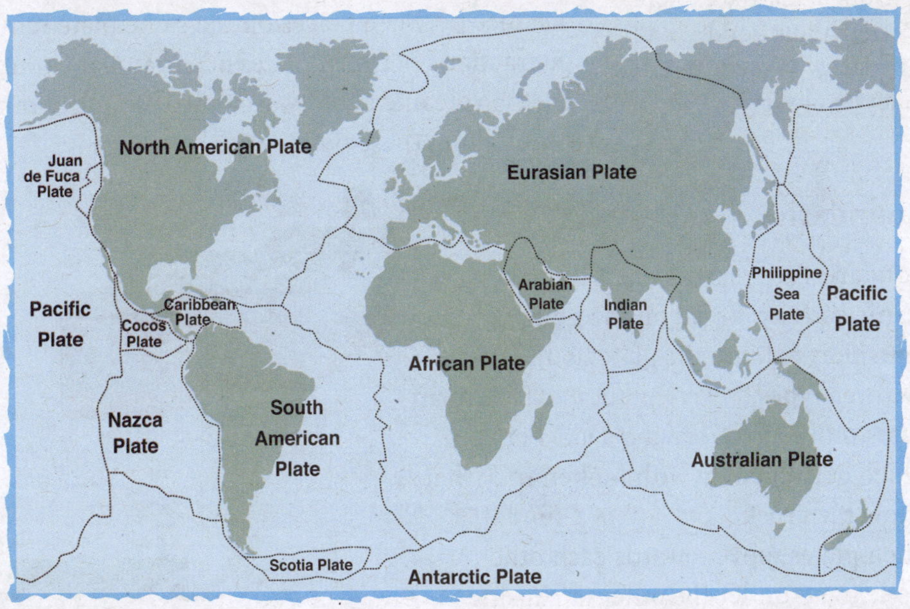

Tectonic plates of the Earth

Movements of the Earth

The idea that continents, particularly South America and Africa, fit together like pieces of a puzzle has been around for a very long time. In 1912, Alfred Wegener, a German **geophysicist** and meteorologist suggested the Theory of Continental Drift. In his theory,

geophysicist: a person who studies the physics of the Earth

he suggests that the continents of the Earth's surface move with time. Wegener proposed that a supercontinent, Pangaea (meaning 'all land' in Greek) once existed. About 300 million years ago, the supercontinent began breaking up into smaller continents, which then drifted to their present positions.

CONTINENTAL DRIFT

The single landmass began to crack and divide due to the slow currents of magma beneath it

In the 1950s, evidence from **magnetism** in the ocean floor revealed that the seafloors across the oceans were spreading by a few centimetres each year. This indicated movement of large parts of the Earth's crust, which we now call tectonic plates. The scientific theory that describes the large-scale motions of the lithosphere is known as the Theory of Plate Tectonics. The lithosphere is broken into a number of plates known as the lithospheric plates that slide on top of the magma. Because of the high temperature and pressure below the crust, it produces a trace of melting that allows the plates to move on this layer into new **configurations**.

Green Earth

With the constant rising of temperatures in the Arctic and Antarctic, it is feared that melting ice would raise the level of the sea. This rise in sea level would submerge many low-lying continental parts.

Among all the tectonic plates that have been identified, the Pacific plate is the largest and consists of mostly the ocean floor. All the other plates consist of both continents and oceans. The plates move as one distinct unit. As the plates move, the distance between places on the same plate remains the same. All major interactions between plates occur at plate boundaries. Most of the Earth's volcanic activity, earthquakes and mountain-building activities occur along these boundaries.

Apply it!

Using Google Earth, explore your neighbourhood and nearby places. Write a report on what you observe.

Plate Boundaries

Plate boundaries are regions of earthquakes and volcanic activity. Based on the types of movements they exhibit, the plate boundaries can be of three types. Divergent boundaries form when plates move apart, leaving a gap between them, which gets filled up with molten rock that oozes below the crust. Convergent boundaries occur when plates move towards each other, causing one to go under the other or causing plates to collide forming mountains. Transform boundaries occur when plates slide past each other, scraping and deforming as they pass.

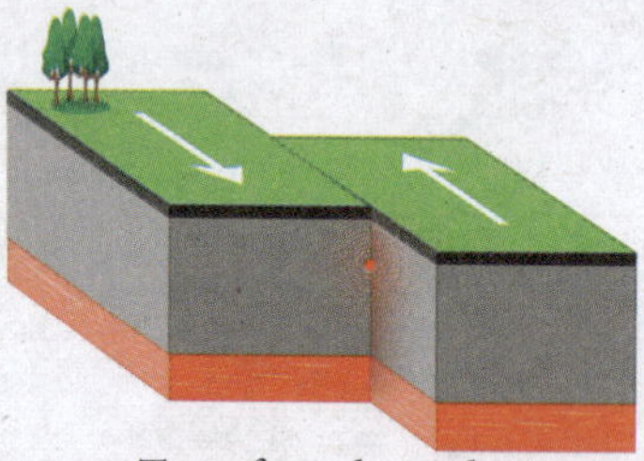

Transform boundaries

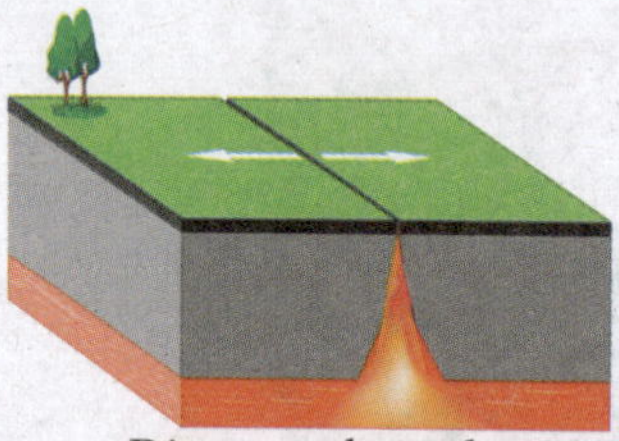

Divergent boundaries

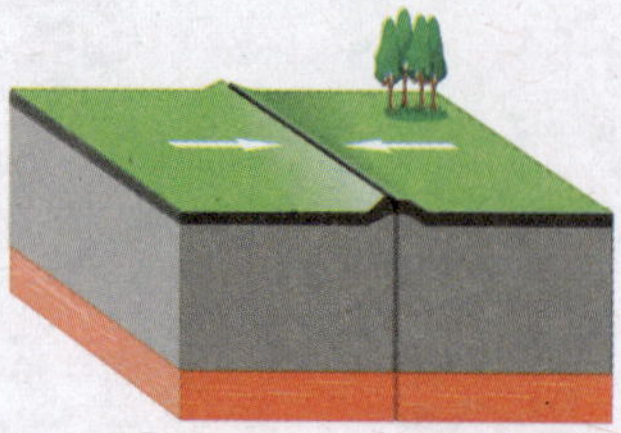

Convergent boundaries

Types of plate boundaries

magnetism: the property of attraction displayed by magnets; configuration: an arrangement of parts or elements in a particular form, figure or combination

Formation of Landforms

The movement of tectonic plates causes the creation of landforms. The world's highest mountains—the Himalayas, and the world's deepest sea trench—the Mariana Trench, were formed this way. Volcanoes, mountains and earthquakes occur at the edges of tectonic plates. Their creation depends on the direction in which the plates are moving.

Formation of Mountains

The formation of mountains is caused by the movement of lithospheric plates, giving rise to horizontal or **orogenic** movements. Such movements result in folding and faulting of the Earth's crust and are responsible for the formation of mountains.

Folding: Folds are formed due to the bending or buckling of horizontal or flat layers of rock. The **deformation** of the layers of rocks is known as folding, and the mountains that are formed in this manner are known as fold mountains. Horizontal compression results in the formation of **upfolds** called anticlines and **downfolds** called synclines. Mountain ranges like the Aravallis in India, the Urals in Russia and the Appalachians in the USA were formed several hundred years ago and are known as the old fold mountains. The mountains that were formed during the last few million years and are still growing are known as young fold mountains. The Himalayas, the Rockies, the Alps and Andes are some young fold mountains. The old fold mountains are lower than the young fold mountains and have rounded peaks and gentler slopes, whereas the young fold mountains have pointed peaks and rugged features like steeper slopes and deeper valleys.

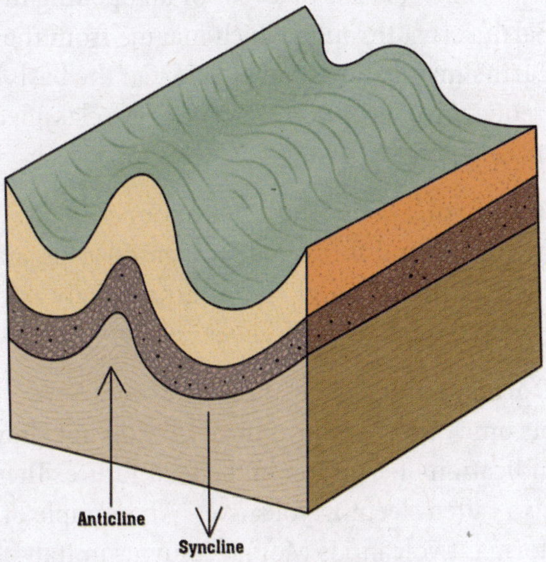

Anticline and syncline

Faulting: Faults are formed when the surface of the Earth is cracked apart by tectonic plates moving away. When parallel cracks or faults occur, blocks of the Earth between the faults may be raised or lowered.

Block Mountains may be formed in two ways. When two roughly parallel faults occur, the block of the Earth between them may be raised, forming a steep-sided block mountain. A block mountain may also be formed by the sinking of the crust on either side of the two parallel faults. The Vosges and the Black Forest are examples of block mountains.

Rift Valleys: When two roughly parallel faults occur, the crust between long, parallel cracks or faults may sink, thus forming narrow steep-sided valleys known as rift valleys. The Great Rift Valley of Africa and the Rhine Rift Valley of Germany are two examples of rift valleys.

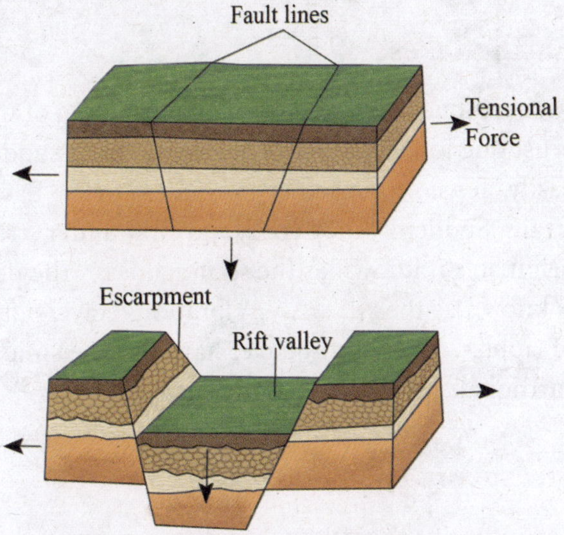

Rift valley

orogenic: a process in which a section of the Earth's crust is folded and deformed by compression to form a mountain range; deformation: the action or process of deforming or distorting; upfolds: something that folds up; downfolds: something that folds down

Landforms on the Earth's surface are ever-changing under the influence of the following two forces:

- Endogenic or internal forces
- Exogenic or external forces

The forces that act on the interior of the Earth are called endogenic forces and the forces that work on the surface of the Earth are called exogenic forces. Endogenic forces, sometimes, produce sudden movements and at other times produce slow movements. Sudden movements such as earthquakes and volcanoes cause mass destruction to the surface of the Earth.

Volcano

A volcano consists of a vent or an opening in the Earth's crust through which magma from the Earth's mantle flows out as lava. On the basis of the frequency of eruption, volcanoes are classified into three types:

Active volcanoes: These volcanoes erupt frequently and throw out lava, gases, ashes and rocks. Stromboli and Mount Etna in Italy are examples of active volcanoes.

Dormant volcanoes: These volcanoes have become quiet after erupting. They do not show any indication of eruption in the near future. They are also called sleeping volcanoes. An example of a dormant volcano is Mount Vesuvius in Italy.

Extinct volcanoes: These volcanoes have not erupted for hundreds of years. There is no possibility of any eruption in the future. These volcanoes are also called dead volcanoes. Mount Kilimanjaro in Africa is an example.

What's in the picture?

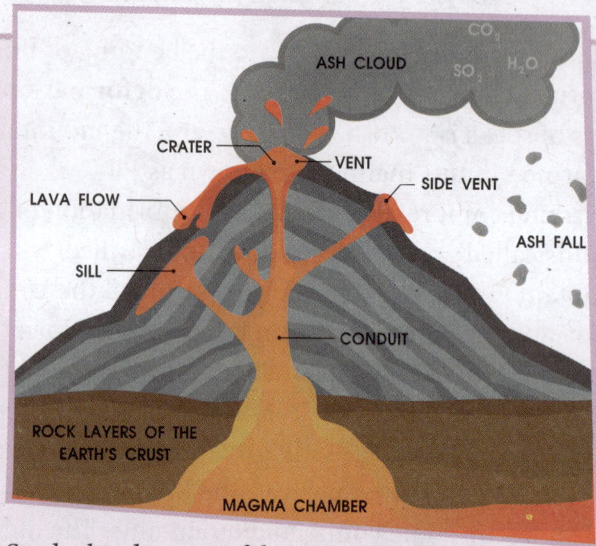

Study this diagram of the structure of a volcano and explain the steps in your own words.

Earthquakes

An earthquake is a sudden violent shaking of the ground. It is caused by sudden movements in the Earth's crust due to the release of energy as rocks suddenly break or shift under stress. Rocks do not bend or break easily. Tension, caused by movement of the Earth's plates, builds up until the rocks cannot withstand the strain. Suddenly, they crack and shift under stress. The place below the Earth's surface where an earthquake originates is known as the seismic focus. The point on the Earth's surface directly above the seismic focus is known as the epicentre. Vibrations travel outward in all directions from the seismic focus in the form of ripples. Most earthquakes have their seismic focus at depths of less than 60 km. The impact of the earthquake is felt most at the epicentre.

Measuring Earthquakes

The intensity of earthquake waves is measured on the Richter Scale. Earthquake tremors are recorded by an instrument called seismograph. The science that deals with the study of earthquakes is called seismology and the scientists who study earthquakes are called seismologists. The Richter scale ranges from 0 to 9.

Distribution in India

In India, the Himalayan region and the Ganga–Brahmaputra valley are prone to earthquakes. Although earthquakes cannot be predicted, the impact can certainly be minimized if we are prepared beforehand. Even the regions in and around the Deccan Plateau have experienced tremors in the past. India has been divided into five earthquake zones. Some common earthquake prediction methods adopted locally by people include studying animal behaviour. For instance, fish in ponds get agitated and snakes come to the surface.

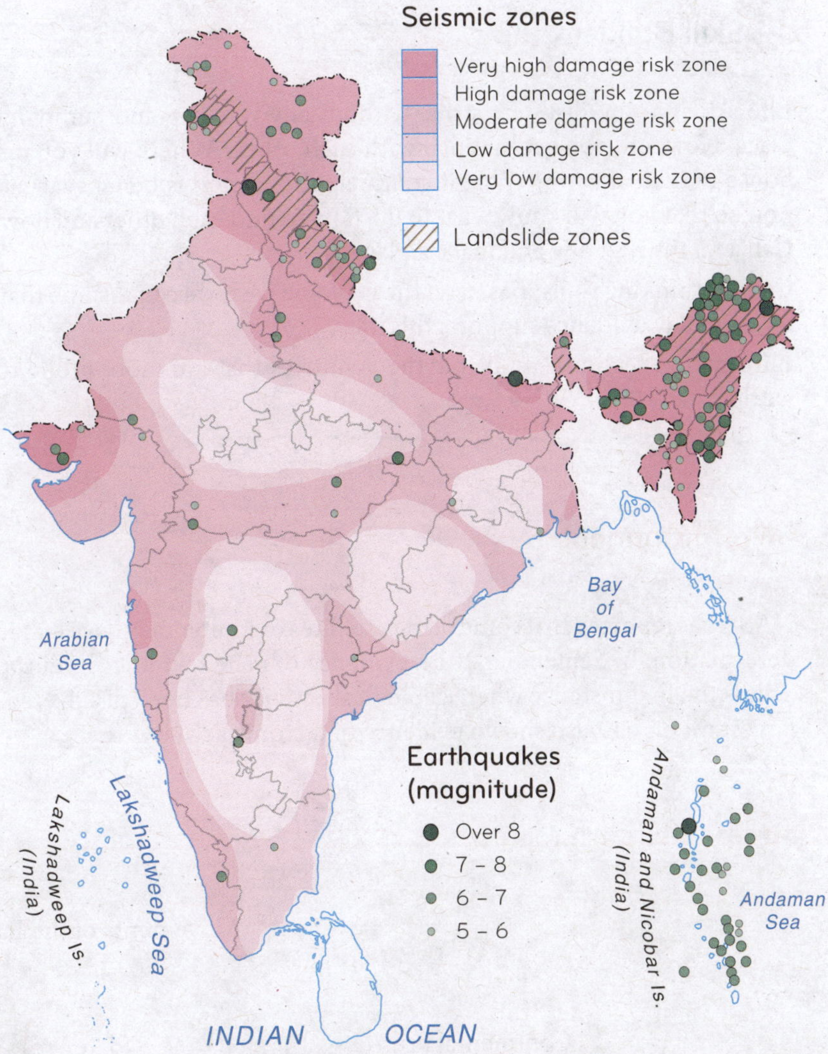

India earthquakes and seismic zones

Preparedness and Preventive Measures for Earthquakes

If indoors:

- Stand against the wall near the centre of the building, in the doorway or underneath wooden furniture.
- Stay away from windows, glass furniture and wall hangings.

If outdoors:

- Stay away from power lines, lamp posts and telephone lines.
- Find a clear spot, away from buildings and bridges.

Geography skills

Working from this map, mark the earthquake prone areas on an outline map of India.

Green Earth

Generally, before and after a large earthquake there will be smaller earthquakes. The ones that happen before are called foreshocks. The ones that happen after are called aftershocks.

If in a car:

- Slow down and find a safe place.
- Stay in the car until the tremors stop.
- Watch out for power lines, broken gas pipes and cracks on the roads.

Skill Builder

Life skills: Some disasters strike without any warning and family members may not all be in the same place. How will you get in touch with each other? Where will you meet? How will you get out of your house in case of a fire? What if your neighbourhood is being evacuated? It's important to make a plan now so that you will know what to do, how to find each other and how to communicate in an emergency. Call a family meeting and make a plan.

Critical thinking skills: Based on the geologic past, we can assume that the Earth is always changing. What modern-day evidence supports this idea?

Information technology: Name the countries that are more prone to earthquakes and volcanoes in the world.

World Connect

NASA has reported that some of the satellites of Jupiter may have features that are related to plate-tectonic style deformation. In September 2014, evidence of plate tectonics in Europa, a satellite of Jupiter, was discovered. This is the first instance where geological activity has been discovered on world other than the Earth. Saturn's largest moon has also shown evidence of tectonic activity.

Wind up

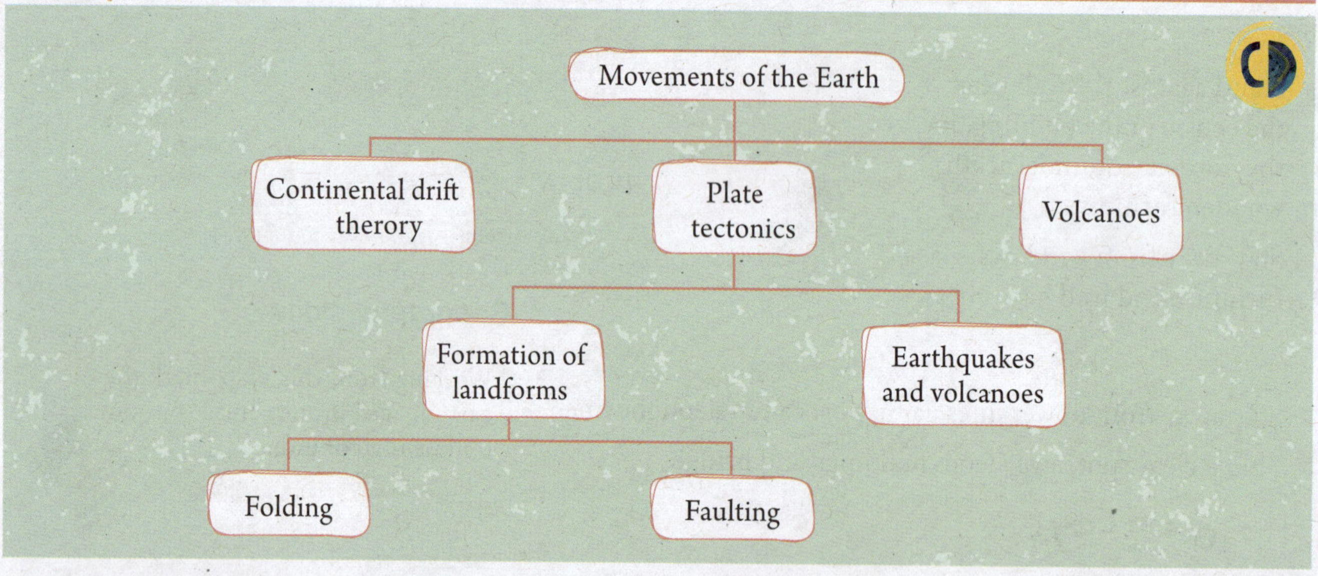

Exercises

A. Fill in the blanks.

1. The place below the Earth's surface where an earthquake originates is known as the ....
2. .... are formed when the surface of the Earth is cracked apart by tectonic plates moving away.
3. The Himalayas are an example of .... fold mountains.
4. .... boundaries occur when plates slide past each other, scraping and deforming as they pass.
5. The forces that act in the interior of the Earth are called ....

B. Choose the correct answers.

1. An active volcano
   a. Stromboli
   b Mount Etna
   c. Mount Rainier
   d. Mount Vesuvius
2. Folding is caused by the force of
   a. gravity
   b. compression
   c. tension
   d. upliftment
3. A dormant volcano
   a. Mount Kilimanjaro
   b. Mount Etna
   c. Nanda Devi
   d. Mount Vesuvius
4. Alfred Wegener was a German
   a. geophysicist
   b. geographer
   c. meteorologist
   d. seismologist

C. Write T for true and F or false.

1. Transform plate movements lead to earthquakes. ☐
2. Mount Kilimanjaro is an active volcano. ☐
3. The Richter Scale ranges in magnitude from 1 to 9. ☐
4. Anticline and syncline are associated with block mountains. ☐

D. Answer these questions in brief.

1. Define an earthquake.
2. Name the instrument used to measure earthquake waves.
3. Which regions in India are prone to earthqakes?
4. What are the three types of plate tectonics?
5. Which instrument is used to record the tremors of an earthquake?

E. Answer these questions in detail.

1. Explain the types of volcanoes.
2. Explain the three types of plate movements. Illustrate your answer with suitable diagrams.
3. List the preparedness and preventive measures for earthquakes.
4. Differentiate between folding and faulting.

Think Big

Integrate with architecture

Collect information about the plan and building materials used in constructing houses in Japan. Discuss why these buildings are made that way.

Learning Tools

List the important points under each title for swift recap of the chapter.

Movements of the Earth

→ ....

→ ....

→ ....

→ ....

→ ....

Formation of mountains

→ ....

→ ....

→ ....

→ ....

→ ....

Volcano

→ ....

→ ....

→ ....

→ ....

→ ....

Define:

Divergent boundaries: ....

....

Convergent boundaries: ....

....

Transform boundaries: ....

....

Anticlines: ....

....

Synclines: ....

....

Earthquakes

....

....

....

....

....

....

....

Web links:

https://oceanservice.noaa.gov/facts/tectonics.html

https://www.bgs.ac.uk/discovering-geology/earth-hazards/earthquakes/what-causes-earthquakes/

Last accessed on 31 August 2021

4. External Processes and Changing Landforms

Warm up

Avner was looking at some old photographs and he came across a beautiful church. It was built of stone, surmounted by a spire. One part of its walls was completely covered in vines and climbers, which really gave it a rustic and elegant look. 'Grandfather, this is such a beautiful church. Where is it located?' asked Avner. 'This church is the one we always pass by when we visit Uncle Ben's place. The year 1897 saw a massive earthquake and that church, one of the oldest in Shillong, collapsed. Another one was rebuilt in its place and stands still today,' said grandfather. Anver was shocked! Even the area surrounding it looks different. How did he not recognize the locality?

Continents, mountains, plateaus, plains, ridges are some of the landforms that exist on the Earth. To fully understand the surface of the Earth, we need to first understand what goes on inside it. We have already learnt about how landforms like mountains and valleys are formed as tectonic plates collide into one another. These landforms do not last forever. The Earth's surface is constantly being broken down and reshaped. With time, these landforms age and wear away. Heat, rain, climate, pollution, acid rain, water, ice and waves slowly cause the tearing down of the Earth's landforms.

The extent to which a landscape is modified depends on many factors such as internal processes, external forces, nature of rocks and the length of time these processes have been taking place.

Major Landforms

While landforms are formed by internal and external processes like weathering, erosion, deposition and other natural processes together level the Earth's surface. The surface of the land is reduced to an even plain. Areas with higher altitudes are worn down and depressions are filled over a period of time.

Green Earth

Keeping adequate vegetation cover is the most important erosion control principle. Bare soil can be washed away with rain.

Gradation

Gravity is the driving force behind the movement of materials from high areas to low areas, thus reducing the height differences between them. The process occurs when rocks are **eroded** into smaller pieces. They are then transported and deposited elsewhere. This process of weathering, erosion and deposition is known as gradation.

eroded: broken

Weathering: The wearing away or breaking down of rocks by natural agents or factors such as temperature changes, moisture and frost is known as weathering. When rocks, soil, minerals, wood and artificial materials on the surface of the Earth are exposed to the atmosphere, they decay or disintegrate.

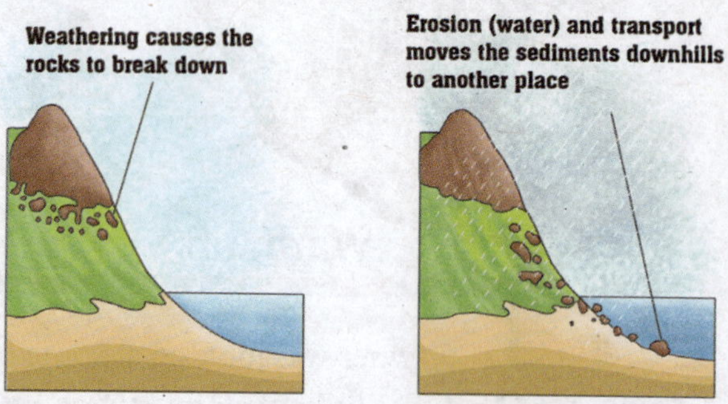

Weathering

There are two types of weathering—mechanical weathering and chemical weathering. Mechanical weathering occurs when rocks are broken down by physical agents like ice, wind or water, and chemical weathering occurs when rocks are broken down by chemical reactions.

Erosion: The wearing away of rocks by agents on the surface of the Earth like running water, moving ice, wind and waves and transporting them away to other locations is called erosion.

Deposition: Deposition is a process in which sediments, soil and rocks are added to a landform or landmass. Wind, ice, water, and gravity transport previously weathered surface materials and deposit these adding layers of sediment.

Agents of Gradation

Rivers, waves, ice and wind all contribute in changing landforms on the Earth. They are also called the agents of gradation. Let us learn about how some landforms are formed.

Rivers

Rivers form a large variety of landforms through erosion, transportation and deposition throughout its course from its source to the mouth.

Waterfall: When the river falls down almost vertically from a sufficient height along its course, it forms a waterfall. Waterfalls cause erosion because of the force with which the water drops.

Meanders: As the land is almost flat, the river slowly flows without eroding much and forms sweeping loops and bends. These large bends are known as meanders. Meanders also cause gradation as the water in such bodies flows.

Oxbow lake: An oxbow lake is formed when a meander forms an almost complete circle and the meandering river cuts across the narrow neck of the land. In due course of time, the neck of the river cuts off from the river and forms a cut-off lake, also called an oxbow lake.

Flood plains: Rivers often overflow their banks, thereby causing floods. The fine alluvial soil brought by such rivers is deposited on the valley floor. This fertile part is called a flood plain. In a flood plain, the coarse materials are deposited along the banks of the river. Thus, long ridges of low height are formed along the banks. These are called natural levees.

Delta: When the river reaches its mouth, it flows very slowly. This is because the land is almost flat. The river also flows **sluggishly** due to the heavy load it carries. The excess load is deposited in the wide river channel. This divides the main channel into several channels called distributaries. In this stage, a triangular-shaped land is formed between the distributaries due to the deposition of sediments. This is called a delta. The largest delta in the world is the delta formed by the rivers Ganga and Brahmaputra.

sluggishly: to move slowly or be inactive

Sea Waves

The processes of erosion and deposition of sea waves give rise to coastal landforms.

Cliff: A steep slope facing the sea is known as a cliff.

Cave: A cave may develop at the base of cliffs that have been subjected to the action of waves over a long period of time. It is a cylindrical tunnel that extends into the cliff.

Sea coves and headlands: Sometimes the coast is made of softer rock separated by harder rock. The waves cut the softer rock to form sea coves and the harder rocks remain as narrow projections or **headlands.**

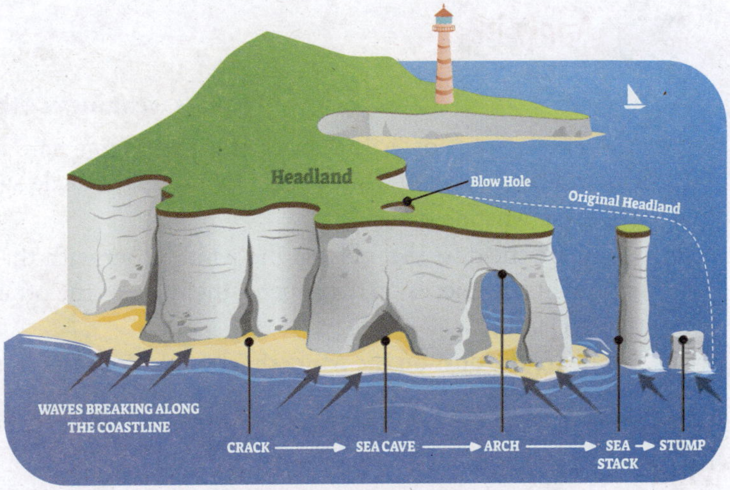

Erosional work of sea waves

Sea stack: Continued erosion of the headland may cause the arch to fall in, leaving behind an isolated column known as a sea stack. The depositional work of the sea waves is a slow process. Beaches are formed by the deposition of sand, gravel and pebbles on the shore. They are generally formed when the sea is calm and winds are of low velocity.

Sand bars: When the broken rock materials are deposited on the sea floor near the coast, sand bars are formed. Sometimes, the sea water is enclosed between the coast and the sand bar. It then becomes a partially enclosed lake near the sea, which is called a lagoon.

Sea arch: Waves may act on a headland from both sides, forming sea caves. When two caves on opposite sides meet, a sea arch forms.

Sea arch

Moving Ice

A glacier is a huge mass of ice that moves slowly over land. Glaciers are often called 'rivers of ice'. They erode the land with rocks stuck to their bottom to expose the solid rock below. A glacier erodes both the bed and the sides of its valley at the same time, thus forming a U-shaped valley with a flat base and very steep sides. In the mountains, a glacier carves deep hollows, forming armchair-shaped depressions known as corrie or cirque. Thereafter, when the ice melts, the basin or hollow is filled with water forming a lake known as a corrie lake or tarn. When two or more glaciers form corries on either sides of the same mountain, they ultimately form a pointed peak called a pyramidal peak.

The glacier carries a number of small as well as big rocks, which it brings down from the mountains. When the glacier melts, these rocks get deposited there. These deposits are known as moraines.

FACT CHECK

A névé is a mass of porous ice, formed from snow, that has not yet become frozen into glacier ice.

headlands: narrow area of land jutting out into a sea, lake, etc.

Apply it!

Rocks wear away other rocks

You will need a piece of shale, a sheet of paper, a large hard rock and one teaspoon of soil. Hold the piece of shale over a large sheet of white paper. Then, rub the shale against the hard rock.

- Describe what happens.
- Compare the dust that falls on the white paper with the shale and the larger rock. What would you say represents the pieces on the paper—the shale or the other rock? How might rocks be broken up in a river and on land?
- Compare the dust on the white sheet of paper to the teaspoon of soil. Is soil made of rock material?

Wind

Moving air, like moving water and ice, is capable of picking up loose **debris** and transporting them elsewhere. The action of the wind is most widespread in deserts. The dryness and lack of vegetation in deserts make it easier for winds to pick up, transport and deposit large quantities of sediment. Wind erosion attacks rock masses and sculpts them into varied shapes. Winds erode the lower section of the rock more than the upper part. Therefore, such rocks have narrower bases and wider tops. They are known as mushroom rocks. Deposition by wind produces extensive dunes. A dune is a hill or a mound of sand deposited by the wind.

What's in the picture?

- What shape do these rocks resemble?
- How did these rocks get this shape?
- What kind of erosion did these rocks go through? Explain the process.

A sand dune begins to build where there is an obstruction like a large rock or bush. Sand is deposited near the obstruction. Once the deposition has started, the sand dune grows rapidly. When the grains of sand are very fine and light, the wind can carry them over very long distances. When this sand is deposited in large areas, it is called a loess. Large deposits of loesses are found in China.

Skill Builder

21ST CENTURY SKILLS

Collaboration: Discuss in class about the possibility of landslides in mountainous areas: what causes them and how are rescue operations carried out.

Critical thinking skills: Would gradation have been possible if there were no wind, moving water or glaciers? What would have been the consequences in such a case?

debris: fragments or remnants of something destroyed or broken

World Connect

22nd March is World Water Day. This was celebrated to create an awareness amongst the people so that they may reflect on the state of the world's freshwater. One of the most used and disputed waterways of the Earth, the Colorado river, provides water to 30 million people and has an innumerable number of dams and diversions. However, due to its heavy utilization, for purposes like agriculture, industry and municipal uses along its 2,333-kilometre course, it does not reach its delta and the Gulf of California. Mexico receives about one-tenth of the river's former flow.

Wind up

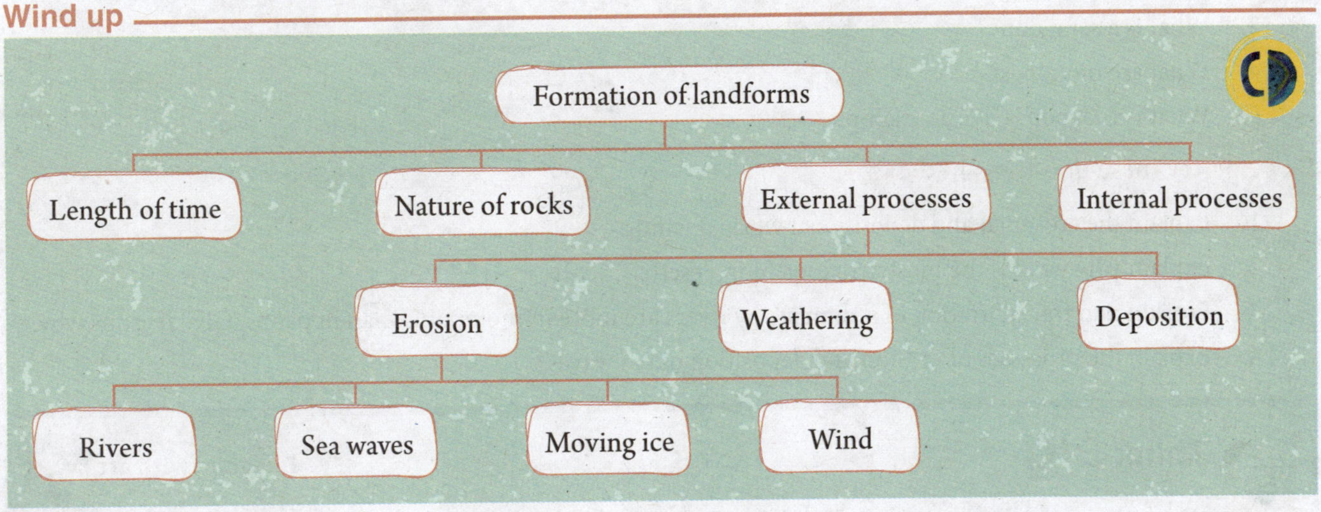

Exercises

A. Choose the correct answers.

1. Which of the following features is not formed by a river?
   a. Delta　b. Mountain　c. Meander　d. Waterfall
2. A valley formed by a glacier resembles the letter
   a. V　b. U　c. I　d. L
3. Loess is a type of
   a. soil　b. rock　c. lake　d. sand dune
4. As the land is almost flat, the river slowly flows without eroding much and forms sweeping loops and bends. These large bends are known as
   a. waterfalls　b. meanders　c. sea arches　d. deltas

B. Fill in the blanks.

1. .... is the largest delta in the world.
2. .... is an agent of erosion in the desert.
3. Large deposits of loesses are found in ....
4. Waterfalls cause erosion because of the .... by which the water drops.
5. A .... is a hill or a mound of sand deposited by winds.

C. Write T for true and F or false.

1. A steep slope facing the sea is known as a cliff. ☐

2. A beach is a depositional feature formed by sea waves. ☐

3. Mushroom rocks are common in desert regions. ☐

4. A dune is a hill or a mound of sand deposited by the wind. ☐

5. A glacier is a huge mass of ice that moves slowly on rivers. ☐

D. Answer these questions in brief.

1. How are oxbow lakes formed?
2. How are flood plains formed?
3. What is a sand dune?
4. What are moraines?
5. What is a lagoon? Give an example.

E. Answer these questions in detail.

1. Explain the erosional and depositional work of winds.
2. Explain why wind is the most active agent in deserts.
3. Erosion and transportation of sediments by rivers are more in mountains than in plains. Give reasons why.
4. Explain the processes of erosion and deposition of sea waves.

Think Big

Integrate with art

Draw three posters showing the landforms formed by the erosional works of sea waves and winds.

Learning Tools

Complete the concept map given below to check your understanding of the chapter.

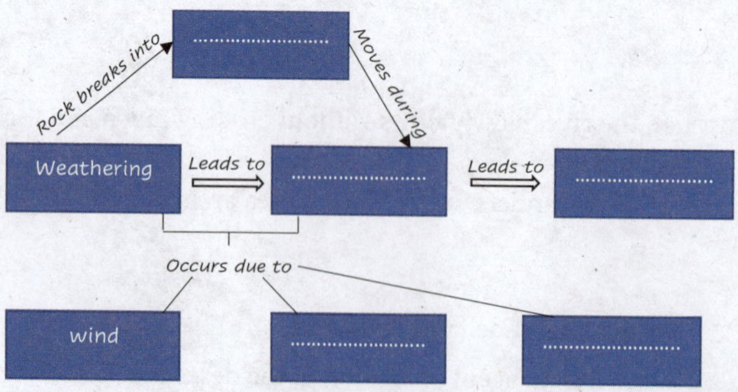

Web links:

http://www.onegeology.org/extra/kids/earthprocesses/weathering.html
https://www.nationalgeographic.com/science/article/weathering-erosion

Last accessed on 31 August 2021

5. The Atmosphere

Warm up

The Earth was formed close to 4.6 billion years ago. Ever since, the atmosphere of the Earth has changed significantly. Initially, the atmosphere of the Earth primarily contained hydrogen and a few other gases such as methane and ammonia. The eruption of volcanoes imparted nitrogen and carbon dioxide to the Earth's atmosphere. Till about 2.4 billion years ago, the atmosphere of the Earth lacked free oxygen. The blue–green algae were the first microscopic organisms to produce oxygen through photosynthesis. This led to the accumulation of free oxygen in the atmosphere. Findings reveal that about three billion years ago, the Sun was only 70 per cent as bright as it is today. This is because greenhouse gases like methane and carbon dioxide present in the atmosphere prevent the heat that comes from the Sun from leaving the atmosphere.

You have already learnt that the Earth is surrounded by a thick blanket of gases called the atmosphere. The atmosphere extends at least 500 kilometres above the Earth's surface and although it is invisible to us, we cannot live without it. It keeps the land warm at night when the Sun has set and protects us from the harmful ultraviolet rays of the Sun. Human beings need oxygen present in the air to breathe.

Green Earth

Air pollution disrupts the balance of carbon dioxide and oxygen present in the air. The level of carbon dioxide present in the air increases because of air pollution.

Composition of the Atmosphere

Based on volume, the gases present in the atmosphere are:

- Nitrogen (78%)
- Oxygen (21%)
- Argon (0.9%)
- Carbon dioxide (0.03%)
- Other mixed gases (0.1%), including neon, helium, hydrogen, methane, xenon, ozone and krypton.
- Besides these gases, the atmosphere contains small amounts of water vapour, dust particles and smoke.

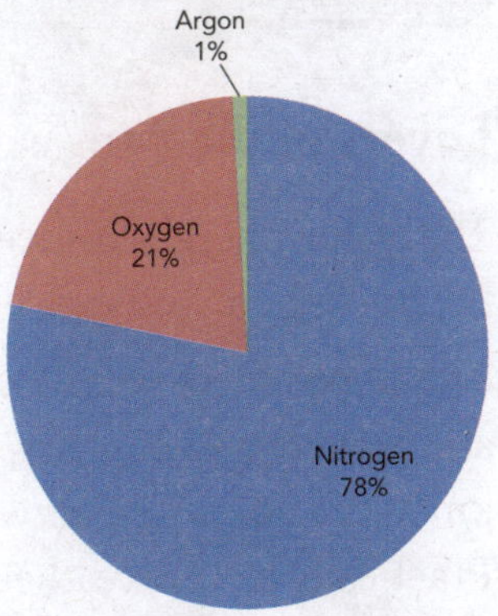

Composition of the atmosphere

Apply it!

When you see leaves rustling outside, what are you actually seeing? ....

Close your mouth and take a deep breath through your nose. What are you smelling? ....

Go outside, close your eyes and listen. What do you hear? ....

Significance of the Atmosphere

We know that living things inhale oxygen while breathing. Green plants produce oxygen during photosynthesis so that the amount of oxygen in the air remains constant. They use the carbon dioxide that humans and animals release into the air to make their food and in turn, release oxygen.

> **FACT CHECK**
> The Earth's atmosphere also safeguards it from various impact events. The Earth's atmosphere burns up all the meteorites and space junk before it reaches the Earth's surface.

Greenhouse Effect

During the day, when the Sun's energy reaches the Earth's atmosphere, most of it goes right through. The incoming solar radiation is known as insolation. Some bounces off, back into space. At night, most of the Sun's energy escapes back into space. However, some energy is trapped inside the atmosphere by the greenhouse gases and water vapour, further warming the Earth.

What's in the picture?

What do you see in the picture? Is this good for the atmosphere? How it is impacting our atmosphere?

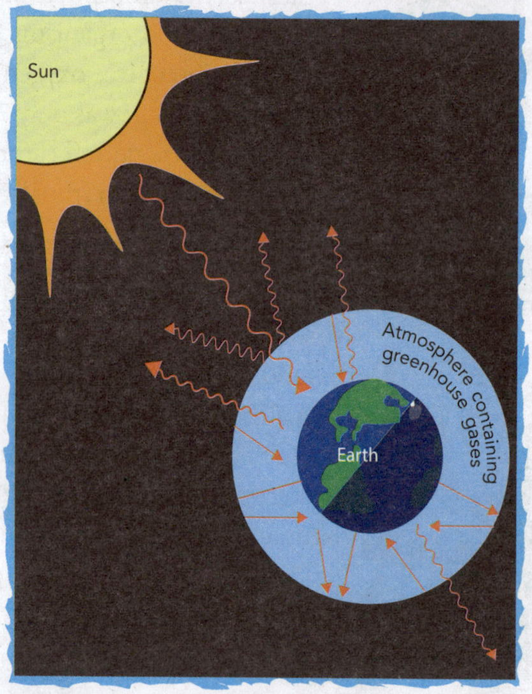

Greenhouse effect

Layers of the Atmosphere

The atmosphere is divided into five concentric layers—troposphere, stratosphere, mesosphere, thermosphere and exosphere.

The troposphere is the lowest layer of the atmosphere. It makes up approximately 75% of the total mass of the atmosphere and contains 99% of the atmosphere's water. It extends to a height of 18 km at the Equator and 8 km at the poles. The air we breathe exists here. The troposphere contains most of the water vapour and dust. Practically all the weather phenomena like cloud formation, rainfall, fog, hailstorm, etc. take place in this layer. The jet stream, which is a narrow, fast-moving 'river' of wind, flows at the upper edge of this layer. The air temperature in this layer typically decreases as altitude increases due to radiation, conduction and convection.

The stratosphere is the second layer of the atmosphere. It extends to a height of 50 km above the Earth's surface. It contains ozone layer, which absorbs the ultra-violet radiation of the Sun and prevents it from reaching the Earth's surface. So, temperature increases in this layer with increasing altitude. This layer is free from clouds and associated weather phenomena thus providing ideal flying conditions for jet planes.

The mesosphere lies above the stratosphere. Meteors, which we commonly call 'shooting stars', burns up in the sky in this layer of the atmosphere. It is the coldest layer of the atmosphere because of the low concentration of ozone causing very less solar radiation to be absorbed in this layer. Due to this, the water vapour present is frozen. This forms ice clouds, which are a mixture of ice particles dispersed in air.

Temperatures rise up to 4500 Fahrenheit in the thermosphere as gas molecules absorb X-ray radiation, resulting in the breaking up of gas molecules into positively charged and negatively charged particles called ions. These particles facilitate wireless communication on the Earth. Due to the presence of ions, this layer is also known as ionosphere. Satellites move around our planet in the thermosphere. One can find the International Space Station in this layer of the atmosphere.

The exosphere is the uppermost layer of the atmosphere. This layer separates the Earth's atmosphere from outer space. It is very thin with only traces of hydrogen and helium present in it. This layer is extremely cold.

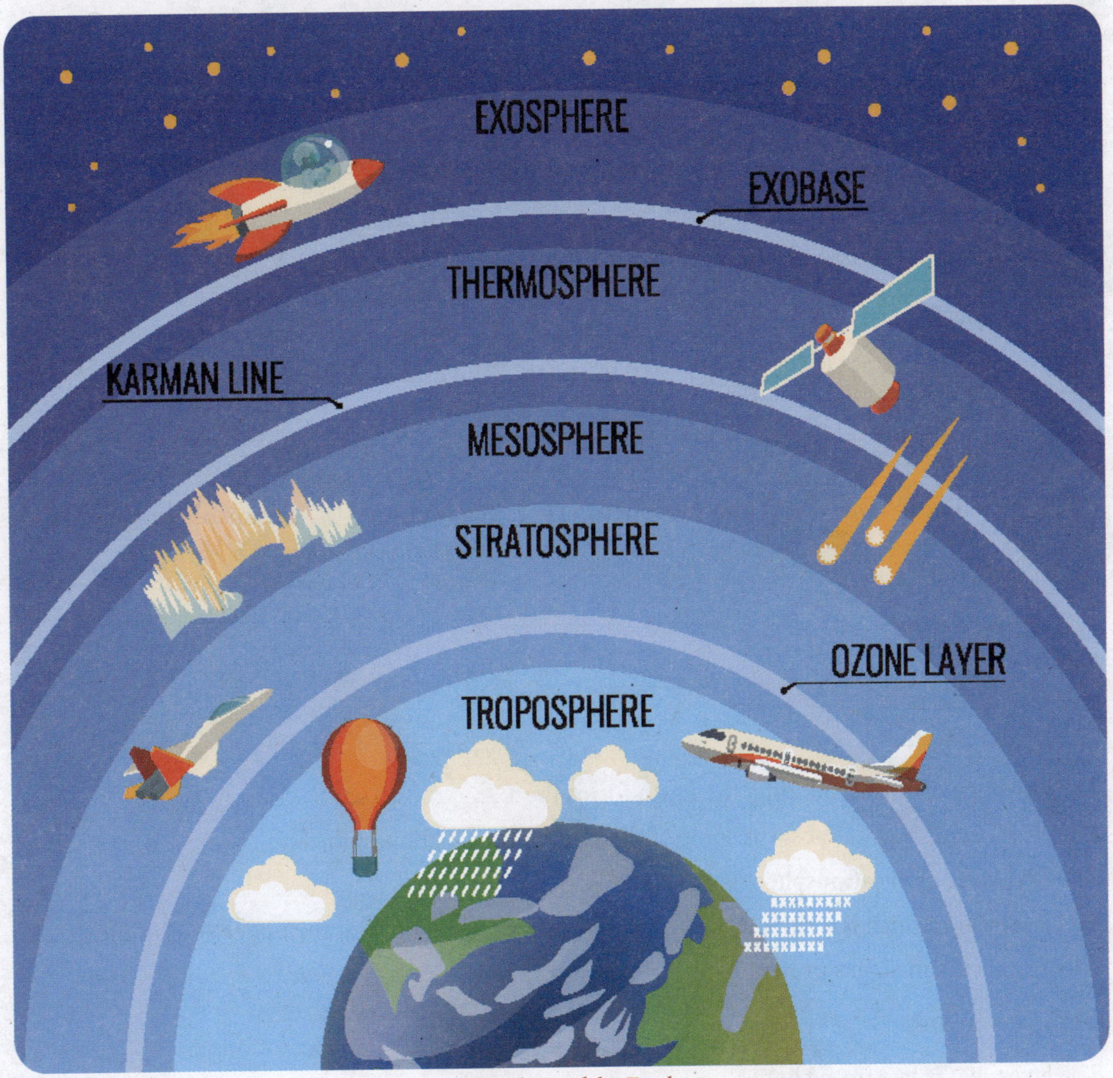

Atmosphere of the Earth

Skill Builder

21ST CENTURY SKILLS

Critical thinking skills: Why does a jet plane flying high in the sky leave behind a white trail?

Collaboration: Conduct a debate in the class on the topic: 'The ozone layer is both a boon and a curse to life.' Discuss in relation to the troposphere and stratospheric ozone.

Life skills: What is global warming? How is it affected by green house gases? Suggest a few measures that can be taken to reduce global warming.

World Connect

In July 2016, NASA kicked off the first stage of a large-scale, airborne greenhouse gas study, the Atmospheric Carbon and Transport–America project. It focuses on the movement of two specific greenhouse gases—carbon dioxide and methane. By tracking and studying how exactly these two gases cycle through our atmosphere, scientists hope to understand how they contribute to climate change.

Wind up

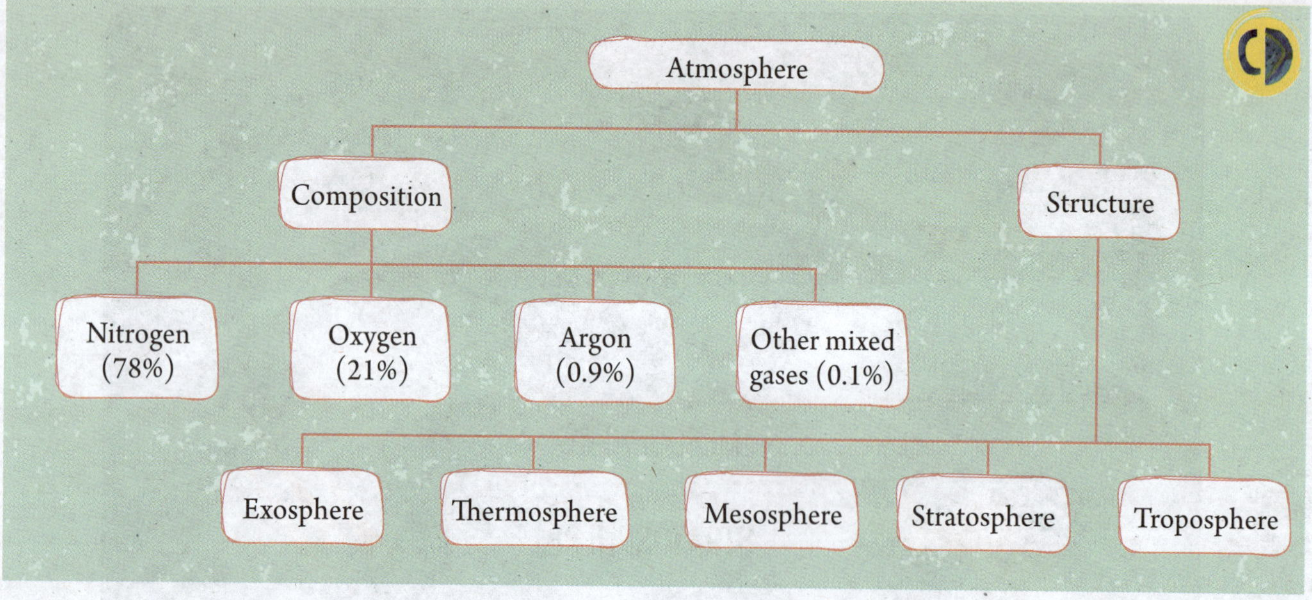

Exercises

A. Fill in the blanks.

1. The envelope of air surrounding the Earth forms the ....
2. The .... gas absorbs some of the ultraviolet radiation of the Sun.
3. The first layer of the atmosphere is the ....
4. The jet stream, which is a narrow, fast-moving 'river' of wind, flows at the upper edge of the ....
5. Nitrogen is the main gas present in air, constituting about ....

B. Answer in one word.

1. The layer that is free from clouds: ....
2. Meteors burn up in this layer of the atmosphere: ....
3. Ozone is present in this layer of the atmosphere: ....
4. The incoming solar heat: ....

C. Choose the correct answers.

1. The atmosphere of Earth is the
   a. layer of gases that surrounds the Earth
   b. layer of Earth's crust
   c. both a and b
   d. none of these

2. The atmosphere of the Earth is retained by
   a. Earth's gravity   b. Earth's core   c. both (A) and (B)   d. none of the above

3. The atmosphere protects life on Earth
   a. by creating pressure allowing for liquid water to exist on the Earth's surface
   b. by absorbing ultraviolet radiations
   c. by warming the surface through greenhouse effect
   d. all of the above

4. The temperature in the thermosphere
   a. decreases   b. increases
   c. remains constant   d. first decreases then increases

5. The atmosphere
   a. becomes thicker with increasing altitude
   b. becomes thinner with increasing altitude
   c. remains the same with increasing altitude
   d. none of the above

D. Write T for true and F for false.

1. Hydrogen constitutes about 21% of the air.
2. In the stratosphere, the temperature decreases with increasing height.
3. Electrically charged particles are called ions.
4. The lower part of the exosphere is called ionosphere.
5. The mesosphere protects the Earth from meteors.

E. Answer these questions in brief.

1. What is the troposphere?
2. In which layer of atmosphere do all the weather conditions occur?
3. What is the ozone layer?
4. What is insolation?
5. What is the composition of the atmosphere?

F. Answer these questions in detail.

1. Describe the structure of the atmosphere.
2. How is the troposphere important to us?
3. Why is the thermosphere also called ionosphere?
4. Distinguish between the mesosphere and the thermosphere.

Think Big Integrate with science

Discuss the importance of green plants and their role in conserving the air around us. Go through science journals and find out about the nitrogen cycle and the oxygen cycle.

Learning Tools

List the important points under each title for swift recap of the chapter.

Atmosphere

Significance

....

....

....

....

....

Composition

....

....

....

....

....

....

....

Layers

→ ....

→ ....

→ ....

→ ....

→ ....

Greenhouse effect

....

....

....

....

Important points

....

....

....

....

Web links:

https://www.nationalgeographic.org/encyclopedia/atmosphere/

https://climatekids.nasa.gov/greenhouse-effect/

Last accessed on 31 August 2021

6. Weather and Climate

Warm up

Tanvi lives in a hilly town in Meghalaya. As she was getting ready for school, her brother turned on the radio to check the weather forecast before heading out. This is a regular practice as it rains heavily in that region. The siblings learnt from the radio report that they should be cautious while venturing out, as there is a likelihood of a storm with heavy rainfall. Their parents told them to stay at home that day as the weather is so unpredictable. Weather and climate are two different terms. Let us learn how!

Weather is the name given to the ever-changing conditions of the atmosphere at a specific place over a short period of time. Weather conditions include hot and cold air, winds and storms. Weather might change continuously and is not the same everywhere. It may be hot and sunny during the day but the evening might be freezing due to heavy rainfall on the same day. Thus, weather may change from moment to moment. The average weather conditions of a particular region over a thirty-year period are called **climate**.

Different places on Earth have different types of climates. Temperature, location on the Earth, humidity, wind, amount of sunlight received, atmospheric phenomenon and precipitation or rainfall are all taken into account to determine the climate of a place.

Temperature

The degree of hotness or coldness of the air is called **temperature**. It is determined by the amount of heat present in the air. To measure temperature, we use a thermometer. Most thermometers are marked with degrees on a scale called celsius. On this scale, water freezes at 0° C and boils at 100° C.

Heat Zones

The Earth is divided into three heat zones on the basis of the amount of sunlight and heat it receives from the Sun. These are the Torrid Zone, the Temperate Zone and the Frigid Zone.

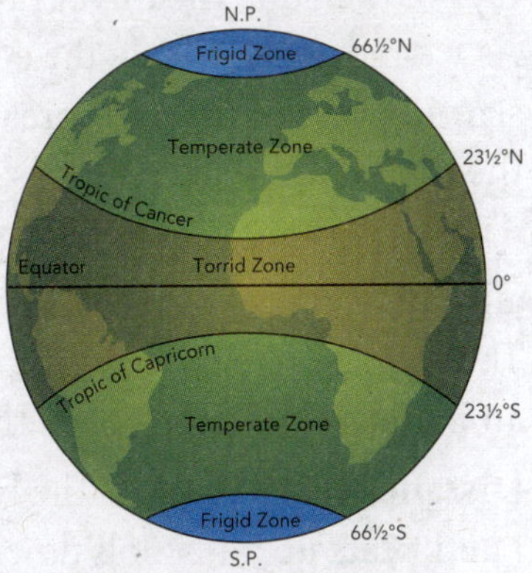

Heat zones of the Earth

Torrid Zone: The area lying between the equator and each of the two tropics, the Tropic of Cancer and the Tropic of Capricorn, is called the Torrid Zone. The Torrid Zone receives the maximum amount of the Sun's heat and sunlight throughout the year. Indonesia, Malaysia, Thailand, Vietnam, Taiwan, Burma, Sri Lanka, India, Bangladesh, Ghana, Madagascar, Chile, Brazil, Argentina and Mexico are some countries that are located in this zone.

Apply it! HC E

How does the air get heated?

Air is generally warmed by the heat from the Earth's surface. The heat on the Earth's surface comes from the Sun. Insolation is the incoming solar energy received by the Earth's surface.

Perform this experiment to find out why there is a difference in temperatures in different places.

1. Hold a torch and shine it vertically on a ball.
2. Observe the area covered and brightness of the patch.
3. Now shine the beam of light at a slant.

Compare the area and brightness of the patch with the brightness formed by the vertical beam. As the beam is slanted, it spreads over a larger area and its brightness decreases. The brightness decreases because the same amount of light is now distributed over a large surface.

- The same theory applies in the heating up of the Earth's surface.

Temperate Zone: This zone extends from the Tropic of Cancer to the Arctic Circle in the Northern Hemisphere and from the Tropic of Capricorn to the Antarctic Circle in the Southern Hemisphere. The regions that fall in this zone receive moderate **insolation** because the sunlight that falls in these areas is slanting. This makes the temperature in these regions moderate. Countries that fall in this zone are the United States of America, European countries, India, Canada, Japan, New Zealand, Middle East countries and North African countries.

Frigid Zone: The Frigid Zone lies between the Arctic Circle and the North Pole in the Northern Hemisphere and between the Antarctic Circle and the South Pole in the Southern Hemisphere. This zone receives the least insolation, that is, low intensity of sunlight. As a result, this area experiences an extremely cold climate. Alaska, Sweden, Finland, Greenland and Northern Russia are some countries lying in the Frigid Zone.

Factors Affecting Temperature

There are several factors that affect the temperature of a place.

Latitude: The latitude at which a place is located affects the temperature of the place. The curvature of the Earth heats the different parts of the Earth at varying degrees. The regions near the equator get more direct rays of the Sun. The direct rays are concentrated over a smaller area, and so, they heat up the region more. As we move away from the equator, due to the **curvature,** the Sun's rays fall on the Earth at an angle. The slanting rays of the Sun spread the heat over a larger area, and so, they do not heat the regions a lot. Thus, the temperature decreases as the distance from the equator increases.

Altitude: The Earth's atmosphere is heated by the energy absorbed by the molecules of gases. As the altitude increases, the density of air decreases. Thus, the amount of heat absorbed decreases with height. The average rate of change of temperature is 1°C for every 165 m of height in the troposphere. Thus, with an increase in height above the surface of the Earth, the temperature decreases.

Distance from the sea: The heating of the Earth's surface directly influences the heating of the air above. Land heats up and cools down faster than water. So, the land is warmer than the ocean in the summer and cooler than oceans in winter. Therefore, places near the sea are cool in summer and warm in winter. On the contrary, as the distance from the sea increases, in the interior of the continents, the temperature conditions become harsh. For instance, Delhi experiences harsh winters and summers.

insolation: the incoming solar radiation from the Sun to the Earth's surface; curvature: the fact of being curved or the degree to which something is curved

Prevailing winds: Winds that blow from the equator and lower latitudes, like the Westerlies, are warm and make the place they blow into warmer. On the other hand, winds that blow from the poles and higher latitudes, for example, the cold polar winds, are cold and make the place they blow into colder. Winds that blow from the sea, called on-shore winds, bring plenty of rain, especially if they are warm winds. Offshore winds hardly bring any rain.

Slope of the land: In the northern hemisphere, the southern slopes of the mountains receive direct heat from the Sun and are hotter when compared to the slopes of the mountains in the north. Hence, the southern slopes are favourable for the purpose of agriculture and human settlements.

Ocean currents: The currents from the low latitudes are warm currents and have a warming effect on the coastal areas. This makes the coast and seaports ice-free in winter. When the cold currents from the Arctic regions move towards the south at lower latitudes, they freeze the coast and many ports.

Atmospheric Pressure

The air has weight, and it exerts pressure. Atmospheric pressure is the pressure that the atmosphere exerts on the surface of the Earth.

What's in the picture?

Which factors do you think are most effective in controlling the weather and climate of this place?

Factors Affecting Atmospheric Pressure

Altitude: Air pressure is the highest at sea level and decreases with altitude. As one goes up, the density of air decreases and so does the pressure exerted by it.

Temperature: When temperature increases, the air expands, and its density decreases. As a result, air becomes lighter and exerts less pressure. In contrast, cold air is dense and heavier. Therefore, it exerts more pressure.

Water vapour: Air containing more water vapour is lighter than air that has little or no water vapour. Thus, moist air exerts less pressure than dry air.

Pressure Belts

Air pressure is measured by a barometer. Can we feel air pressure? No, not usually, as it is countered by an equal pressure from inside our body. However, when you go up or down a hill or you are in an aircraft, your ears get blocked due to the change of air pressure.

Since different latitudes receive different amounts of heat from the Sun, there exist a number of pressure belts:

Equatorial Low-Pressure Belt (5° N and 5° S): This area gets vertical rays of the Sun, therefore, it is very hot in this region. Warm air being lighter rises up, thus, the region experiences a low atmospheric pressure.

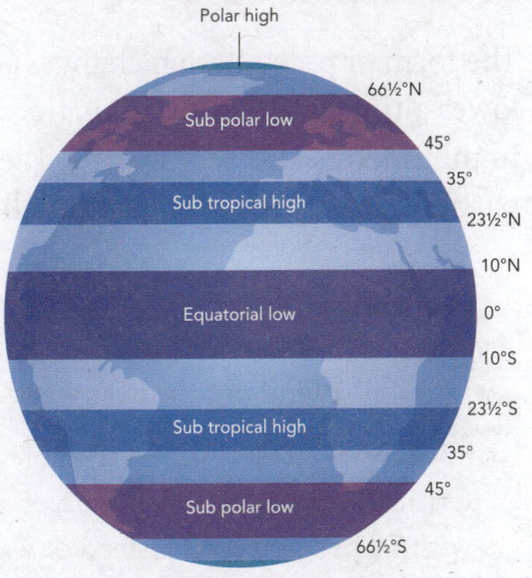

Pressure belts

Subtropical High-Pressure Belt (30° N and 30° S): Ascending air from the equatorial low-pressure belt cools and descends, creating a high-pressure region. It is also called the Horse Latitude.

Subpolar Low-Pressure Belt (60° N and 60° S): As the warm air from the tropical regions comes in contact with the cold polar regions, the warm air rises above the cold air. This leads to low pressure in this region. Also, the bulk of the air is pushed towards the equator.

Polar High-Pressure Belts: Extremely low temperatures cause cooling and contraction of dense air at the poles, which sink to form the high pressure in this belt.

Winds

Moving air is called wind. They always blow from high-pressure to low-pressure regions. The main cause of wind is the unequal heating of the atmosphere by the Sun resulting in differences in the pressure between places. How do you think scientists and meteorologists study wind? They do so by measuring the wind's direction and speed. An anemometer is used for measuring the speed of the wind. A wind vane is used to determine the direction of the wind. Winds are usually named after the direction they originate from.

> **FACT CHECK**
>
> *Loo* is a strong dusty wind that blows over North India during the day time in summers. It causes low humidity and high temperature in the entire Indo-Gangetic Plain.

Local winds: Local winds are created as a result of mountains, vegetation and water bodies. Good examples of local winds are sea breezes and land breezes. Local winds cover very short distances.

Permanent winds: These are large air masses that are created mainly as a result of the Earth's rotation, and the pressure belts created due to the uneven heating of the Earth's surface. They blow constantly in a particular direction throughout the year. Some examples of permanent winds are trade winds, westerlies and the polar easterlies.

Seasonal winds: Seasonal winds are driven by changes in the weather patterns. These winds change their directions with the change in seasons. Seasonal winds occur in many locations throughout the world. An example is the monsoon wind.

Humidity

Humidity increases or decreases with the change in air temperature. For example, at a temperature of 0 °C, one cubic meter of air may contain 4.8 g of vapour. At a temperature of 30° C, it will increase to 30.4 g. We can infer that the higher the temperature of the air, the more moisture it can absorb. Thus, warm air blowing over oceans and seas picks up moisture, which brings much needed rainfall.

Precipitation

The form of precipitation changes with the change in temperature. For example, rainfall is common in lower altitudes and snowfall is frequent in the higher altitudes. Rainfall is measured with a rain gauge in millimetres and centimetres. The daily records are added for a year, which is the total rainfall in one particular year. The average rainfall of a place for 35 to 40 years is called the mean annual rainfall.

Skill Builder

21ST CENTURY SKILLS

Life skills: Find out the next week's weather forecast by looking on the Internet.

Creativity: Based on your findings, write a short weather report and read it out in class.

Critical-thinking skills: Have you ever stopped to think what the Earth would be like if it was covered with 70 per cent land instead of water? Write an essay on what would happen.

World Connect

NASA's Hubble Space Telescope has found clues that suggest that two exoplanets may be habitable. The exoplanets, which lie beyond our solar system, Trappist-1b and Trappist-1c, are believed to have atmospheres unlike the hydrogen-dominated atmospheres found on gaseous planets. Both exoplanets lack the hydrogen-helium envelope, which would create a dense atmosphere and act like a greenhouse.

Wind up

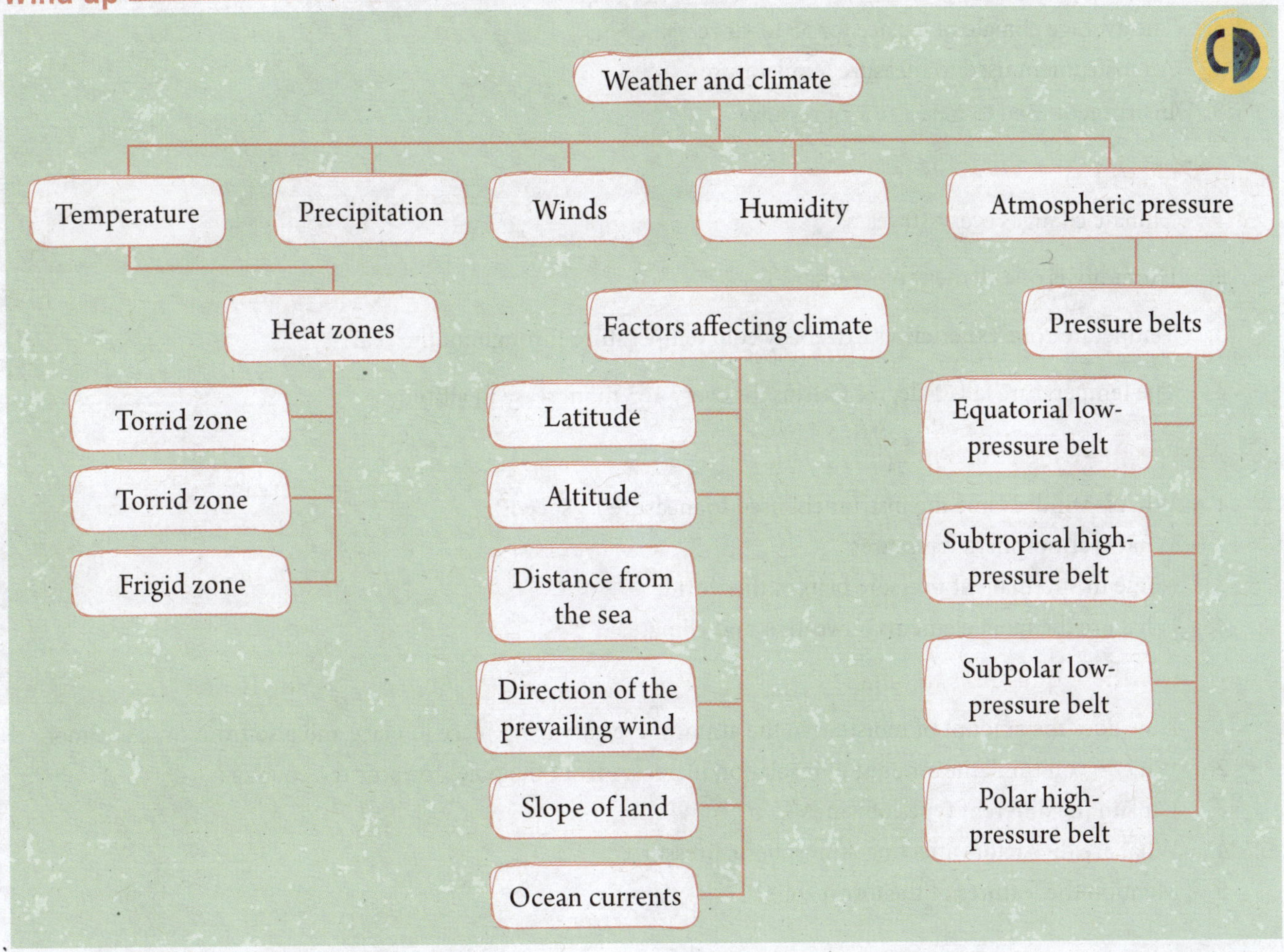

Exercises

A. Choose the correct answers.

1. It increases or decreases with the change in air temperature.
   a. Rainfall b. Humidity c. Wind d. Pressure
2. Monsoon wind is an example of a
   a. permanent wind b. seasonal wind c. local wind d. none of these
3. These types of winds cover very short distances
   a. permanent winds b. seasonal winds c. local winds d. none of these

4. Weather changes
   a. week after week
   b. day after day
   c. within a short period
   d. in any of the above time period
5. Rainfall is measured by
   a. a rain gauge
   b. water level increase in ponds
   c. water level increase in water table
   d. none of these

B. Name the following.

1. Moving air: ....
2. An example of a seasonal wind: ....
3. The average climate of a place for 35 to 40 years: ....
4. An instrument used to measure temperature: ....
5. Instrument used to measure air pressure: ....

C. Write T for true and F for false.

1. Climate changes every 10 years. ☐
2. Humidity is one element of weather. ☐
3. Temperate zone experiences extremely cold temperature throughout the year. ☐
4. The temperature falls 1 degree Celsius for every 165 m increase in altitude. ☐

D. Answer these questions in brief.

1. What is wind? Name the instrument used to measure its speed.
2. What is atmospheric pressure?
3. Name the permanent pressure belts of the world.
4. What are the main elements of weather and climate?

E. Answer these questions in detail.

1. How does the amount of moisture in the atmosphere vary from place to place and also from time to time?
2. Why do you think the amount of insolation increases from the poles towards the equator?
3. Explain the different types of winds.
4. What are the factors affecting atmospheric pressure?
5. Mention the features of the torrid zone.

Think Big

Integrate with Science

Balancing balloons!

Air, like most substances, becomes bigger (expands) when it is heated. Blow up two balloons to the same size. Tie each balloon to one end of a long, thin piece of wood. Balance this on a pencil supported by cans or books and mark the balance on the wood.

Next, put one balloon in a cold place, for instance, a fridge and the other in a warm place and watch. Let some air out of the warm balloon and blow some air into the cold balloon, so that they are the same size. Now do they balance?

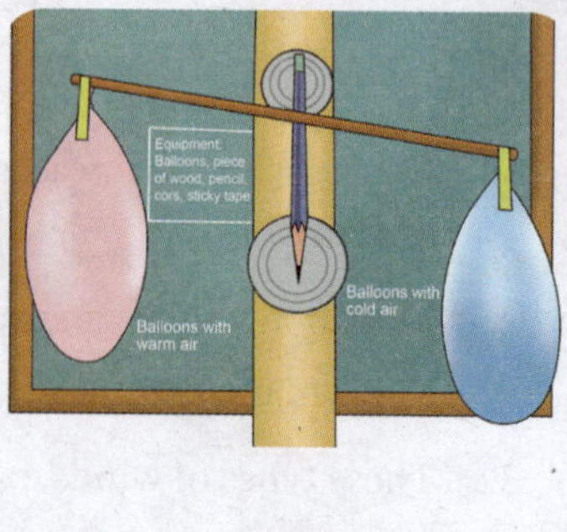

Learning Tools

Complete the following table.

Name of the Pressure belt	Location	Causes	Features
Equatorial low-pressure belt	5° ---5°N & S of Equator	Vertical rays of the Sun	
	30° ---35° N & S		Horse Latitudes
Sub-polar low-pressure belt		Bulk of air is pushed towards the equator	
	70°--90° N & S	Extremely low temperatures cause cooling and contraction of dense air	

Web links:

https://climatekids.nasa.gov/menu/weather-and-climate/
https://www.bbc.co.uk/bitesize/guides/zgyw4qt/revision/1

Last accessed on 31 August 2021

7. Water

Warm up

What makes the Earth unique? It has all the necessities to sustain life. The Earth is made up of 71% water and 29% land. This means that water is more **predominant** than land on the Earth. However, of all the water that exists on the Earth, only one per cent is **potable**. Most of the Earth's water is found in seas and oceans. We already know that the Earth's temperature varies according to the place, the water that is found in each of these places is also different. Water exists in three states—solid, liquid and gas.

The realm of water on the Earth is called the hydrosphere. The hydrosphere consists of all the Earth's water—on the surface, in the ground and in the air. Water is found mostly in the basins of seas and in oceans, where it has a depth of about 3 to 4 km. The oceans account for 97.2% of the Earth's water; rivers and lakes hold about 0.017%—all either existing as freshwater or salt water. In the solid form, water exists in the form of polar caps and ice sheets, which make up 2.15% of the Earth's water. Only 0.0001% of the water is present in the atmosphere in the form of water vapour.

Condensation: It is the process by which water vapour changes into water when it comes in contact with a cold surface. Clouds, fog, mist, dew and frost are some examples of condensation.

Precipitation: It is the process by which condensed water vapour falls on the ground in various forms, such as rain, snow and hail.

Types of Rainfall

Convectional Rainfall: When the land warms up, it heats the air above it. This causes the air to expand and rise. As the air rises, it cools and condenses. If this process continues, then rainfall will occur. This type of rainfall is very common in tropical areas.

Relief Rainfall: It occurs when warm, moist air ascends along the slope of a mountain. The air then condenses and rainfall occurs on the **windward** side. The **leeward** side of the mountain receives very little rainfall. This is called the rain shadow region.

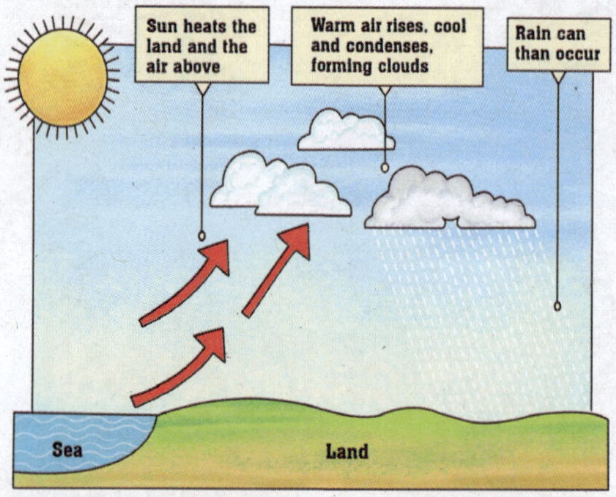

Convectional rainfall

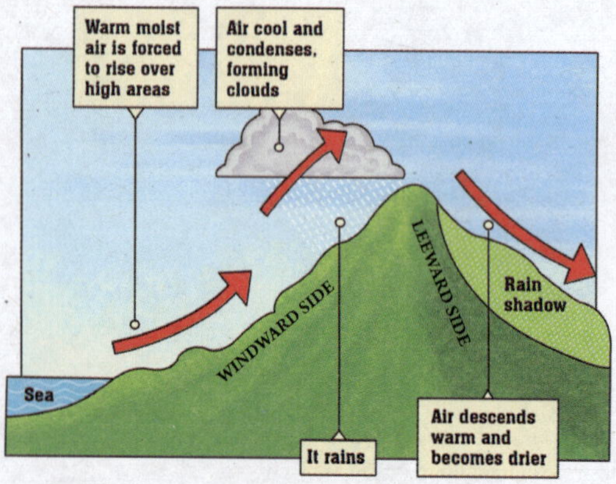

Relief rainfall

predominant: having superiority in power or influence over others; potable: fit to drink; windward: facing the wind or on the side facing the wind; leeward: on or towards the side sheltered from the wind

Cyclonic Rainfall: It is also known as frontal rain. It is caused when two air masses of different temperatures meet. Warm air and cool air do not mix as they have different densities. As the warm air rises over the heavier cool air, it cools and creates a front, then clouds form and produce rain.

Cyclinic rainfall

Water Cycle

Oceans are the primary source of water on the Earth. Water evaporates from the ocean into the atmosphere. Water also enters the atmosphere through evaporation from soil, plants and other water surfaces. The water vapour in the air condenses into clouds. Winds blowing from the ocean, transport the moisture in the cloud. This condensed water vapour comes down as rain and snow mainly over the land. Some of this precipitation that falls is absorbed by plants and soil. The rest of it runs into rivers or seeps into underground streams. This is known as surface run-off. This excess water flows in the form of rivers and streams to reach the sea. From the land, water makes its way back to the sea, and the cycle begins again. Thus, water cycle is the continuous circulation and changes in the form of water across the ocean, seas, land and atmosphere.

Water cycle

Apply it!

Make a rain gauge.

Take an empty milk carton and cut off the top part of it. Bury the carton in the ground, and keep a ruler standing in the carton. Once it rains, you can find out how much it rained.

The actual movement of water can be quite complicated in actuality. For example:

- Some of the water may seep underground and later appear on the surface in the form of a spring at some other place.
- Some of the water may remain frozen and may become part of the cycle only when it melts.
- Some water may become a part of the city water supply before joining this cycle.

Temperature and Salinity of Ocean Water

Ocean water gets heated by the Sun. In general, water is warmer near the equator. The temperature decreases towards the poles. The highest temperatures are recorded in enclosed tropical seas.

Ocean water is **saline** due to the presence of a large amount of dissolved salts. These minerals are brought down by the rivers in the silt they carry. Salinity means the degree of saltiness of the oceans and seas. It is expressed as the number of parts of salt dissolved in a thousand parts of sea water. The average salt content is 35 g/kg of sea water. The Dead Sea has a salinity of 280 parts per thousand. The Arctic Ocean has the lowest salinity of 20 parts per thousand.

Movements in the Ocean

The oceans are never still. They keep moving constantly. There are three different kinds of movements—waves, tides and ocean currents. Winds provide the main force for the horizontal movement of ocean water. This movement is basically due to prevailing winds, differences in temperature and salinity of ocean water and variation in the density of ocean water.

FACT CHECK

The highest point of the wave is called the crest and the lowest is called the trough.

Waves

The up and down movements seen due to rise and fall of ocean waters are called waves. Most waves are caused by wind when it brushes the surface of the sea. Average ocean waves are about 1.5 to 3 m high. In shallow water, near the shore, waves break. Waves have great force and are powerful agents of erosion. Some are triggered by underwater landslides and earthquakes and volcanic eruptions in or near the ocean. These waves can be as high as 20 to 30 m. They are called tsunamis. The most common cause of a tsunami is an undersea earthquake. It causes large areas of the sea floor to rise or subside. This leads to the generation of huge waves with extremely long wavelengths. A tsunami travels at speeds of about 500 to 1,000 km per hour. Its speed reduces as it enters the shallow water near the coast.

What's in the picture?

Identify this movement. What causes it?

Tides

The alternate rise and fall of the ocean waters twice in 24 hours are known as tides. When the water has risen to its highest level, covering much of the shore, it is at high tide. When the water falls to its lowest level and recedes away from the shore, it is low tide.

Tides are caused by the gravitational pull of the Moon and Sun. Since the Moon is much closer to the Earth, it has a more pronounced effect on tide formation. The two major types of tides are:

Spring tide: It occurs when the Sun, Moon and Earth all lie in the same line. Since, the gravitational pull of the Moon and Sun acts together, the tides generated are highest. Thus, it occurs during the new moon and full moon.

Neap tide: It occurs when the Sun and the Moon are not in one line but at right angles to each other. Since the water in this case gets drawn in opposite directions under the influence of the Sun and the Moon, the tides produced are lowest.

saline: of, concerned with, consisting of, or containing common salt

Tides are very important.

- The increased depth of water at high tide helps larger ships to enter the harbour.
- Many ships use the retreating waters of the low tide to leave harbours.
- Tides constantly sweep the coasts, carrying away the silt brought down by rivers, thus keeping the river channels and many harbours free from sediment.
- During high tides, low-lying areas along sea coasts are flooded and this water is used for manufacturing salt. Salt is produced in this manner along the west coast of India.
- Strong tidal currents are also used to generate electricity.
- Fishermen depend on their regular rhythm of high and low tide for their livelihood. At the time of high tides, large-scale fishing is carried on in creeks, bays and lagoons.

Ocean Currents

Streams of water move along the surface of the ocean in definite paths as well as direction. Such more or less permanent streams of water flowing in a definite direction are known as ocean currents.

Ocean currents develop due to the

- variation in the temperature of ocean water.
- variation in the density of ocean water.
- direction of the prevailing wind.
- rotation of the Earth.
- shape and position of the coast.

Ocean currents can be cold or warm. Currents that originate near the equator and flow towards the poles are warm currents. Those that originate in the high latitudes and flow towards the equator are cold currents. The general circulation of ocean currents is clockwise in the Northern Hemisphere and anti-clockwise in the Southern Hemisphere. Some important ocean currents are the Gulf Stream and the Labrador Current.

The Gulf Stream originates in the Gulf of Mexico in the Alantic Ocean. It is a warm current. As it moves across the ocean, it is known as North Atlantic Drift. The Labrador Current flows southwards from the Arctic Ocean along the coast of Canada. This is a cold current as it originates in the Arctic Ocean.

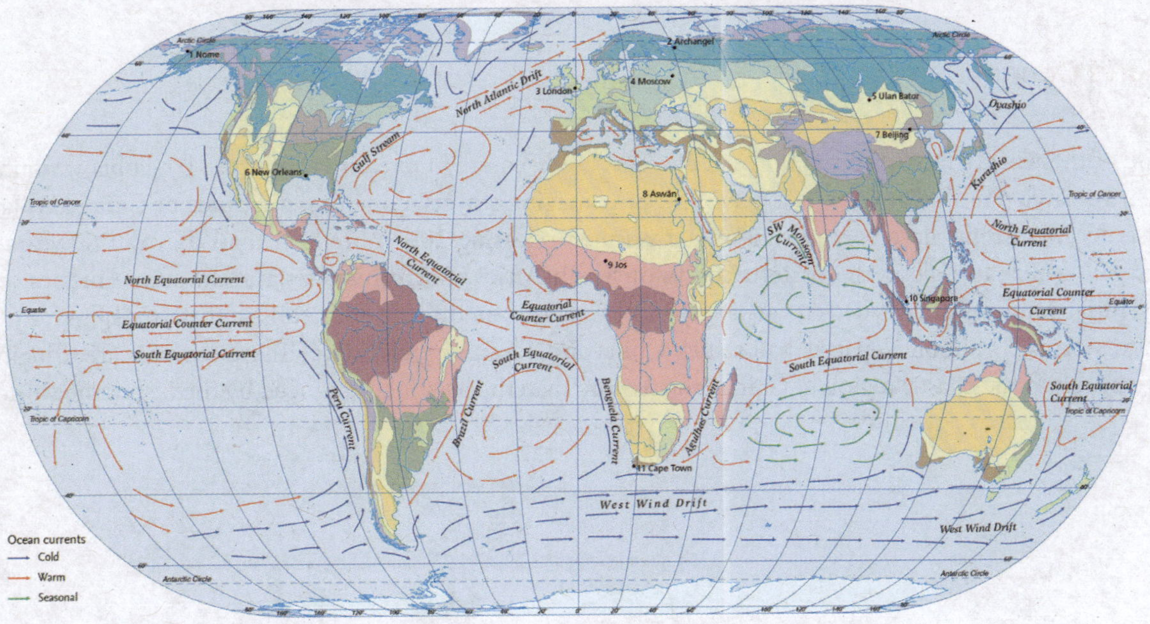

Ocean currents

Effects of Ocean Currents

- Ocean currents influence the distribution of temperature around the Earth. The warm and cold currents increase or decrease the temperature in the coastal areas respectively.
- Warm currents increase the moisture-bearing capacity of the wind and cold currents decrease the same. Deserts are mostly along the western side of the continents where cold currents flow.
- Mixing of cold and warm currents causes dense fog which hampers navigation.
- The best places for fishing are found where warm and cold currents meet, for example, areas around Newfoundland, Canada and Japan.
- Ocean currents help in navigation.
- Warm currents help in keeping the oceans free of ice, which makes it easier for the ports to function.

Geography skills

Working from this map, locate two cold currents, two warm currents and two seasonal currents on an outline map of the world.

Skill Builder

21ST CENTURY SKILLS

Critical thinking skills: Do you think ocean circulation is necessary? Support your arguments with the help of examples.

Life skills: You will need milk cartons, toothbrush and toothpaste to perform this activity.

1. Leave the water running while brushing your teeth. During the same time, ask someone else to fill some glasses with the running water till you finish brushing.
2. Record how many glasses are filled. Then multiply the number of family members you have with the number of times each person brushes his or her teeth.
3. Then, multiply the result with the total number of glasses of water you collected. This is actually how much water your family can save if they turn off the water while brushing!

World Connect

Some of the world's most important ocean currents are becoming increasingly affected by global warming. A recent research shows that there is a grave risk of damaging storms along the coastlines of China and Japan. These ocean currents have been getting much warmer, releasing 20% more heat than they did 50 years ago. Currents, which run along the eastern coasts of South Africa, Asia, Australasia and South America, carry substantial amounts of heat. This is caused by increasing carbon dioxide emissions in the atmosphere and can lead to storms. Typhoon Nepartak had struck China and Taiwan in July, 2016. These currents are bringing in more heat into the coastal region of China, much more than the heat increase faced by the rest of the world.

Wind up

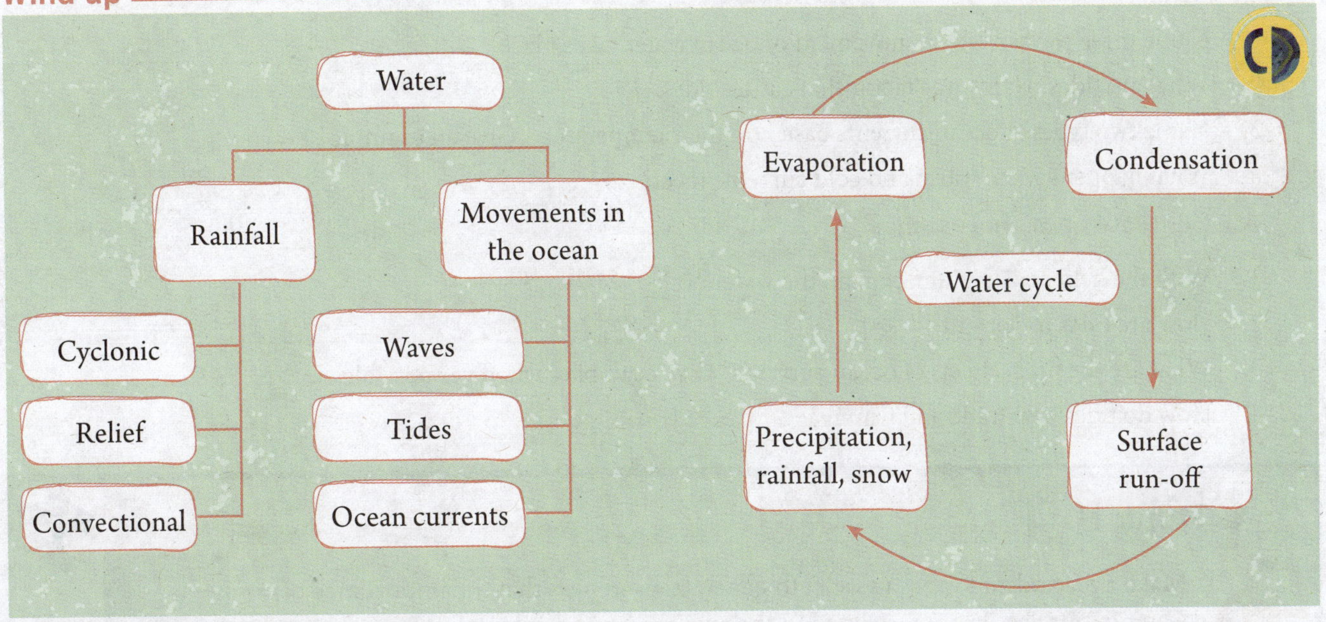

Exercises

A. Fill in the blanks.

1. Waves that are as high as 20 to 30 m are called ....
2. When the water falls to its lowest level, it is a .... tide.
3. The Labrador Current is an .... current.
4. Ocean water is saline due to the presence of a large amount of .... salts.
5. When cold and warm currents mix, it creates a dense ....

B. Choose correct answer.

1. Which is the process through which water continuously changes its form?
   a. Water cycle b. Food cycle c. Rain d. All of these
2. Which water is salty?
   a. River water b. Pond water c. Rain water d. Sea water
3. Mixing of cold and warm currents causes dense fog which hampers
   a. navigation b. communication c. fishing d. none of these
4. Oceans contain
   a. 97.3% of water of Earth b. 2% of water of Earth
   c. 0.68% of water of Earth d. 0.973% of water of Earth
5. Ocean currents influence the distribution of this around the Earth.
   a. rainfall b. temperature c. minerals d. none of these

C. Distinguish between these terms.

1. Waves and tides
2. Condensation and precipitation
3. Relief and cyclonic rainfall
4. High tide and low tide

D. Answer these questions in brief.

1. Name three ways in which movement of ocean water takes place.
2. What are tides? Name one factor that causes tides.
3. Name two types of ocean currents based on their temperature. Give an example of each.
4. What happens when warm and cold currents meet?

E. Answer these questions in detail.

1. With the help of a diagram, explain the water cycle.
2. How are tides important?
3. What are the main effects of ocean currents? Give examples, wherever possible.
4. How do tides help trade and fishing?

Think Big

Integrate with Art

Make a placard and write a slogan to generate awareness that the importance of water in our lives is not restricted to the availability of drinking water.

14 LIFE BELOW WATER

Learning Tools

Define and describe each stage of the water cycle.

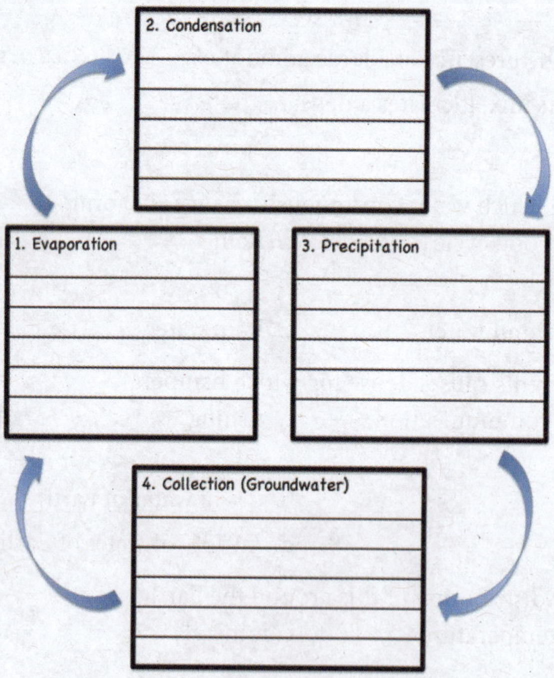

Web links:

https://www.nationalgeographic.org/encyclopedia/hydrosphere/

https://www.nationalgeographic.org/topics/resource-library-ocean-currents/?q=&page=1&per_page=25

Last accessed on 31 August 2021

8. Natural Vegetation and Wildlife

Warm up

The panda, the tiger and the orangutan are the three most endangered animals in Asia. China's forest reserves have some of the last panda habitats of the world. India is trying its best to conserve the Royal Bengal tiger. The orangutan is safe in the less commercialized rainforests of Borneo and Sumatra.

Different forms of wildlife and vegetation are found in different parts of the world. Plants that exist naturally without any human interference are called natural vegetation. Natural vegetation is found in an area called a natural region. A natural region is **homogeneous** with regard to climate, soil and natural vegetation. It is an area of the Earth that has similarities in relief, temperature, rainfall, vegetation and human activity. Different types of natural vegetation interact with wildlife in a natural region. Plants and animals that are found in a particular area are called its ecosystem. They depend on each other for survival.

The natural vegetation of a place is determined by its climatic conditions. For example, forests are found in areas that have a hot and humid climate, shrubs are found in dry areas and grasslands are found in regions that receive moderate rainfall. The altitude of the place, slope of the land, thickness of the soil, temperature and rainfall also affect the vegetation of a place.

Forests

A forest is an ecosystem that consists of a closed formation of trees, shrubs, herbs, microorganisms and animals. The forests of the world are broadly classified into six types.

- Tropical evergreen forests
- Tropical deciduous forests
- Temperate evergreen forests
- Temperate deciduous forests
- Mediterranean forests
- Coniferous forests

Tropical Evergreen Forests

Location: Tropical evergreen forests are found in the equator and regions near the tropics. These forests are also known as rainforests or selvas. The forests are found between 10 °N and 10 °S of the equator. The Amazon Basin and the coast of French Guiana in South America, the Congo Basin, the Guinea Coast of Africa, Malaysia, Indonesia and New Guinea in South Asia have tropical rainforests.

homogeneous: composed of similar or identical parts or elements

Climate: The tropical evergreen forests experience hot climates throughout the year. The Sun is almost always overhead in the sky. This region gets very heavy rainfall, that is, more than 250 cm.

Vegetation: The tropical evergreen forests are covered with dense trees. These trees have broad leaves, which they do not shed all at once, and thus, stay evergreen throughout the year. These trees form a dense **canopy** that prevents the sunlight from reaching the ground.

Mahogany, ebony and rosewood are some of the trees found in these forests. These trees yield hardwood, which is used for making furniture.

FACT CHECK

The world's largest tropical rainforest covers much of the northern part of South America as well as the southern portion of Central America. The region is often called the Amazon basin.

Tropical Deciduous Forests

Location: Tropical deciduous forests are also called monsoon forests. They are found in countries such as India, Pakistan, Bangladesh, Myanmar, Thailand, Vietnam, West Indies, Venezuela and Columbia. The eastern part of Brazil in South America and the northern part of Australia also have these types of forests.

A tropical deciduous forest

Climate: The climate in these regions is marked by a long dry season, which is followed by a season of heavy rainfall. The rainfall ranges from 70 cm to 200 cm.

Vegetation: The trees shed their leaves during the dry season to conserve water. These forests have a thick undergrowth of small trees and shrubs. The trees are not very dense and have a medium height. Some of the trees found in these forests are sal, teak, palm, shisham, sandalwood, neem and bamboo.

Temperate Evergreen Forests

Location: Temperate evergreen forests are mostly found in regions that experience warm summers and cool winters. They are common in coastal regions that have mild winters and heavy rainfall. Temperate evergreen forests are found in many parts of North and South America, Central and Southern Asia, Europe and New Zealand.

A temperate evergreen forest

Climate: These forests experience a moderate climate. The rainfall in these forests is intense in the winters, while the summers are mild and relatively dry.

Vegetation: These forests have mixed vegetation, consisting of both hardwood and softwood trees. Temperate evergreen forests have a variety of trees. Trees with both needle-like and broad leaves are found in these forests. Some of the trees that are found in these forests are pine, cedar, fir, redwood, oak and eucalyptus.

canopy: branches of trees that spread over a forest like a roof

Temperate Deciduous Forests

A temperate deciduous forest

Location: The temperate deciduous forests comprise trees that shed their leaves every year. They are found between 40 °N and 60 °S of the equator. Temperate deciduous forests are found in the eastern United States, parts of Canada, Europe, China and Japan.

Climate: These regions experience hot summers and cold winters.

Vegetation: Temperate deciduous trees shed their leaves in the autumn season and remain leafless throughout the winter season. In spring, new leaves sprout. Oak, ash, beech, elm, poplar, cedar, redwood, fir, maple and birch are some of the trees found in temperate deciduous forests.

Mediterranean Forests

Olive trees in a Mediterranean forest

Location: Mediterranean forests are found in regions with hot and dry summers and cool and moist winters. The areas surrounding the Mediterranean Sea in Europe, Asia, Africa, North America, South America and Australia have these forests.

Climate: These forests have hot and dry summers and mild and wet winters.

Vegetation: Widely spaced trees with broad leaves, thick roots and long roots are found in these forests. The trees are not very tall and many shrubs grow in between them. Trees found in these forests can withstand dry summers without shedding their leaves. Oak, olive, fig, pine, fir, cedar and cypress are the main trees found in these forests. Trees that bear oranges, figs, olives, grapes, peaches and plums grow here.

Coniferous Forests

A coniferous forest

Location: Coniferous forests are also called taiga. These forests are most commonly found in the regions of southern Canada, Norway, Sweden, Poland, Finland and northern Russia.

Climate: The winters are long and severe with temperatures remaining below freezing point for almost six months. The summers are short and cold.

Vegetation: Coniferous trees are tall, straight and evergreen with narrow needle-like leaves. They bear softwood, which is light in weight. There is almost no undergrowth. Spruce, pine, fir, larch, cedar and hemlock are some examples of coniferous trees. Coniferous forests are a source of many valuable products that are of great commercial value. For instance, pulp is used to make paper and other boxes.

Grasslands

They are best understood as a sea of grasses, with grass being the major vegetation of a region. They are found in the interiors of continents that receive low rainfall.

Tropical Grasslands

A savannah

Location: They are found on either side of the equator between the Tropic of Cancer and the Tropic of Capricorn. Tropical grasslands cover most of Africa, parts of the Brazilian plateau in South America, large areas of northern Australia and India. Tropical grasslands have various names. They are called savannah in Africa and campos in Brazil.

Climate: The temperature is mostly hot. The summers are hot and wet, and winters are dry and warm. It rains for 6 to 8 months in these regions. The total rainfall is between 25 cm and 75 cm.

Vegetation: Tall grasses, about 2 m to 4 m in height, grow here along with scattered trees. These grasslands are used extensively for animal grazing and farming.

Temperate Grasslands

A temperate grassland

Location: Temperate grasslands are located in the mid-latitude temperate regions that are found in the interior of the continents. These grasslands are known as the steppes in Europe, pampas in South America, prairies in North America and veld in South Africa and Australia. Temperate grasslands are drier and colder than the tropical grasslands.

Climate: Temperate grasslands have hot summers and cold winters.

Vegetation: The vegetation in these grasslands consists of short grasses as the rainfall received here is not sufficient for the growth of trees.

Deserts

Deserts are large areas that cannot support any vegetation because of inadequate or no precipitation. Some deserts have sparse vegetation. Deserts are of three types—tropical deserts, temperate deserts and the tundra or polar deserts.

Tropical Deserts

Location: Tropical deserts are located along the western margin of continents.

Climate: These areas experience extremely high temperatures and very less rainfall.

Vegetation: These deserts have very scarce vegetation because of very little or no rainfall. The leaves of the plants are modified into thorn-like spines and have a waxy coating to prevent the loss of water. The roots are long and grow deep into the soil to absorb water. The stems are fleshy and store water. Some of the plants that grow in the deserts are date palms, cactus, thorny bushes, coarse grasses and acacia.

Temperate Deserts

Location: These deserts are cold deserts located in the temperate zones, which are located in the interior of the continents. The Gobi desert in Mongolia and the Kyzyl Kum and Taklamakan deserts of Central Asia are temperate deserts.

Climate: The temperate deserts experience extremely high temperatures during the summers. The winters are cold and it snows.

A desert

Tundra or Polar Deserts

Location: These deserts are located in northern Canada, southern Greenland, northern Eurasia and Alaska.

Climate: Winters are very long and cold, while summers are very short and cool. There is very little rainfall. The soil in these regions is permanently frozen and is known as permafrost. The Sun does not rise for months during the winters, and during the summers, it does not set for months.

Vegetation: Very few plants grow in the polar deserts. Most of the plants are short and stunted. Mosses, lichens, dwarfed willows and shrubs grow here.

Wildlife

Wildlife of an area includes undomesticated animal species that exist in the wild. There are different types of wildlife in deserts, rainforests, plains and grasslands.

What's in the picture?

What human quality is this animal associated with? Give reasons why.

Animals of the Tropical Region

The tropical region is covered with dense forests that have tall trees. Most of the animals live on trees and are called arboreal animals. Some of the animals found here are monkeys, apes, sloths, bats, tree lizards and lemurs. The world's largest snake, the anaconda, is found in the tropical evergreen forests of the Amazon rainforest. Turtles, snakes, alligators and crocodiles are found in the marshes and rivers. Tigers, lions, rhinos and leopards are found in monsoon forests.

Animals of the Temperate Regions

Temperate deciduous forests are rich in wildlife. Animals found there include raccoons, bears, red and grey foxes, various species of deer, elk, bison, wolves, coyotes, prairie dogs, amongst many more. Arboreal marsupials, which are found only in these regions, along with different species of frogs and toads, are found here along with a variety of songbirds. There are seasonal changes in these regions that affect these animals too. Migration and hibernation are two ways that help the animals survive the harsh winter months.

Prairie dogs

Animals of the Grasslands

In tropical grasslands, animals like zebras, giraffes, deer, elephants, leopards, panthers and hyenas are found. In temperate grasslands, antelopes, wild asses, wolves and wild dogs are found.

Apply it!

Find out the only continent in the world that does not have any grasslands. Also, find out the flora and fauna found in that continent.

Animals of the Deserts

Because of the heat, most of the animals in deserts are **nocturnal**. Some of them are burrowing animals. The camel is well-adapted to desert conditions. Wild asses, jackals and foxes are also found here.

Reindeer

Animals of the Cold Regions

Animals living in the cold regions have a thick skin and are covered with fur to protect themselves from the cold. Reindeer, musk ox, polar bear, wolf, Arctic fox, seal and walrus are some animals found in these regions. **Migration** is a common phenomenon in the cold or polar regions. During winters, the animals migrate to warmer areas to protect themselves from the extreme weather conditions.

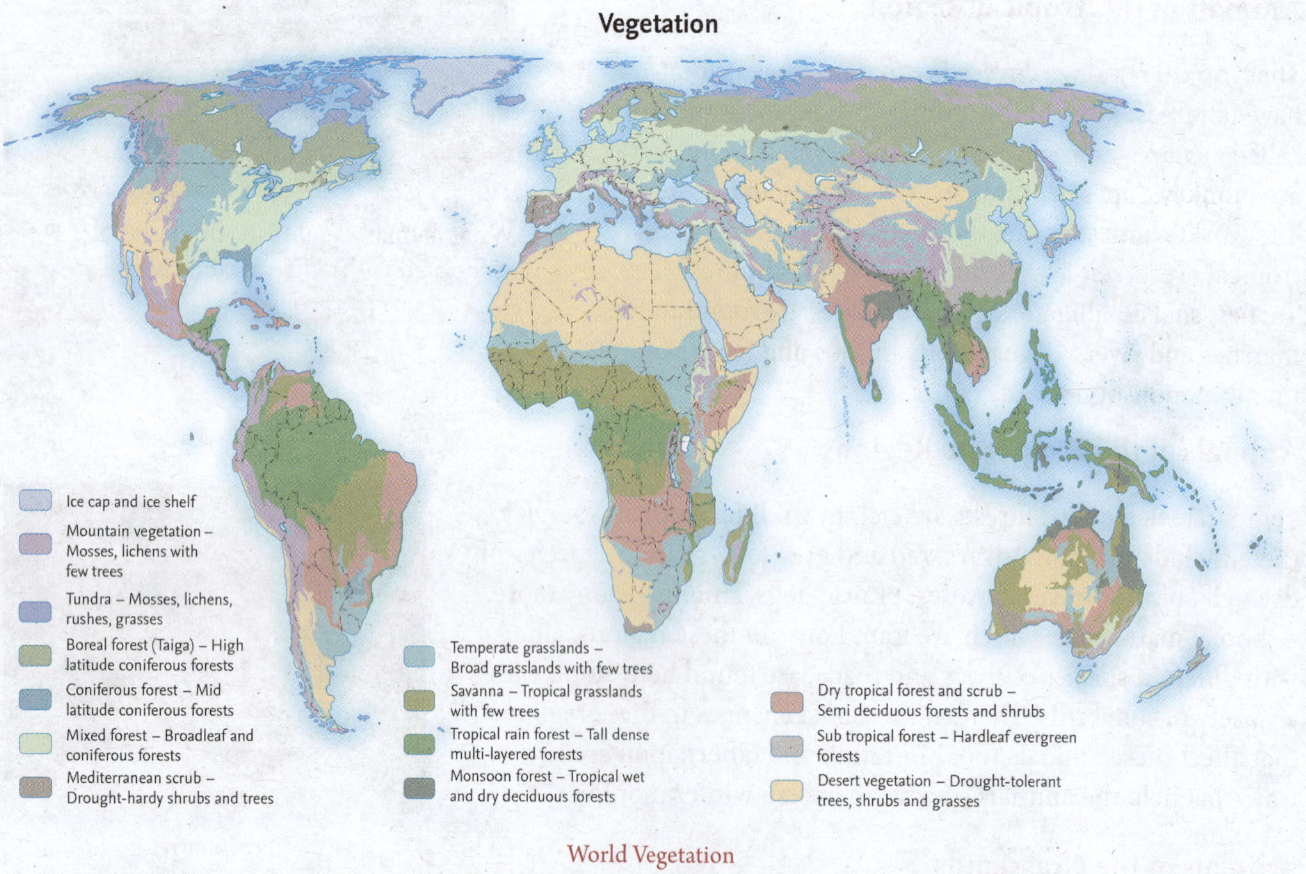

World Vegetation

nocturnal: animals that are active during the night; migration: a periodic or seasonal movement of a large number of animals or birds from one place to another

Skill Builder

21ST CENTURY SKILLS

Critical thinking skills: Explain why there is a uniformly high temperature in the Equatorial regions.

Life skills: We know how plants adapt to the harsh climatic conditions of the polar deserts. Find out how the animals of these regions survive in the extremely cold weather. Select an animal and prepare a PowerPoint presentation on how it copes with the weather in these regions.

Information literacy: Which forest types have more commercially usable trees?

World Connect

World Wildlife Day, 2022

World Wildlife Day is observed on 3rd March every year to increase the awareness about the need to protect animals and plants. It was introduced by the United Nations in 2013. The Convention on International Trade in Endangered Species of Wild Fauna and Flora (CITES) was signed on the same day. The theme of World Wildlife Day (WWD), 2022 has been "Recovering key species for ecosystem restoration". It is an attempt to draw attention to the conservation status of some of the most critically endangered species of wild fauna and flora, and to drive discussions towards imagining and implementing solutions to conserve them.

Wind up

- Forests
  - Tropical evergreen
  - Tropical deciduous
  - Temperate evergreen
  - Temperate deciduous
  - Mediterranean
  - Coniferous
- Deserts
  - Tropical
  - Temperate
  - Tundra
- Grasslands
  - Temperate
  - Tropical

Exercises

A. Choose the correct answer.

1. Very few plants grow in the
   a. temperate deserts
   b. tropical deserts
   c. grasslands
   d. polar deserts
2. Tropical evergreen forests are also called
   a. rainforests
   b. deserts
   c. grasslands
   d. none of these
3. Where are tropical evergreen forests found?
   a. India
   b. Brazil
   c. China
   d. none of these

4. What is the name of the largest snake found in tropical rainforest?
   a. Anaconda b. Black cobra c. Two mouth snake d. None of these

5. Which of the following is not found in tropical deciduous forests?
   a. Tiger b. Elephant c. Silver Fox d. Monkeys

B. Write T for true and F for false.

1. Pine and bamboo are found in the deserts. ☐
2. Eucalyptus and the dwarfed willow are found in the prairies. ☐
3. Most animals of the tropical deserts are nocturnal. ☐
4. Animals living in the tundra deserts are usually covered with fur. ☐

C. Fill in the blanks.

1. .... varies from region to region due to the difference in temperature and moisture.
2. The tropical deciduous forest receive a rainfall of .... cm in a year.
3. .... grow where temperature and rainfall are plentiful to support a tree cover.
4. Monkeys and lemurs are found in the ....
5. .... grasslands occur on either side of the equator and extend till the tropics.

D. Answer these questions in brief.

1. Why do deserts have sparse vegetation?
2. Name three countries where tropical evergreen forests are found.
3. What is the climate like in Mediterranean forests?
4. What are the other names for tropical grasslands?
5. In which regions of the world are coniferous forests located?

E. Answer these questions in detail.

1. Distinguish between the tropical grasslands and temperate grasslands.
2. Describe the natural vegetation of temperate evergreen and temperate deciduous forests.
3. Describe the natural vegetation and the wildlife of tropical rainforests.
4. Describe the location and special features of the Mediterranean forests.
5. How are deciduous forests different from evergreen forests?

Think Big

Integrate with science

A. Listed below are some of the many ways that we can try to save the endangered animals. Make a chart with the given points and display it in class.
   1. Learn more about wildlife by reading books, watching television programmes about nature, visiting zoos and nature preserves.
   2. Try to volunteer for a wildlife organisation.
   3. Do not pet wild animals.
   4. Do not buy products that have been tested on animals.
   5. Try to create awareness about endangered species by writing articles and drawing posters.
   6. Do not disturb the habitats of wild animals.

B. Discuss the ways in which you can help prevent animal extinction in your country.

Learning Tools

Use this foldable sheet to recall whatever you have learnt about the forests, grasslands, deserts and wildlife.

1. Fold a sheet of paper in half.
2. Fold this long rectangle in half.
3. Fold both ends back.
4. On the side, make vertical cuts through one thickness of paper, forming four tabs.

Use this book for data occurring in fours.

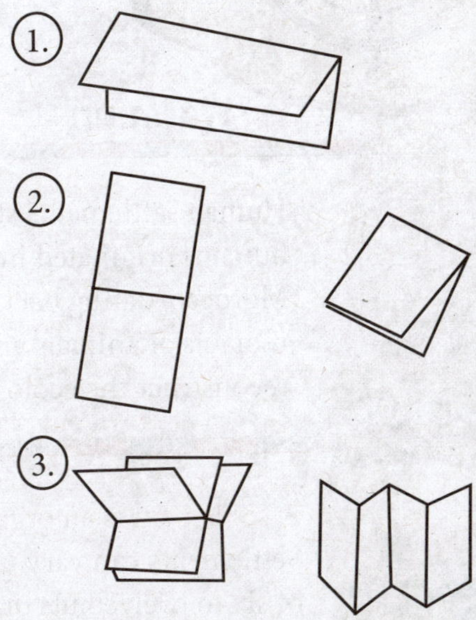

Web links:

https://www.knowledgeuniverseonline.com/ntse/Geography/introduction-natural-vegetation-wild-life.php

Last accessed on 31 August 2021

9. Human Settlements

Warm up

Human settlements started as far back as the Palaeolithic Age. It is believed that humans originated in Africa, and the first known settlement was uncovered in Morocco, dating back to 300,000 years ago. Archaeologists found human skulls, remains of animals and various objects. These archaeological finds helped them reconstruct the ecology of the area during the period.

A settlement is an organized group of human habitation where people build their houses. Settlements can vary in size from very small to extremely large. Clusters of houses, hamlets of six to twelve huts or compact villages accommodating a few hundred houses all are types of human settlements. Bigger settlements are called towns or cities. Large cities are also known as metropolises and are home to millions of people. These can also be either permanent or temporary. An example of a temporary settlement is a refugee camp. Settlements start in different places for different reasons.

Factors Affecting the Location of Settlements

Do you know how the Indus Valley Civilization began? It flourished on the banks of the river Indus because this region had an adequate supply of water and the land surrounding it was fertile. Broadly, the growth and development of a settlement depends on reliable water supply, less susceptibility to natural disasters, defence and availability of building materials, fertile land and shelter from harsh climatic conditions.

Port towns, market towns, religious towns and administrative towns were some of the earliest human settlements. Today, two types of settlements are normally recognized. They are rural settlements and urban settlements.

FACT CHECK

Tokyo is the largest city of the world. It has a population of more than 37 million, which is a quarter of Japan's total population. Cities come in all shapes and sizes. Some cities might have a large area but may not be very populated.

Rural Settlements

Rural settlements are mainly engaged in agriculture and other primary activities such as agriculture, forestry, fishing etc. They are small in size and usually consist of about two to four houses upto a few hundred houses. Rural settlements have small populations. A few modern facilities are available in the rural settlements.

Patterns of Rural Settlements

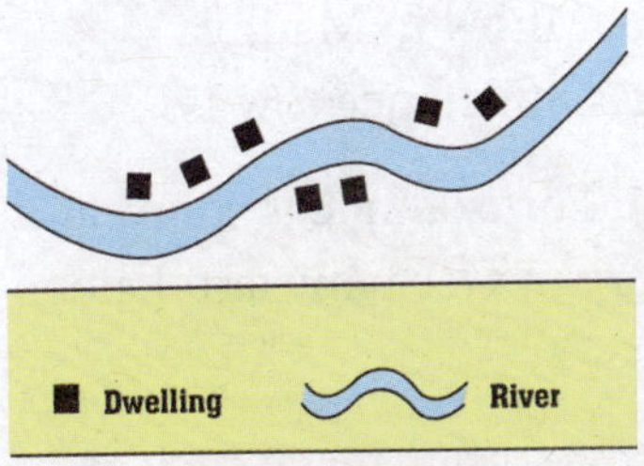

Linear pattern

Rural settlements are identified by five patterns: linear, circular, radial, nucleated and dispersed.

Linear Pattern: These are settlements that form along linear features such as banks of rivers, coasts or transport routes like roads or railways.

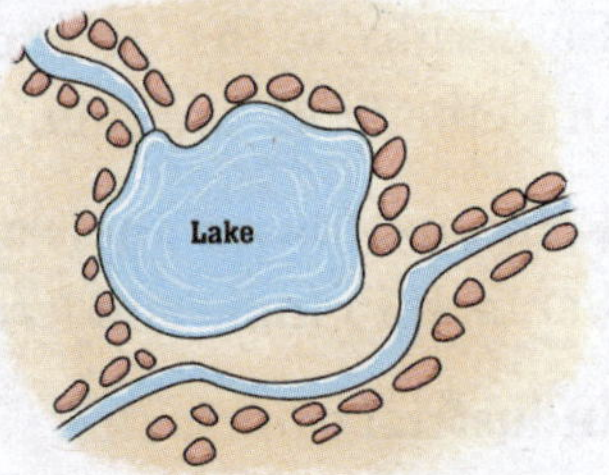

Circular pattern

Circular Pattern: These settlements usually develop in a circle around a waterbody such as a lake, pond or an oasis in a desert.

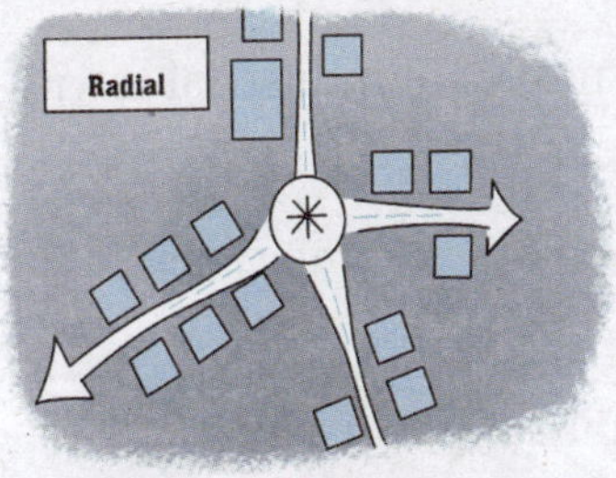

Radial pattern

Radial Pattern: These settlements are built along the streets that spread out in all directions from a central point.

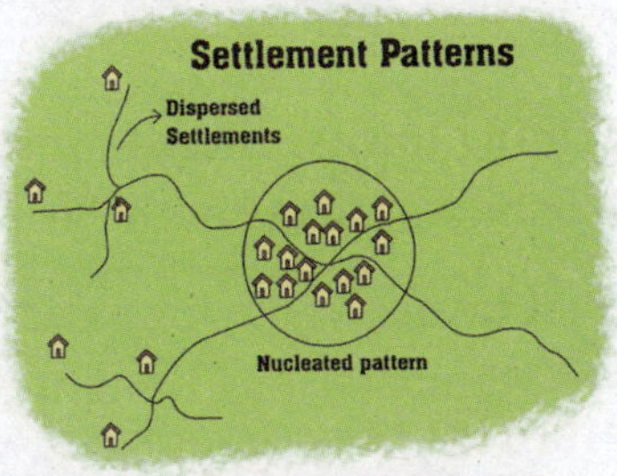

Dispersed and nucleated patterns

Dispersed Pattern: In isolated or dispersed settlements, the villages are scattered over a vast area. There is no specific plan and the settlement is a single village. They are usually found in mountainous highlands, forested areas and deserts. The main occupation of people living in these settlements is cattle rearing and forestry.

Nucleated Pattern: This is a closely built area of dwellings in flat and fertile areas. The houses are located adjacent to each other.

In villages, people build houses with locally available building material that suits their environment. In regions of heavy rainfall, houses have slanting roofs. In places where water accumulates in the rainy season, houses are constructed on raised platforms or stilts. In hot climates, thick-mud walled houses with thatched roofs are common.

What's in the picture?

Identify this type of settlement. Where are you most likely to find these settlements in India and the world?

Apply it!

Open Google maps and locate your city in it. Now, switch on the satellite mode and see your city again. Do it for a number of cities in the world and list which city has the houses closely located to one another.

Urban settlements

Urban settlements are of bigger sizes with populations ranging from thousands to lakhs. No settlement can be called an urban settlement in India until it supports a minimum population of 5,000 people. People are mainly engaged in secondary and tertiary activities like industry, trade, transportation and services. Urban settlements are often equipped with modern facilities like healthcare, education and sanitation. Environment pollution is a pressing problem with urban settlements. Urban settlements are classified on the basis of the economic activities they support.

Administrative towns: These are centres of administration and government. They comprise the capital cities, both at national and state levels. Some examples are New Delhi, Kolkata and Washington D.C.

Defence towns: These towns are centres of military activities. Jalandar in Punjab, Mhow in Madhya Pradesh, Pathankot in Punjab and Barrackpore in West Bengal are some examples of defence towns.

Cultural and educational towns: These are centres of culture, art and education. For example, Oxford and Cambridge in the UK and Santiniketan in India are educational towns; Heidelberg in Germany and Leiden in Netherlands are cultural towns.

Religious towns: These are centres that develop around religious shrines or places of pilgrimage such as Varanasi in India and Jerusalem in Israel.

Industrial towns: These are centres of production and different goods. Some examples of industrial towns are Jamshedpur and Ahmedabad in India, Pittsburgh in the USA and Lancashire in the UK.

Market towns: These are centres for collection and distribution of various goods. Some examples are Burdwan in India and Norwich in England.

Mining towns: These towns develop near mining areas. Some examples are Dhanbad in India and Johannesburg in South Africa.

Port towns: These towns develop around a large port and trading and distribution centres. Some examples are Mumbai, Hong Kong and Singapore.

Resort towns: These are centres of recreation and tourist attraction. Hill stations such as Darjeeling and Ooty in India, St. Moritz in Switzerland and sea-side towns such as Kovalam and Puri are some examples of resort towns.

Junction towns: These are located at the crossroads of major roads or railways. Some examples include Mughalsarai in India and Chicago in the USA.

Residential towns: These are suburbs and small towns where the population is considerably large. Some examples are Chandigarh in India and Richmond in the UK.

Rural—Urban Relationship

Rural and urban areas are dependent on each other. Increasing proportions of people living in urban settings cause scarcity of land, making it increasingly difficult for people to grow their own food. Villages have plenty of land for agriculture, and therefore, they supply food grains, agricultural raw materials and manpower to towns. On the other hand, towns supply industrial goods and employment opportunities for people.

Skill Builder

21ST CENTURY SKILLS

Life skills: Based on what you have learnt, answer these questions.

1. What do people need to survive?
2. How do people decide where to settle?
3. In what ways does humankind change the environment?
4. What happens to the environment when human population grows?

Collaboration: Form groups of four in the class and list and rank eight cities. Determine the state with the least population and the state with the most. Discuss possible reasons why.

Critical thinking skills: Name five activities of rural settlements and five of urban settlements.

World Connect

Leipzig was on its way to becoming a metropolis that attracted people from all over Europe due to its centralized location. It was one of the major European centres of learning and culture in music and publishing. After World War II, it became a major urban and trade centre in East Germany. However, Leipzig suffered economic drawbacks and declines resulting in a change in landscape, infrastructure and geography. Today, Leipzig is considered a 'shrinking city' because of its rapid population decline and infrastructure devastation. While Leipzig is one of the most liveable cities in East Germany and is a prominent cultural centre, it is still suffering the repercussions of the last World War, economically, politically and socially.

Wind up

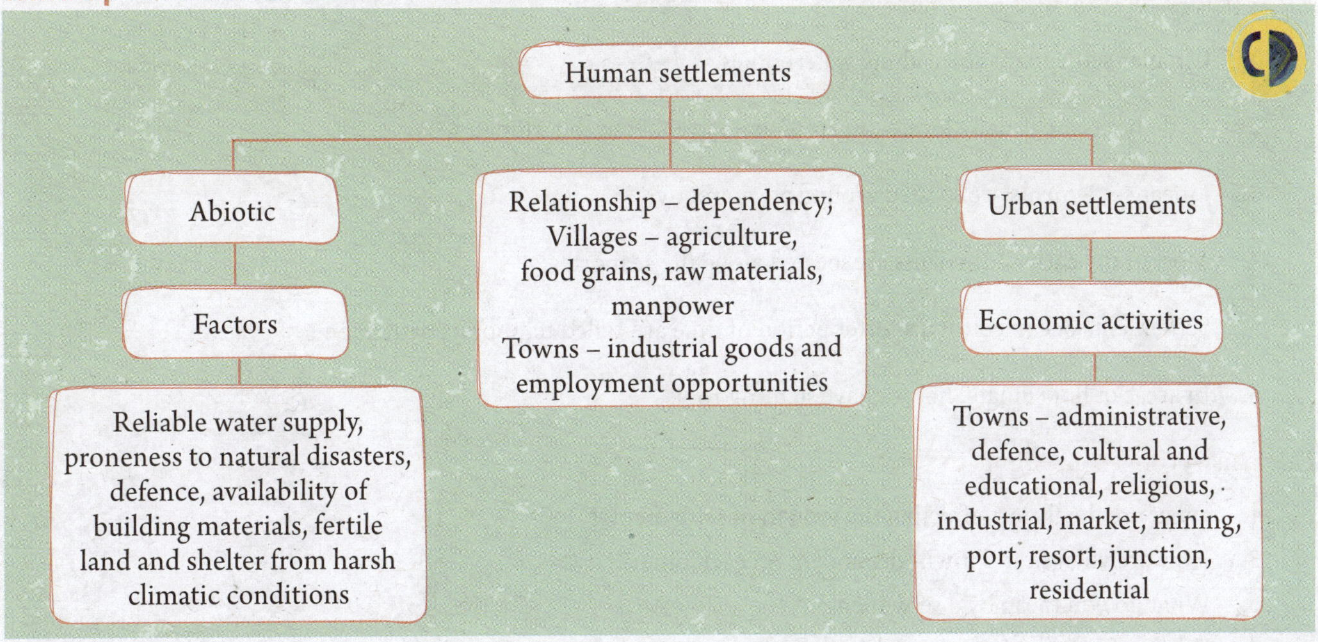

Exercises

A. Fill in the blanks.

1. .... towns are located at the crossroads of major roads or railways.
2. In regions of heavy rainfall, houses have .... roofs.
3. .... settlements have small populations.
4. .... towns are centres of collection and distribution of goods.
5. People in urban settlements are mostly engaged in .... and .... activities..

B. Choose the correct answers.

1. Which type of settlement is occupied for a short time?
   a. Permanent settlements
   b. Temporary settlements
   c. Both (a) and (b)
   d. None of these
2. The natural conditions for selection of an ideal site are
   a. favourite climate
   b. availability of water
   c. suitable land
   d. all of these

3. In which environment do people build slanting roofs of their houses?
   a. Places with heavy rainfall
   b. Places that are hot
   c. Places that are cold
   d. None of these
4. In which of the following settlements are the people engaged in activities like fishing, agriculture, handicraft, etc.?
   a. Rural settlements
   b. Urban settlements
   c. Forestry settlements
   d. None of these
5. Mumbai is a
   a. port town
   b. mining town
   c. resort town
   d. religious town

C. Write T for true and F for false.

1. Circular settlements form along waterbodies. ☐
2. Settlements are usually located in areas that have favourable climates. ☐
3. Linear settlements are located around a waterbody. ☐
4. Most of the early settlements are located along the seaports. ☐
5. Settlements occupied for a shorter period of time are called temporary settlements. ☐
6. In areas of hot climate, houses have slanting roofs. ☐

D. Answer these questions in brief.

1. What are the factors affecting the growth of settlements?
2. How are villages and towns dependent on each other?
3. What do you mean by a settlement?
4. What are cultural towns?
5. Name two educational towns.

E. Answer these questions in detail.

1. Distinguish between rural and urban settlements.
2. Classify the types of towns using examples from places in India.
3. Name and explain the various types of rural settlements.
4. What are port towns? How are they important?
5. Classify urban settlements on the basis of the economic activities they support. Give examples for each.

Think Big

Integrate with art

Using clay, make models of houses found in different parts of India that experience different climatic conditions.

Learning Tools

Create a usable timeline by using an Accordion Book Foldable. Insert the names of rural settlement patterns in one and the types of urban settlements in another. Add characteristics of each group to help you remember the chapter.

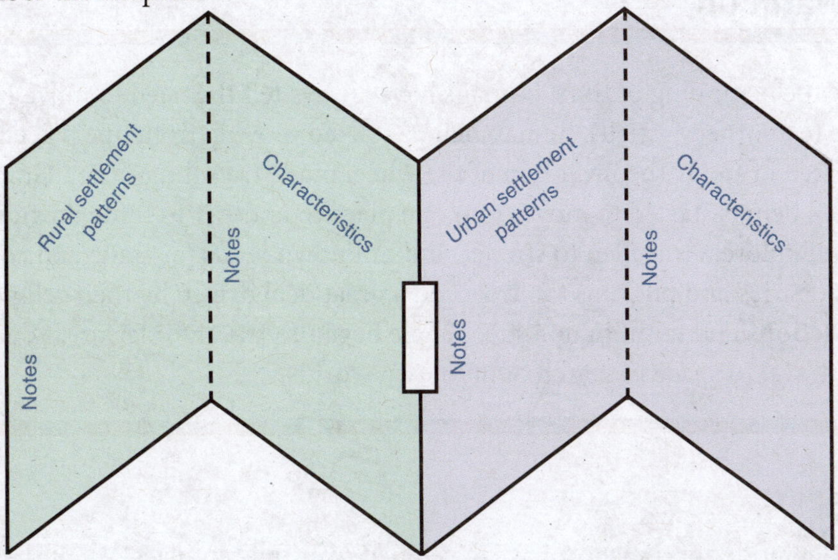

Web links:

https://geography-revision.co.uk/gcse/urbanisation/human-settlements-types-and-patterns/

Last accessed on 31 August 2021

10. Transport and Communication

Warm up

Since the beginning of time, humans have always felt the need to move from one place to another. Initially, human beings started moving from one place to another in search of food. The invention of the wheel made travelling easier. Gradually, human beings started to move from one place to another to settle down in better areas. Explorers travelled to strange and unknown lands for trade and commerce. Missionaries and pilgrims too travelled a great deal driven by their religious **convictions** and faith. In no time, people began to travel for leisure. Today, humans even travel to space in search of unknown worlds.

Transport

Different modes of transport have developed over the centuries. All of these forms of transport have become easily accessible. The four major means of transport are roadways, railways, waterways and airways.

Roadways

The oldest constructed roads date back to 4,000 BCE and were discovered in Mesopotamia, in modern-day Iraq. Roadways are an important means of transport for short distances. They are classified into metalled and unmetalled. The plains have a dense network of roads. However, roads can also be built in mountains, deserts and forests. One of the highest roadways is the Manali–Leh highway in the Himalayas. When roads are built underground, they are known as subways or underpaths. Roads built on raised structures are known as flyovers.

Today, most countries have modern highways.These are named differently in different countries—motorways in UK, freeways in the USA, autobahns in Germany and auto routes in France. Trans-continental roads link different parts of various countries within a continent. For example, the Trans-African Highway connects Cairo and Cape Town and the Trans-Canada Highway connects Victoria in British Columbia to St. John's in Newfoundland and Labrador.

In India, roads are essential for the progress of the nation. This is primarily because India is predominantly an agricultural nation and farmers require roads for the transport of their goods to markets. The Northern Plains of India have a good network of roads and cities, towns and villages are well connected. Highways and freeways have been built to connect important cities to remote villages. The Golden Quadrilateral highway network in India connects the four metropolitan cities—Delhi, Mumbai, Kolkata and Chennai.

convictions: firmly held beliefs or opinions

Railways

The Circum–Baikal railroad, Trans-Siberian Railway

The railways constitute the principal mode of transportation for **freight** and passengers. It brings people from the farthest corners of the country together for different purposes like, conducting business, sightseeing and even as a means of travel for people who are on a pilgrimage. The earliest engines worked on steam, but as technology improved, these were replaced by diesel and electric engines. Nowadays, superfast trains have been introduced for faster travel. These trains are called bullet trains or Shinkansen trains and are found in Japan. The Indian Railways has the largest network of trains in Asia. The current fastest train in India is the Vande Bharat Express that operates between Delhi and Varanasi and between Delhi and Katra at a maximum speed of 130 km/h.

The Transcontinental Railways refer to a long-distance railway network built across a continent. The Trans-Siberian Railway is the longest railway system connecting St. Petersburg in Western Russia to Vladivostok on the Pacific Coast. The Canadian Pacific Railway connects Halifax in the Atlantic coast to Vancouver in the Pacific coast. The Trans-Andean railway line links Buenos Aires in Argentina with Valparaiso in Chile. The Trans-Australian railway line runs between Sydney and Perth.

FACT CHECK

The Orient Express was one of first transcontinental trains in the world. It connected Paris with Istanbul.

In India, the Northern Plains are most suitable for the construction of railway lines with their level land, high population density and rich agriculture. This region has the maximum concentration of railway lines in the country. India's first high-speed railway was commissioned to Japan in the year 2016. The planned railway would run approximately 500 kilometres (310 miles) between India's financial capital, Mumbai and the western city of Ahmedabad at a speed of 320 km/h.

Waterways

Waterways are the cheapest and the most widely used means of transport. They are most operational in carrying bulky goods over long distances. Inland waterways and sea routes constitute waterways.

An International Container Cargo ship in the open sea

Navigable rivers, lakes and canals are used as inland waterways. The Ganga–Brahmaputra river system in India, the Great Lakes in North America and the river Nile in Egypt are the most important inland waterways. Heavy and bulky goods are transported from one continent to another. Ocean and sea routes are connected with ports. London, Singapore, Mumbai, Hong Kong, Karachi, Cairo, Durban and Cape Town are some of the important seaports of the world.

freight: goods transported in bulk via roadways, railways, waterways or flight

Airways

In the early 20th century, the development of airways started. It is the fastest means of transport and is also the most expensive.

> **Apply it!**
>
> The Suez Canal is one of the busiest waterways in the world. Find out what happened when a ship named Ever Given blocked it for nearly a week.

While airways have become much more affordable in today's world, fog, storms, unpredictable weather phenomena and at times events like volcanic eruptions continue to disrupt air travel.

Airways can reach the remotest and most inaccessible areas, where there are no roads and railways. Helicopters are widely used to help people at times of natural disasters for distributing food, water, clothes and medicines. Some important airports are Mumbai, Delhi, London, Paris, Frankfurt and Cairo.

Communication

Communication is the means of conveying messages or ideas from one person to other. Different modes of communication are used to provide information, to educate and to entertain. Communications tools can be physical and **virtual** devices and systems employed for the main purpose of communication.

The invention of the radio and television introduced a wireless medium of communication. It also enabled communication with millions of people at the same time. This is called mass media. The introduction of the telegraph, cablegram, telephone and radar have created an efficient system of communication. The introduction of computers has revolutionized the communication system, transforming the entire range of communications systems and industries. All production systems are now built around computers. Digital information can be shared across all digital systems. E-mails can send messages instantly through a computer. The Internet is a source of information on almost any topic. Satellites have made communication easier and faster. They help in weather forecasting, oil exploration, survey of forests, underground water and mineral wealth exploration, weather forecast and disaster warning.

What's in the picture?

What are these people doing? Is this common nowadays?

Personal communication is used between two people or when a few people are involved, for example, post office, telegraph, teleprinter, telephone, fax and e-mail. The means of communication include books, magazines, newspapers, radio, television and films.

Skill Builder (21st Century Skills)

Critical-thinking skills: What impact does transportation have on air quality?

Initiative and Self-Direction: The Internet has ushered in new ways for people to communicate. Write down ten points on how you can stay safe on the Internet.

Life skills: Imagine if a COVID-19 pandemic like situation would have occurred in the 1950s, how would the life of the people would have been affected? Think from the point of view of transport and communication.

virtual: existing in an electronic domain

World Connect

NASA has partnered with experts from the aircraft industry to design a new passenger jet that can fly at supersonic speeds. These superfast planes are expected to travel faster than the speed of sound. NASA visualises a 'low boom' plane that releases a supersonic 'heartbeat,' or a 'soft thump'. The QueSST jet will be the first in a series of X-planes that will receive funding in NASA's fiscal 2017 budget. The project aims at making future planes safer, greener and more efficient, improving standards by measuring the results of fuel use, emissions and noise. The first flights are expected to begin in the year 2020.

Wind up

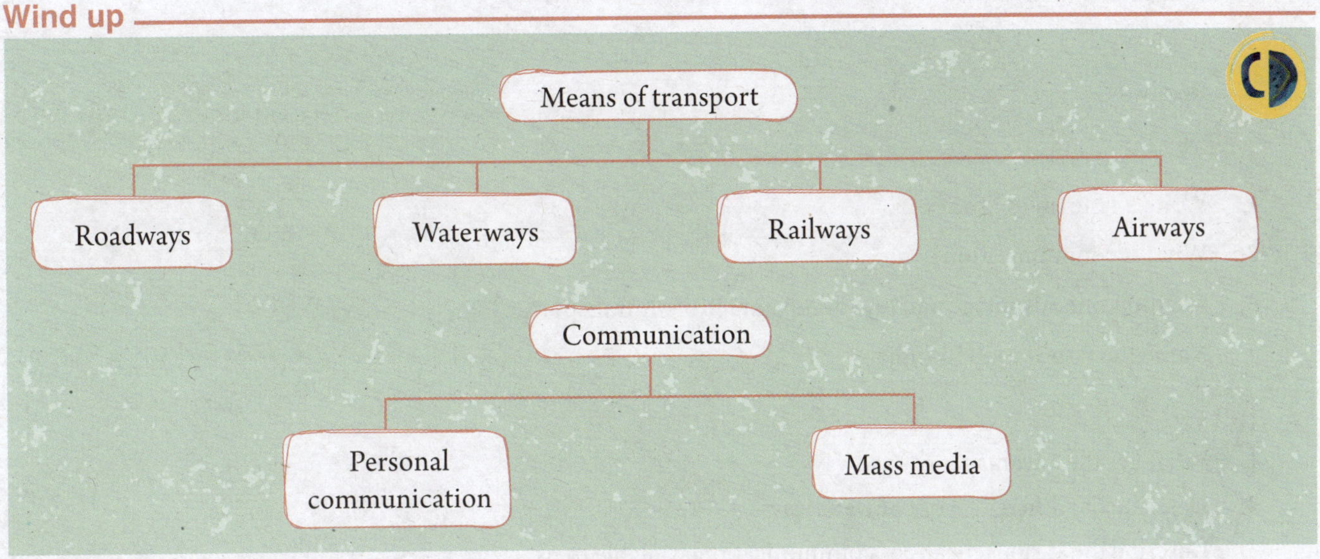

Exercises

A. Fill in the blanks.

1. .... are the cheapest mode of transport.
2. Radio is an example of .... communication.
3. In Germany, highways are called ....
4. The Trans-Canada Highway connects Victoria in British Columbia to .... in Newfoundland and Labrador.
5. The bullet trains found in Japan are called ....

B. Choose the correct answer.

1. The Trans-African highway connects Cairo and
   a. Siberia
   b. Cape Town
   c. Durban
   d. Bulawayo
2. The Trans-Siberian railway runs between Vladivostok and
   a. Moscow
   b. Paris
   c. St. Petersburg
   d. Kiev
3. Which region in India has a dense network of railways and roadways?
   a. Deccan Plateau
   b. Northern Mountains
   c. Coastal regions
   d. Northern plains

4. Which of the following is the cheapest mode of transporting goods in bulk over long distances?
   a. Roadways
   b. Railways
   c. Waterways
   d. Airways
5. Which of the following cities is not connected by Golden Quadrilateral highway?
   a. Kolkata
   b. Delhi
   c. Hyderabad
   d. Chennai

C. Write short notes describing each of these.

1. Inland waterways
2. Communication
3. Railways
4. Roadways

D. Answer these questions in brief.

1. Write a note on roadways.
2. What is communication?
3. Mention one advantage and one disadvantage of air transport.
4. Name the fastest train in India.

E. Answer these questions in detail.

1. What are the advantages of roadways?
2. Describe the different types of waterways.
3. Describe the various means of communication available to us.
4. Give an account of the railway networks of the different continents.
5. Write short notes on:
   a. inland waterways
   b. the railway network of India

Think Big

Integrate with language

An entire class of pupils in Bosnia are being taught sign language so they can communicate with a deaf classmate. Their teacher Sanela Ljumanovic decided to help the children in her class at Sarajevo's Osman Nakas primary school learn to sign, after noticing that six-year-old Zejd Coralic had become isolated from his peers. It comes after Bosnia adopted laws in 2003 that meant children with disabilities should be fully integrated into the classroom. Would you say that sign language is a means of communication? Find out how the blind read books and the history behind it.

Learning Tools

Make a multi-page pocket book and record notes about the Roadways, Railways, Waterways, Airways and communication. Organize the notes in the appropriate pockets.

1. Fold a sheet of paper (8 1/2” _ 11”) in half like a *hamburger*.
2. Open the folded paper and fold one of the long sides up two inches to form a pocket. Refold along the *hamburger* fold so that the newly formed pockets are on the inside.
3. Glue the outer edges of the two-inch fold with a small amount of glue.
4. Make it a multi-page booklet by gluing several pockets side-by-side. Glue a cover around the multi-paged *pocket book*.

Use 3” _ 5” index cards and quarter-sheets of note-book paper inside the pockets to record your notes.

Web links:

https://www.encyclopedia.com/history/encyclopedias-almanacs-transcripts-and-maps/communication-and-transportation

Last accessed on 31 August 2021

11. Life in the Deserts

Warm up

When you think of a desert, what do you imagine? Camels, sand dunes, oases and warm weather conditions usually come to mind. However, there are some deserts that are nothing like the deserts that we imagine. They are icy, cold and even rocky.

A desert is defined as a place that receives very less rainfall and has scanty vegetation. These regions are extremely hot or cold with **sporadic** rainfall. Depending on the temperature, the deserts can be classified as hot deserts or cold deserts. Hot deserts are located in the tropical areas, while the cold deserts lie in the temperate and polar regions.

The Hot Desert—Sahara

Tropical deserts lie between 30° N and 30° S of the equator. These deserts are located on the western margins of the continents. Some examples of tropical deserts are the Sahara Desert, the Thar Desert, the Great Basin Desert and the Chihuahuan Desert. The Sahara is the largest tropical desert in the world.

What's in the picture?

By looking at the colours on this map, can you identify which part of Africa is covered by the Sahara Desert?

Location

The Sahara covers about one-fourth of the African continent. The Sahara Desert is bounded by the Atlantic Ocean in the west, the Mediterranean Sea in the north and the Red Sea in the east. It covers an area of about 8.5 million sq km. The Atlas Mountains are located to its north–west. The Sahara Desert is spread across eleven countries—Morocco, Algeria, Libya, Egypt, Tunisia, Sudan, Chad, Mali, Mauritania, Niger and West Sahara. The river Nile passes through Egypt and empties into the Mediterranean Sea. Important cities located in the Sahara include Nouakchott, Timbuktu and Mali.

Climate

There is lack of moisture in the air and skies are cloudless over the Sahara. The day temperature is as high as 55 °C, and the temperatures drop to –15 °C during the night.

sporadic: occurring at irregular intervals or only in a few places

Hot and dry winds blow across the region. The annual rainfall in the Sahara is as low as 25 cm. The Libyan Desert is the hottest region of the Sahara. Sandstorms are common and dusty winds, such as the khamsin, sirocco, harmattan and simoon, blow throughout the desert.

Natural Vegetation and Animal Life

The hot and dry conditions in the Sahara support little vegetation. The plants that do grow here obtain and conserve water in different ways. Animals that can survive with very little water live here. Some of the plants that grow here are cactus, acacia, baobab and date palms. Date palms mostly grow near oases. The spotted hyena, jerboa, dama gazelle, common jackal, chameleon, crocodile and sand fox are some animals found in the Sahara.

A jerboa

People and Economic Activities

The important nomadic tribes of the Sahara are the Bedouins and Tuaregs. They rear animals, such as sheep, goats and camels. These animals provide milk and meat. The tribes move from one place to another and live in temporary tents. Near the oases, there are people who cultivate crops. They lead settled lives, especially in the Nile valley in Egypt. The farmers of the Nile valley are known as the Fellahins. The main crops cultivated are rice, maize, millet, beans, sugarcane and dates. Cotton is the most important crop. A few vegetables are also grown here.

A person from the Tuareg tribe

The houses are made of mud walls, which are best suited to the hot climate because they are cooler than the houses built using other materials. The roofs are flat. The diet of the fellahin is made up of maize flour and a dish of beans called 'ful'. The people mostly wear loose flowing robes with a turban to protect them from the heat.

Apply it!

E

Storing Water

15 LIFE ON LAND

You will need a piece of sponge, two plastic cups, waxed paper, a weighing machine and some water.

- Cut the sponge into two equal pieces and weigh them.
- Take two plastic cups and fill one-fourth of them with water. Soak one piece of sponge in each cup.
- Carefully remove each sponge and weigh them again. You will notice that each sponge has gained weight.
- Cover one of the sponges with waxed paper and set both the sponges aside to dry for a couple of days. Weigh each of the sponges after two days. You will find that there is a difference in the weights of the two sponges. The sponge covered with a waxed paper weighs more as it retains water. This shows how the waxy coating on the leaves of the desert plants prevents the loss of water.

A Cold Desert—Ladakh

Ladakh is a cold and barren desert. The Ladakh Range, with an average height of approximately 6,000 m, does not have a major peak. There are several mountain passes such as the Karakoram Pass and Zoji La Pass. The region is drained by the river Indus and its tributaries—Shyok, Zanskar, Nubra and Suru. There are many glaciers in the region, particularly in the Karakoram Range. There are two lakes—Pangong Tso and Tso Moriri.

Ladakh

Location

Ladakh is a union territory located in India. It lies to the north of the Greater Himalayas. It is bounded by the Karakoram Range in the north and by the Zanskar mountains in the south. Ladakh starts from the Shyok River and extends till the Tibetan border.

Climate

Ladakh is situated at a high altitude. Therfore, the climate is cold and dry. The day temperature during the summer season is just above 0 °C, while the night temperature is about –25 °C. Winters are extremely cold and the temperature drops to about –40 °C. The winds blowing through the mountain pass bring heavy snowfall during the winters.

The Himalayas prevent the moisture-laden winds to bring rainfall here. Thus, rainfall is as low as 10 cm every year. During summer, the melting snow supplies water to the entire region.

Vegetation and Animals

Due to inadequate rainfall, Ladakh has an almost treeless and rocky **terrain**. The mountains are barren. In the low-lying areas, there are a few trees such as willow, poplar, cedar, elm, cypress, juniper and yew. Apple, walnut and apricot trees grow in the summer season. The important animals found here are yak, wild goats, wild sheep and a variety of dogs. The main bird species found here are robins, snowcocks and ravens. Yak is an important animal and is domesticated for milk and wool.

Geography skills

On an outline map of the world, highlight the hot deserts in yellow and the cold deserts in red.

People and Economic Activities

Agriculture, handicrafts and tourism are the main occupations of the people of Ladakh. Agriculture is the main activity of the people during the summer. Barley, potatoes, peas, beans and turnip are some of the vegetables grown here. The climate in the winter months is too harsh for the cultivation of crops. Tourism is the source of livelihood for the people during the summers. Because there is scarcity of resources, such as water and fuel, Ladakhis have learnt to use the available resources judiciously.

Ladakhi women

terrain: a stretch of land, especially with regard to its physical features

Skill Builder

21ST CENTURY SKILLS

Life skills: Do you live in a wet, dry, or moderate climate? Select some plants that are native to your area. What kind of adaptations do they exhibit that help them survive in your climate?

Critical-thinking skills: How is sand formed?

World Connect

The Lut Desert, or Dasht-e Lut, is located in the southeastern part of Iran. It is believed be to be the driest place on the Earth. A scorching surface temperature of 70 °C has been recorded here. It was named a World Heritage Site by UNESCO in July, 2016.

Wind up

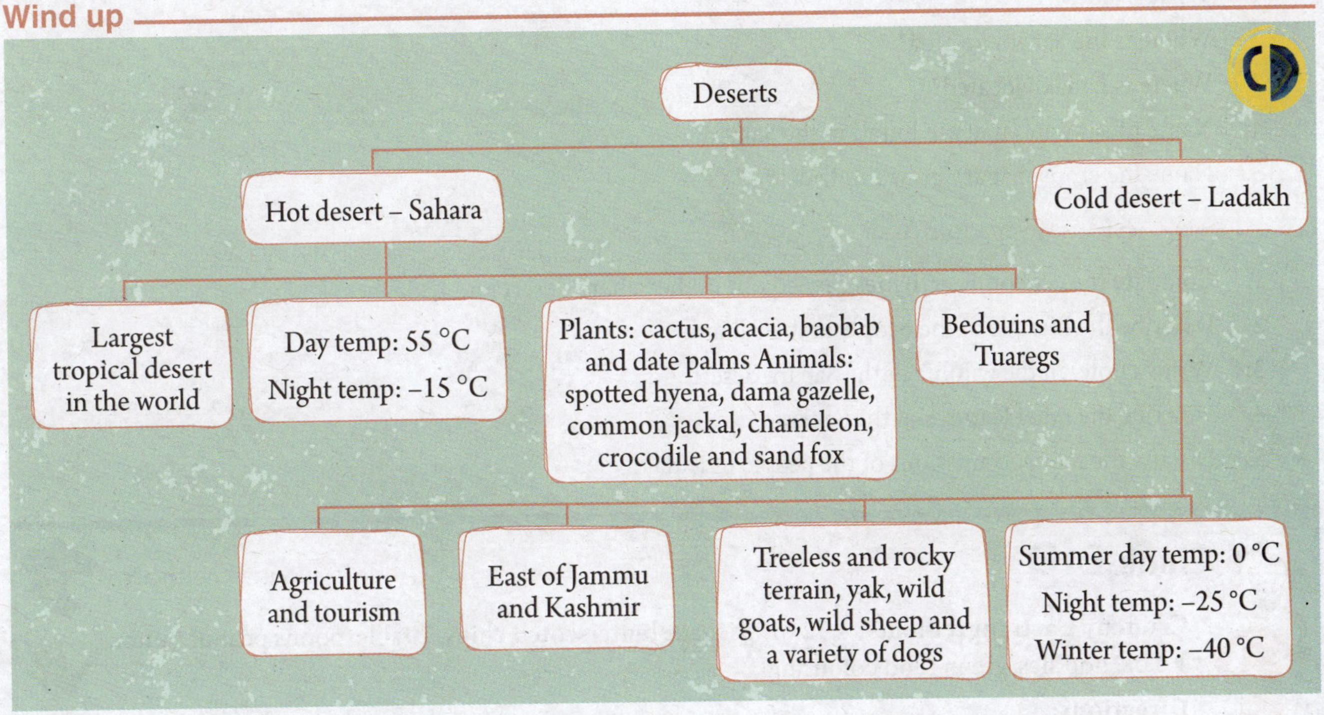

Exercises

A. Choose the correct answers.

1. Which region is characterised by extremely high or low temperature and has scarce vegetation?
   a. Desert b. Fertile land c. Grassland d. None of these
2. Which of these trees is not found in the Sahara desert?
   a. Mango b. Date palm c. Acacia d. All of these
3. How many countries touch the Sahara desert?
   a. Eleven b. Thirteen c. Sixteen d. Twenty
4. Ladakh starts from the Shyok River and extends till the
   a. Thar Desert b. Tibetan border c. Sundarbans d. Islands

B. Match the columns.

	Column A		Column B
1.	Fellahins	a.	tree of Ladakh
2.	Khamsin	b.	Depression with water in deserts
3.	Pangong	c.	farmers of the Nile valley
4.	Willow	d.	dusty storm of Sahara
5.	Yak	e.	Lake in Ladakh
6.	Oasis	f.	important animal of Ladakh

C. Give reasons:

1. Houses are made up of mud walls in the hot deserts.
2. People mostly wear flowing robes and turbans in hot deserts.
3. Ladakh is a treeless region.
4. Tourism in summer is the main source of livelihood in Ladakh.

D. Answer these questions in brief.

1. What is a desert?
2. Where is the Sahara located?
3. Where is Ladakh located?
4. Name the animals that are found in the Sahara.
5. Name the crops that are grown in Ladakh.

E. Answer these questions in detail.

1. Compare the economic activities carried out in the Sahara desert and Ladakh.
2. Describe the lifestyle of the people of the Sahara.
3. Write a note on the wildlife of the Sahara desert.
4. Describe the relief features of the Sahara.
5. Discuss the main occupations of the people of Ladakh.

Think Big

Integrate with art

Crunchy Cacti Ingredients: 1 12 oz. package butterscotch chips, 2 tablespoons peanut butter, 1 6 oz. noodles, green food colouring

Directions:

- Melt the chips with the help of an adult.
- Stir in the peanut butter and food colouring.
- Boil the noodles and let them cool.
- Once cool, add the noodles to the butterscotch and peanut butter mixture and coat well.
- Remove from heat. Work atop wax paper and fashion a golf ball-sized portion of the mixture into a cactus shape.
- Cool it to harden, peel the cactus from the paper and chow down.

Makes appropriately 15 to 20 crunchy cacti.

Learning Tools

Taking notes

After reading the chapter, use major headings of the section to create an outline of the chapter.

I. *Hot desert (Explain in your own words)*

i. *Location: (Highlight the important points of each sub heading)*

ii. *Climate ...*

iii. *Natural vegetation and animal life ...*

iv. *People and Economic activities ...*

II. *Cold deserts (Explain in your own words)*

i.

ii.

iii.

iv.

Web links:

https://www.worldwildlife.org/habitats/deserts
https://www.nationalgeographic.com/environment/article/deserts

Last accessed on 31 August 2021

12. Life in the Tropical and Sub-Tropical Regions

Warm up

Farah was excited. She is going on a wildlife safari with her cousins in Hemis national park in Ladakh. They started very early in the morning and Farah was ready with her phone to capture photographs of wild animals. Just then, one of the passengers clicked a photograph of a snow leopard. The tour guide told that passenger, 'Please turn off your flash as it may disturb the animals'. Farah stopped to think, 'I wonder if animals get disturbed by tourists ... '

The Amazon Basin

South America from space

Often referred to as the 'lungs of the Earth', the Amazon is the world's largest tropical rainforest. It covers over five and a half million square kilometres, covering over 40 per cent of Brazil's geographical area. Besides Brazil, this great rainforest is also located in other South American countries including Peru, Venezuela, Ecuador, Colombia, Guyana, Bolivia, Suriname and French Guiana. It is located on the equatorial region between 10° N and 10° S. The Amazon River, which flows through this region, is the world's largest and second longest river with over 1,100 tributaries. It flows eastwards and empties into the Atlantic Ocean. The Amazon River is about 6,400 km long.

What's in the picture?

Name the river that flows through this forest. Why is it famous?

Climate

The closeness of the region to the Equator results in a hot, wet and humid climate throughout the year. There are hardly any seasonal changes except in some areas where the winter months can be typically cold due to the Antarctic winds coming in from the south. Rainfall is very high and it rains every day. The temperature drops at night but humidity remains high.

Vegetation

Green Earth

Clearing of the rainforests began in the past 100 years to make way for farm land.

The Amazon is one of the richest areas of the world in animal and plant diversity and is home to more than half the world's total plant and animal **species**. The hot and wet lowlands of the Amazon basin and the Orinoco Basin are covered with evergreen rainforests known as selva. These forests are very dense with thick undergrowth. The trees grow very close together so that their branches form a canopy at the top that keeps the sunlight from reaching the ground, making the forests dark with less than 1 per cent of the available sunlight making it through the tree canopy above. Over 200 species of trees can be found in one hectare of Amazon rainforest. The trees do not shed the leaves at any particular time of the year since there is plenty of rain. These forests yield tall hardwood trees. The wood of some South American trees is so dense that it does not float. Rubber, mahogany, ebony, Brazil nuts and chuckle are some of the trees that grow in the region.

The Amazon rainforests have the largest variety of animals in the continent. It is home to the anaconda, one of the world's largest snakes. The armadillo and the giant anteater are also found here. Piranha, a flesh-eating fish, lives in the Amazon River. The selvas is home to a huge variety of wildlife. Monkeys, crocodiles, snakes and thousands of insects share this forest. So far, around 40,000 plant species, 1,300 bird species, 3,000 types of fish, 430 mammals and 2.5 million different insects have been identified, yet the range of plant and animal species in the Amazon remains largely unknown. Scientists estimate that only 40 per cent of all insect species have so far been identified.

An armadillo

People and Economic Activities

Due to its inaccessibility, it remains one of the most thinly populated areas in the Equatorial region. There are scattered settlements distributed over a few large cities such as in Iquitos, Peru, Manaus and Belém, which are situated on the banks of the Amazon River and other major rivers. In many regions, the forest has been cleared for soya bean plantations and ranching, the most extensive non-forest use of the land. Some of the inhabitants harvest wild rubber latex and Brazil nuts. This is a form of extractive farming where the trees are not cut down. These are relatively **sustainable** operations in contrast to lumbering or agriculture, which are dependent on the clearing of the rainforest. The natives live in thatched huts made from leaves of grasses and palms. The hammock, a hanging network couch made from the bark of the hamaca tree, is an invention that came from this region. The women grow crops like yams, sweet potatoes and bananas. This keeps the families going, especially on days when hunting and fishing are unsuccessful. The people build traditional houses called maloca.

Native Brazilian tribe

A dwelling in the Amazon rainforest

species: a group into which animals, plants, etc. are divided; sustainable: conserving an ecological balance by avoiding depletion of natural resources

Apply it!

How rainforests create wet climates

You will need two-litre bottles, stones, potting soil, plant cuttings and a plastic bag.

- Place a layer of stones at the bottom of each bottle.
- Add a two-inch layer of potting soil on top of the rocks in each bottle.
- Plant a few plant cuttings, making sure all roots are covered.
- Water the plants until the soil is moist.
- Cover one of the bottles, from the base to the top with a plastic bag. Use a thread to secure the plastic bag.
- Place the bottles in a warm, sunlit area.
- Observe what happens in the bottle everyday during the unit.
- You will notice water droplets on the plastic bag. What do you think this means?

The Ganga–Brahmaputra Basin

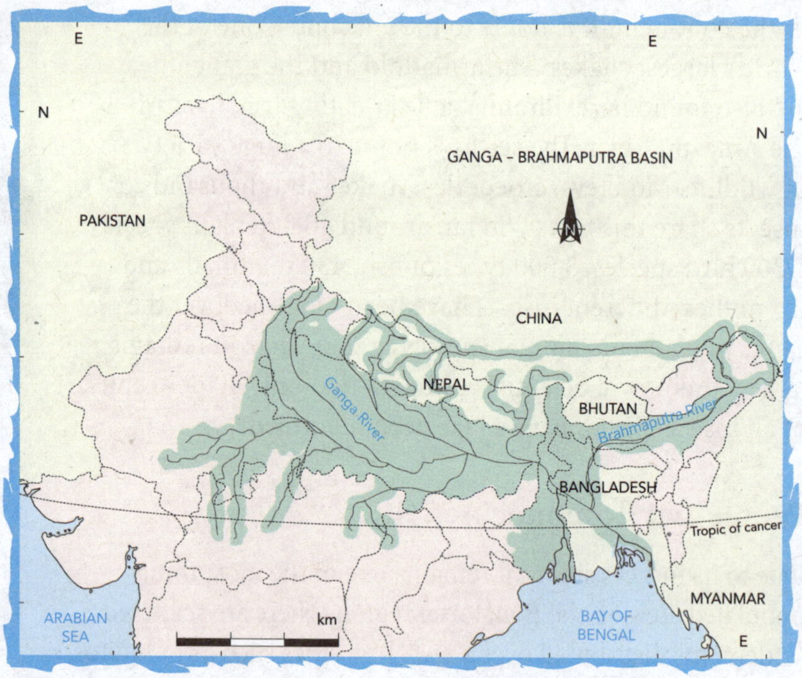

The Ganga–Brahmaputra Basin

The Ganga–Brahmaputra basin is located between 10° N and 30° N in a sub-tropical region. The Ganga and the Brahmaputra along with their tributaries form this river basin. The Northern Plains lie to the south of the Himalayas. These plains are the most extensive and fertile plains of the world. This is caused by the deposition of sediments brought down by these rivers.

Location

This basin extends from the Ganga River in the west to the Brahmaputra River in the east. The Ganga originates from the Gangotri glacier in the Himalayas. The Ganga basin stretches from Delhi to Kolkata. The river and its tributaries together flow through the states of Haryana, Uttar Pradesh, Uttarakhand, Bihar, West Bengal, Rajasthan and Madhya Pradesh.

The Brahmaputa basin lies to the north–east of India. It originates near Lake Mansarovar in Tibet. It is known as Tsangpo in Tibet and Dihang in Assam. The Ganga and the Brahmaputra rivers join together and form the largest and most fertile delta of the world known as the Sundarbans.

Climate

This plain has a monsoon type of climate. The features are hot summers, wet monsoons and cold winters. Most of the rainfall occurs in the summer season, falling heavily in the areas surrounding the Brahmaputra and then slowly decreasing as we move towards the Ganga. Floods are highly prevalent during the monsoon season causing huge loss to life and property.

Vegetation

A clouded leopard

Tropical deciduous forests make up the Ganga–Brahmaputra Basin. Sal, teak, *peepal* and bamboo are some of the trees found here. The vegetation includes tropical deciduous trees in the plains, mangroves in the Sundarbans and coniferous trees in the cold and hilly regions of Sikkim, Arunachal Pradesh and Uttarakhand. The delta region has mangrove forests with breathing roots. Towards the Himalayas, coniferous forests are more common.

Wildlife

> **FACT CHECK**
> The local species of mangrove trees growing in the Sundarbans are called *Sundari*.

There are many national parks and wildlife sanctuaries. Elephants, rhinoceros, tigers, deer and monkeys and a great variety of fish are found here. In the delta region, in the Sundarbans forest in particular, the endangered Royal Bengal Tiger is found. Animals in the delta include the Indian python, clouded leopard, Indian elephant and crocodiles, which live in the Sundarbans. The one-horned rhino inhabits the Brahmaputra plains. The chital, kingfishers and eagles are found in this region in abundance. The Ganges river dolphin and the Irrawaddy dolphin are **endemic** to the territory.

Sadly, most of the wildlife that exists in the region is endangered due to poaching, hunting and various human activities. Today, it is believed that there are only 1,200 Royal Bengal tigers living in the wild in the Sundarbans. While the government is stepping up efforts to prevent further decline in the tiger population, people are still involved in large-scale poaching. Large areas of forests have been almost cleared and only a small area is dedicated to the conservation of these animals.

People and Economic Activities

The Ganga–Brahmaputra Basin is one of the most densely populated regions in the country. Agriculture is the main occupation of the people as the soil is fertile and suitable for growing crops. There are plenty of perennial rivers that drain the region and the land is flat and low, enabling abundant produce. The main crops grown are wheat, maize, sorghum, tea and jute. The industries are mainly agro-based industries, like the jute industry, the sugar industry and the silk industry. In the rural areas, small-scale and cottage industries have also developed.

Most of the people in the Ganga–Brahmaputra basin live in villages. The plains are densely populated and there are a number of cities with a population of more than 10 lakhs. Some of them are Kanpur, Allahabad, Varanasi, Patna, Kolkata and Guwahati. This region has a dense network of rail and roadways, which developed with the growth of trade, industries and tourism.

endemic: regularly found among particular people or in a certain area

Skill Builder

21ST CENTURY SKILLS

Life skills: Research and make a list of the products that we obtain from rainforests. Can human civilization survive without these products?

Critical-thinking skills: Give reasons for the following.

1. Equatorial rainforests are not commercially exploited.
2. Floods occur frequently in the Ganga–Brahmaputra basin.
3. Wildlife is almost absent in the Ganga–Brahmaputra basin.
4. Evergreen forests are found in the equatorial regions.

World Connect

Deforestation in the Amazon has been a growing problem over the past five decades, with ranchers leading the way in clearing rainforest for cattle and cultivation. But while Brazil, the largest country in South America, seems on track to reduce deforestation, other major Amazonian countries like Peru are increasingly struggling to protect their share of the world's largest rainforest.

In fact, a new wave of deforestation is underway in the Huanuco region of central Peru, which now has the highest concentration of the deforestation in the country, according to an Amazon Conservation Association (ACA) report. The report is based on **algorithms** of satellite data from 2013 through 2015 and points to cattle grazing as the main culprit, Matt Finer, a senior research specialist at the ACA told ThinkProgress. 'We just hadn't really dealt with that driver before. You hear that more in the context of Brazil'.

Wind up

- Tropical and sub-tropical regions
  - Amazon Basin
    - Largest tropical rainforest
    - Hot, wet and humid climate
    - One of the richest areas of the world in animal and plant diversity and is home to more than half the world's total plant and animal species
    - Soya bean plantations and ranching
  - Ganga-Brahmaputra Basin
    - Hot summers, wet monsoons and cold winters
    - Indian python, clouded leopard, Indian elephant and crocodiles, one-horned rhino, Bengal tiger, Irrawaddy dolphin
    - Tropical deciduous trees in the plains, mangroves in the Sundarban and coniferous trees in the cold and hilly regions
    - Extends from the Sutlej River in the west River Ganga in the west to river Brahmaputra in the east

algorithm: a process or set of rules to be followed in calculations or other problem-solving operations, especially by a computer

Exercises

A. Fill in the blanks.

1. The Ganga basin experiences a .... type of climate.
2. The Amazon river drains in the ....
3. The delta region has .... forests with breathing roots.
4. The main occupation of the people of the Ganga–Brahmaputra basin is ....
5. The Ganga river originates from the ....

B. Choose the correct answer.

1. The staple food of the Ganga–Brahmaputra basin is
   a. fish b. wheat c. rice d. Both a and c
2. The Brahmaputa basin originates near Lake Mansarovar in
   a. Nepal b. Assam c. Tibet d. Both b and c
3. Traditional houses in the Amazon rainforest are known as
   a. Armadillo b. Iquitos c. Maloca d. Orinoco
4. The climate of the Amazon basin is
   a. wet monsoon b. dry c. cold d. hot and wet
5. In the Ganga-Brahmaputra basin, people are still involved in this activity despite the government is stepping up efforts to prevent further decline in tiger population.
   a. hunting b. poaching c. fishing d. animal rearing

C. Write T for true and F for false.

1. Cotton is grown in the Amazon basin on a commercial scale. ☐
2. The Sundarbans are home to the Asiatic Lion. ☐
3. The Ganga basin stretches from Delhi to Kanpur. ☐
4. The tropical rainforests of the Amazon Basin yield softwood. ☐
5. Brazil nuts are harvested in the Amazon rainforest. ☐

D. Answer these questions in brief.

1. State the location of the equatorial rainforests.
2. What is the latitudinal extent of the the Ganga–Brahmaputra basin.
3. Name the trees found in the equatorial rainforests.
4. Name the type of fauna found in the equatorial rainforests.

E. Answer these questions in detail.

1. Distinguish between the flora of the Amazon basin and the Ganga–Brahmaputa basin.
2. Explain the relationship between the climatic conditions and the natural vegetation of the Amazon basin.
3. Explain the process of agriculture in the Amazon forest area.
4. What are the factors affecting the growth of agriculture in the Ganga–Brahmaputra basin?
5. Describe the forests of the Amazon basin.

Think Big

Integrate with science and art

Make a terrarium

You will need a glass jar, pebbles, potting soil and small plants.

Put pebbles and potting soil in the bottom half of the glass jar. Plant some small plants and water it sparingly. Watch your terrarium thrive.

Learning Tools

Highlight the important points you have learnt about the tropical rainforest from this chapter to create your own study guide.

Characteristics	Amazon Basin	Ganga–Brahmaputra Basin
Location		
Climate		
Vegetation		
Wildlife		
People and economic activities		

Web links:

https://www.britannica.com/science/tropical-rainforest

https://www.nationalgeographic.org/encyclopedia/rain-forest/

Last accessed on 31 August 2021

13. Life in the Temperate Grasslands

Warm up

Grasslands around the world have different names. African grasslands are called savannas, North American grasslands are called prairies, South American grasslands are called velds and Eurasian grasslands are called steppes. They make up 70 per cent of the world's total land area. However, these regions are going through a swift decline. Unsustainable agricultural practices, overgrazing and crop clearing are some of the causes.

Temperate grasslands and savannahs are **biomes** whose **predominant** vegetation consists of grass and/or shrubs. A biome is a specific environment that is home to living things suited for that place and climate. For instance, a desert biome is great for a lizard, but a koala needs the leafy greens of a forest biome. Located to the north of the Tropic of Cancer and south of the Tropic of Capricorn, temperate grasslands are found in the interior of continents in both the hemispheres. The major temperate grasslands include the steppes in Europe and Asia, the pampas in South America, the prairies in North America, the veld in South Africa and the downs in Australia.

The Prairies

Prairies

The prairies are vast stretches of flat grassland with moderate temperatures, moderate rainfall and a few trees. They usually bring to mind the golden, wheat-covered land located in the interior lowlands in the heart of North America. The prairies include the Great Plains in the United States of America and parts of central Canada. The Great Plains region includes all or parts of Texas, New Mexico, Oklahoma, Kansas, Colorado, Nebraska, Wyoming, South Dakota, North Dakota, Montana, Alberta, Saskatchewan and Manitoba. The soil in these areas is rich and extremely fertile and is suitable for extensive agricultural purposes. Some lakes that drain the region are Lake Winnipeg and Lake Manitoba, and some rivers are Missouri, Mississipi, Athabasca and Red. The prairies of Canada are drained by the tributaries of the Saskatchewan River.

Climate

This region has extremes of temperature since it is far away from the moderating influence of the sea. Such a climate is also known as a continental type of climate. Winters are

biome: a large naturally occurring community of flora and fauna occupying a major habitat, e.g. forest or tundra;
predominant: present as the strongest or main element

extremely cold with plenty of snow, while summers are generally hot and humid. Rainfall is moderate and mostly occurs in the spring and summer seasons. Rainfall decreases from the east to the west, thereby creating different types of prairies in the region. The chinook wind, which is a warm and dry local wind blowing down the east side of the Rocky Mountains at the end of winter, partly melts the snow, making the region slightly warmer in the cold winter months.

Vegetation

The prairies do not receive adequate rainfall for trees to grow. These vast plains in the middle of the continent are covered with rich tall grass. A few trees grow on hill slopes that get more rainfall. While there is a variety of vegetation, there is no abundance of vegetation. The type of grass changes according to season and climate. The southern part of the prairies is mainly grassland, and the northern part has trees like aspen and poplar. The lake areas and the wetlands are the most abundant in vegetation with oak and aspen trees and different types of shrubs.

Today, there has been a **drastic** shift from grassland to cropland in the prairies. This has diminished the natural vegetation and has increased losses of organic matter and plant nutrients from the soil. Only a small portion remains in its native state.

Animals

The prairies are home to many different species of wildlife. Coyotes, gophers, black bears, moose, beavers, red foxes, rabbits and prairie dogs are found here. The region is home to a large number of ducks—almost half in amount of the total number of ducks in North America. The bison (American Buffalo) is the most important animal for the Native Americans and once dominated this region. It became almost extinct due to **indiscriminate** slaughter. Today, it is a protected animal. With the advent of agriculture and the transition from grassland to crop land, a number of species are becoming extinct. Agriculture destroys natural habitats and damages the food of the animals because of the use of pesticides and fertilizers. The quantity of fish is also diminishing vastly due to recreational activities like over-fishing. Low ranching cost and easy transportation in rural areas make ranching an attractive economic activity.

A bison

People

The prairies were originally inhabited by prairie Indians who had learnt to respect and support the natural life cycles. The prairies are richer than any other natural region in terms of natural resources. It has extensive land suitable for cultivation and a wide variety of minerals. These gifts of nature are well utilized by its people, who are hard working and make use of science and technology. This has made the USA and Canada two of the most advanced and modern countries in the world.

Although only 10 per cent of the land is under cultivation, North America is a surplus food producer. Tractors, harvesters and other machines and scientific methods of cultivation are extensively used. North America is the world's largest producer of maize, wheat and soyabeans. It is the largest producer of barley and oats. Dairy farming refers to rearing cattle for milk.

drastic: likely to have a strong or far-reaching effect; indiscriminate: done at random or without careful judgement

The dairy belt extends from the cooler and humid parts of the prairies through the Great Lakes area to the north–east region along the Atlantic coast. Milk, butter and cheese are the chief products. Large mineral deposits, particularly of coal and iron ore and a good network of roads, railways and canals in this region have made it the most industrialized region in the world.

FACT CHECK

A safari is an overland journey, usually a trip within Africa. In the past, the trip was often a big-game hunt, but today, a safari often refers to trips to observe and photograph wildlife or hiking and sight-seeing.

The Velds

South Africa is a country rich in natural resources, climatic environments and diverse ethnic groups. The veld is the temperate grassland of Africa. It covers the countries of South Africa, Lesotho, Swaziland, Zimbabwe, Botswana and Namibia. This region is marked by scanty trees, tall grasses and shrubs and land, which is mostly used for **pasturage** and farmland.

There are different types of velds in South Africa depending on altitude, type of vegetation found and climate. There are three types of veld differentiated on the basis of elevation. They are the high veld (1200–1800 m), the middle veld (600–1200 m) and the low veld (150–600 m).

What's in the picture?

Name the animals found in such regions.

Climate

Being far away from the sea, it experiences a highly variable climate with large differences between the summer and the winter temperatures. A small amount of rainfall is distributed throughout the year. The summers are usually hot, while the winters are cold with variations in daily temperatures. Precipitation usually occurs during the summer months. The low velds receive more precipitation than the high velds. Temperatures are greatly influenced by the elevation of a place.

Apply it!

Grasslands are the granaries of the world. Prairies are the bread basket of the world. What do you understand from these two sentences? Do you think without the prairies, the USA would have been a major producer of wheat in the world?

Vegetation

The veld is mostly an open treeless plain. The rainfall here is not sufficient for trees to grow. Hence, short grass grows everywhere, along with thorny bushes and shrubs. The grass is shorter and less coarse than the grass found in the savannah. On hill slopes, where there is more rain, some trees like the willow and poplar are common. The veld regions support an enormous variety of natural vegetation.

Wildlife

The region has a diverse and varied wildlife. Animals found here are lions, cheetahs, leopards, giraffes, elephants, hippopotamuses, oryxes, kudus, elands, sable antelopes and roan antelopes amongst many more. However, most of these creatures can survive only on or near protected areas. A rare species endemic

pasturage: the practice of pasturing grazing animals

to the veld is the vervet monkey. Mass slaughter, poaching, trophy hunting and intrusions of farmers and agriculturists into animal habitats have diminished wildlife populations immensely. Wildlife conservation efforts in Southern Africa have been carried out towards the creation of large, international conservation areas to preserve the wildlife that currently thrives in the veld.

Vervet monkey

People

The occupation of the people living in the velds are mining and cattle rearing. Agriculture is carried out wherever fertile land is available. The main crops are maize, wheat, barley, oats and potato. Cash crops like tobacco, sugarcane and cotton are also grown. The grasslands have ideal conditions for cattle and sheep rearing. Cattle are reared in the warmer and the wetter eastern part. They are reared for milk and meat. Frozen meat and beef are mainly exported to the countries of South Europe. Sheep rearing is the main occupation in the veld. Sheep are reared for the production of wool. The sheep are of fine quality and consist mainly of the merino breed. The Angora goats yield mohair and leather. South Africa is the largest producer of **mohair** in the world. It is also the second largest exporter of merino wool in the world after Australia. Mining is an important occupation of the veld. The minerals are gold, diamonds, iron ore and coal. The mining centres are Johannesburg and Kimberley, which have well-developed networks of transport and communication.

Skill Builder

21ST CENTURY SKILLS

Critical-thinking skills: The prairies in North America were formed due to movements in the Earth's interior. Because of their height, the Rocky Mountains create a huge rain shadow area on their leeward side. There is a lack of rainfall in the rain shadow area. This lack of rainfall prevented trees from growing extensively east of the mountains, thereby causing the growth of tall grasses and shrubs in the prairie region. The weather is moderate and there are very few trees to move to create agricultural land. What can you understand about the effects of weather and climate on an area?

Information literacy: Prepare a short report about black-footed ferrets that are found in the prairies. Write down their physical appearance and characteristics, habitat and behaviour.

Life skills: Grassland degradation is an environmental disturbance in which grass struggles to grow due to causes like overgrazing, climate change and human action. Make a list of some restorative methods that would prevent this in the years to come.

World Connect

The black-footed ferrets, believed to be extinct but then rediscovered 35 years ago, will be restored to a pair of western Wyoming ranches. These ferrets were bred at a facility outside Fort Collins in northern Colorado. These species are a member of the weasel family and are long and sleek in appearance. These endangered species feed on prairie dogs and are **nocturnal**.

mohair: the hair of the angora goat; nocturnal: done, occurring, or active at night

Wind up

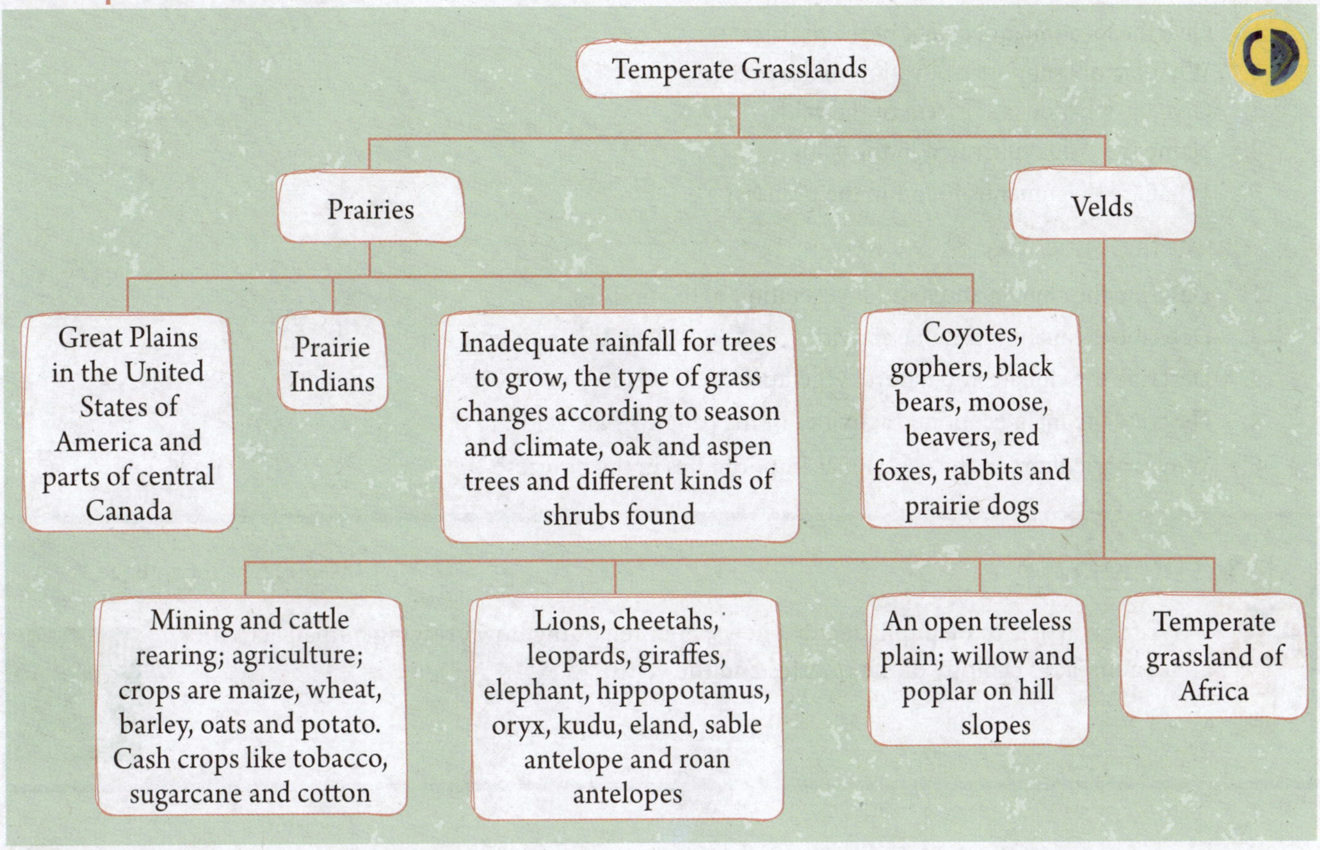

Exercises

A. Fill in the blanks.

1. The temperate grasslands of South America are known as ....
2. The Canadian prairies are drained by the river .... and its tributaries.
3. A local warm wind in the prairies is known as ....
4. South Africa is the largest producer of .... in the world.

B. Match the columns.

	A		B
1.	The Great Plains	a.	Largest Amazon rainforest cover
2.	Brazil	b.	mining
3.	Saskatchewan	c.	Canadian Prairies
4.	Lesotho	d.	the USA
5.	Johannesburg	e.	velds

C. Write T for true and F for false.

1. The veld experiences occasional droughts. ☐
2. Sheep rearing is more important than cattle rearing in the veld. ☐
3. Terraced farming is practised in the prairies of North America. ☐
4. Grass in the velds is less short and coarse than in the savannah. ☐

D. Answer these questions in brief.

1. Give the location and extent of the prairies.
2. What factors support cultivation in the prairies?
3. Give the location and extent of the velds.
4. Name the crops cultivated in the velds.
5. What are the minerals found in the prairies?

E. Answer these questions in detail.

1. Describe the climate and natural vegetation of the prairies.
2. Describe the main economic activities of the people in the prairies.
3. Describe the climate and natural vegetation of the velds.
4. Describe the main economic activities of the people in the velds.
5. Why is agriculture in the veld not as important as in the prairies?

Think Big

Integrate with language

Write an article to be published in a newspaper regarding how growing human activities are a threat to ecology of the prairies and the velds.

15 LIFE ON LAND

Learning Tools

Write the important points about the prairies and the velds in the table below.

Characteristics	Prairies	Velds
Location		
Climate		
Vegetation		
Animals		
Life of people and economic activities		

Web links:

https://www.worldwildlife.org/biomes/temperate-grasslands-savannas-and-shrublands

Last accessed on 31 August 2021

1. Democracy

Warm up

Cleisthenes was an Athenian leader in the 6th century BCE who was considered to be the father of democracy. He introduced many reforms to correct the inequalities of the early Athenian society. Today, the form of democracy practised in the world is very different, dynamic and ever evolving.

Every country needs some form of government to manage its internal and external affairs. There are different systems of government in the world, like democracy and monarchy. As time progressed, these forms have also evolved and undergone changes. Kings and queens are still in power in some countries, but in most cases, the countries have become constitutional monarchies, where a constitution is in place to limit the powers of the monarchs.

Democracy, as a preferred form of government, is widespread in the world. The basic principles of democracy continue to give power to the people and provide equal treatment for all. However, the understanding of democracy has deepened everywhere. People have become aware of their rights and have opinions on a wide range of national and international issues.

Key Elements of a Representative Democracy

A government can be called democratic if it empowers the people to play a role in decision making. There are many reasons why democracy has gained an edge over other systems of government.

- People are able to elect their representatives. As the size of the population has increased worldwide, a large number of views and opinions need to be considered by governments. When making laws and policies, the government must bear in mind the interests of all communities in the country, whether they are in a majority or minority. For this purpose, a democratic country conducts elections in which people vote and elect their representatives. These elected representatives together form the government.
- For the purpose of electing representatives, a democracy must hold free and fair elections. This means that equal opportunities should be given to the people to contest in elections. In India, every citizen is guaranteed the universal adult franchise, which means that everyone who is 18 years and above enjoys the right to vote in order to elect the representatives.
- The active participation of the people in the affairs of their country makes a democracy successful. When people are allowed to participate in the government, they take more interest in the functioning of the system.

Universal adult franchise

- As the government depends on the support of the majority, it is accountable and answerable to the people. As elections happen regularly after a fixed term, the government makes laws that accommodate the different communities. It is always sensitive to the rights of the citizens.

India's Journey as a Democracy

India became a democratic country after almost 200 years of British rule. The constitution declared India to be a **sovereign**, socialist, **secular**, democratic **republic**. The constitution is the primary source of laws and powers in India. It is the lengthiest constitution in the world. In a democracy, the people need to be safeguarded against the misuse of power by those who exercise political power. The constitution provides those essential safeguards to all the citizens in the form of rights. It also provides the basic structure to our democracy.

26 January, 1950 | India Becomes a Republic

On 26 January 1950, India declared herself a republic. The *New York Times* wrote, 'Assumption of the status of a sovereign democratic republic brings in to force the new Constitution, which abolishes untouchability and includes the most detailed document of fundamental rights of any constitution.'

Democracy, a Popular Form of Government

The number of countries that have adopted democracy as a form of government has steadily increased in the past. A primary reason for this is the respect for basic human rights, which democracy promises to the citizens. People in countries like Nepal, South Africa, Malaysia and South Korea had opted for democracy to break away from autocratic regimes or military rule.

History is evidence that people were discriminated against in different parts of the world for reasons like race, gender, caste, religion, language and economic status. Such inequality led to struggles for dignity and equality on the part of the **downtrodden**.

Liberty, freedom, dignity and equality are the values that make democracy a popular choice.

What's in the picture?

1. What do these statues represent?
2. Was India a democratic nation then?
3. In a democracy, do people have the right to protest?

Democracy is an **ideology**, and it requires institutions to become a reality for the people. In India, all the political offices and posts, like those of the president, the prime minister, ministers, members of the parliament, chief ministers, political parties and the election commission, are some of the institutions that play a key role in the proper functioning of the government.

sovereign: possessing supreme or ultimate power; secular: not connected with religious or spiritual matters; republic: supreme power is held by the people and their elected representatives and there is an elected or nominated president; downtrodden: oppressed or treated badly by people in power; ideology: a system of ideas and ideals, especially one that forms the basis of economic or political theory and policy;

Political Parties

Political party canvassing

India follows a multi-party system, which means that different political parties are allowed to form and function. A political party is formed by a group of people who possess similar ideologies about how to approach and tackle national issues. Political parties represent the different viewpoints and opinions of the people. They contest elections and thus engage people in the political process. They also form the government that helps in making, implementing and enforcing laws. When elections are conducted, parties and candidates contest with each other to win the maximum number of votes from their constituencies. The party that wins a majority can form the government. If no political party wins a majority, parties have to come together to attain the minimum number of seats required to form the government. This coming together of various political parties to form a government is called a **coalition**.

National Parties

Political parties that have a presence in the whole country are called national parties. There are eight national parties that have presence and support throughout the country.

- Bharatiya Janata Party
- Indian National Congress
- Communist Party of India (Marxist)
- Communist Party of India
- Bahujan Samaj Party
- Nationalist Congress Party
- All India Trinamool Congress
- National People's Party

Geography skills

On an outline map of the world, mark the countries that have adopted democracy as a form of governance.

State Parties

There are many state parties in India, which only function in their respective states. There are almost 50 state parties in India, as recognized by the election commission. These parties are instrumental in representing the demands of the people in their state and thus assist in the expansion of democracy in the country. Some well-known state parties are Asom Gana Parishad, Shiromani Akali Dal, Telugu Desam Party and Aam Aadmi Party.

FACT CHECK

The indelible ink, which is used to mark a voter's finger, contains silver nitrate that gets darker with exposure to light.

Election Commission

The election commission of India is responsible for holding elections in India. Its primary role is to ensure that elections are free and fair. It is independent of the control of the organs of the government such as the legislature, the executive and the judiciary. The chief election commissioner heads the commission.

Green Earth

The National Air Quality Index (NAQI) was launched by the government to keep a close watch on the quality of air in the country. This will help create awareness about the dangerously rising levels of pollutants in the air. The right to clean environment was granted by the Supreme Court as a part of the right to life.

Electoral Reforms: The election commission of India has introduced several reforms to make the process of election better and free of malpractices. Electronic Voting machines (EVMs) were introduced to improve the efficiency of the casting

coalition: the coming together of various political parties to form a government and counting of votes. Electoral rolls, which contain the names of all eligible voters of an area, are now computerized to minimize errors. Issuing election photo identity cards or EPIC, was also one such reform that ensured that the voters had an identity proof while casting votes.

Apply it!

The Symbol of NOTA

The right to vote is an important right given to the people in our country. Earlier, many people did not exercise their right to vote because they did not support any particular candidate or political party contesting the elections. The option of 'None of the Above' was introduced on 18th September 2015. It empowers the citizens to not vote for anyone, if they feel none of the candidates contesting elections are worthy of their vote. On the directive of the Supreme Court, the Election Commission of India included the option of NOTA in the Electronic Voting Machines. The right to reject was upheld by the Supreme Court as an electoral reform required to make the politicians more responsible.

1. What does NOTA mean?
2. Why was it introduced?
3. How has it made India's democracy better?

Skill Builder

21ST CENTURY SKILLS

Critical thinking skills: Carry out a debate in the class on the topic: 'Is democracy the best form of government?'

Life skills: If a country's Parliament or a state building is attacked, why is it considered an attack on democracy?

Information literacy: Find out which forms of government the following countries have adopted.

1. Afghanistan ....
2. Australia ....
3. Brunei ....
4. United Kingdom ....
5. Denmark ....
6. Bhutan ....
7. Thailand ....
8. China ....

World Connect

'Four score and seven years ago, our fathers brought forth on this continent, a new nation, conceived in liberty, and dedicated to the proposition that all men are created equal.

Now we are engaged in a great civil war, we are met on a great battle-field of that war. We have come to dedicate a portion of that field, as a final resting place for those who here gave their lives, that that nation might live. The world will little note, nor long remember, what we say here, but it can never forget what they did here. It is for us the living, rather, to be dedicated here to the unfinished work which they who fought here, have thus far so nobly advanced. It is rather for us to be here dedicated to the great task remaining before us—that from these honored dead we take increased devotion to that cause for which they gave the last full measure of devotion—that we here highly resolve that these dead shall not have died in vain—that this nation, under God, shall have a new birth of freedom—and that government of the people, by the people, for the people, shall not perish from the earth.'

Abraham Lincoln at the Gettysburg Address

-Excerpt from the famous Gettysburg Address of Abraham Lincoln, in which he gave the most widely accepted definition of democracy, 19th November 1863.

Wind up

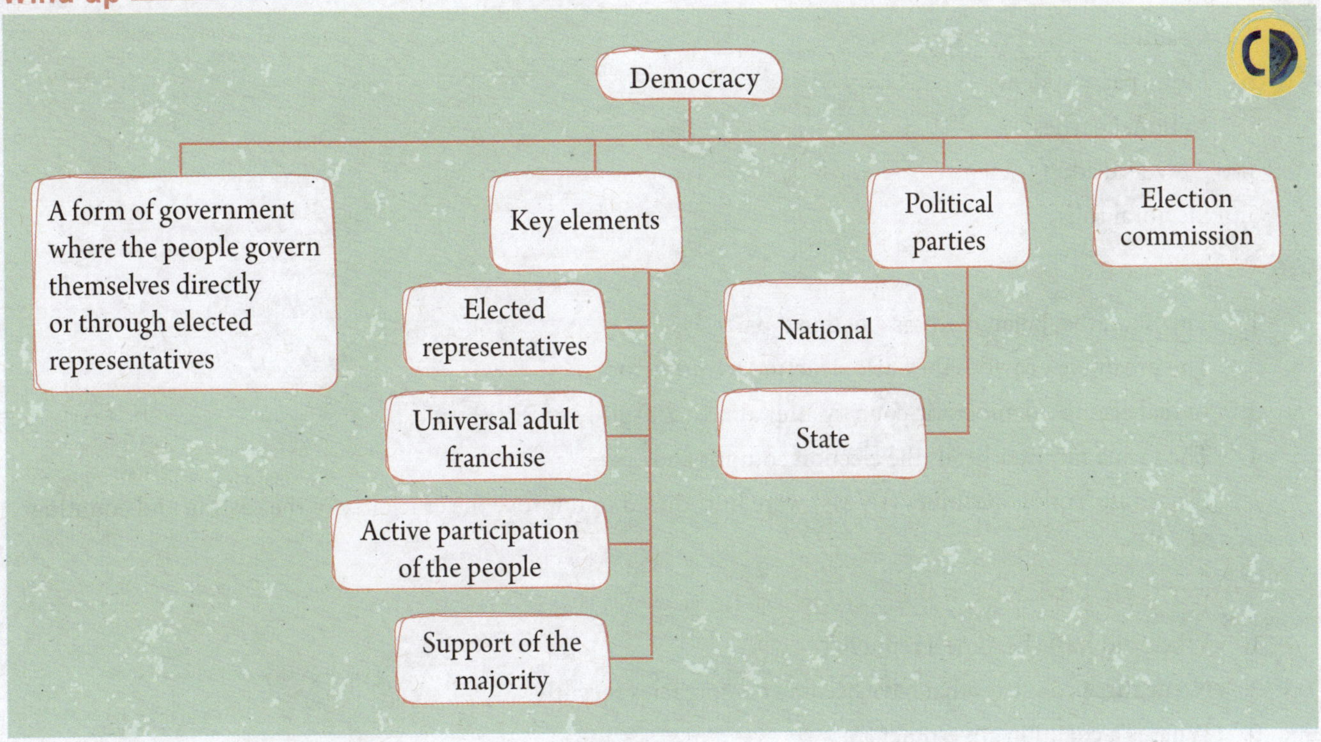

Exercises

A. Choose the correct answers.

1. Political parties that have a presence in the whole country are called
   a. national parties
   b. state parties
   c. coalitions
   d. regional parties
2. As a form of government, democracy has become
   a. unpopular
   b. new
   c. popular
   d. old
3. Electoral rolls contain
   a. the names of political leaders
   b. the names of all eligible voters of an area
   c. the names of political parties
   d. the names of government employees eligible for voting
4. This body is responsible for holding elections in the country
   a. central government
   b. state government
   c. election commission
   d. political parties

B. Define the following terms.

1. Coalition
2. Multi-party system
3. National parties
4. Universal adult franchise
5. Electoral rolls

C. Write T for true and F for false.

1. The Bharatiya Janata Party is a national party.
2. The preamble provides the basic structure to our democracy.
3. India became a democratic country after almost 200 years of British rule.
4. The prime minister heads the election commission.
5. Electronic Voting machines (EVMs) were introduced to improve the efficiency of the casting and counting of votes.

D. Answer these questions in brief.

1. When did India become a republic?
2. Name three countries that have become democracies recently.
3. What is a coalition government?
4. What is universal adult franchise?
5. What are the values that make democracy a popular choice?

E. Answer these questions in detail.

1. What are the key elements of a democracy?
2. List three electoral reforms introduced in the recent years.
3. State parties perform an important role in our country. Explain.
4. Read the passage and answer the questions.

   India became a democratic country after almost 200 years of British rule. The constitution declared India to be a sovereign, socialist, secular, democratic, republic. It is the primary source of law and power in India. It is the lengthiest constitution in the world. In a democracy people need to be safeguarded against the misuse of power by those who exercise political power.

   i. Who exercises political power in our country?

   ii. Why is the constitution important?

Think Big

Art integration

Choose any one national party in India and make a poster on its symbol, flag and the number of times it has been in the government.

Learning Tools

A. Conduct this quiz in the class.

1. What form of government exists in this country?
2. Does the government have a written constitution?
3. How long has the government structure been in place?
4. Does the constitution limit the power of the government?
5. Does the constitution permit one part of the government to check or balance another?
6. Does the constitution provide individual rights?

B. Follow the steps below to make a foldable and create your own study guide based on what you have learnt. Use this book with data occurring in threes.

1. Fold a sheet of paper into half with the paper horizontal.
2. Fold the right side toward the centre, trying to cover one half of the paper.

NOTE: If you fold the right edge over first, the final graphic organizer will open and close like a book.

3. Fold the left side over the right side to make a book with three folds.
4. Open the folded book. Place your hands between the two thicknesses of paper and cut up the two valleys on one side only. This will form three tabs.

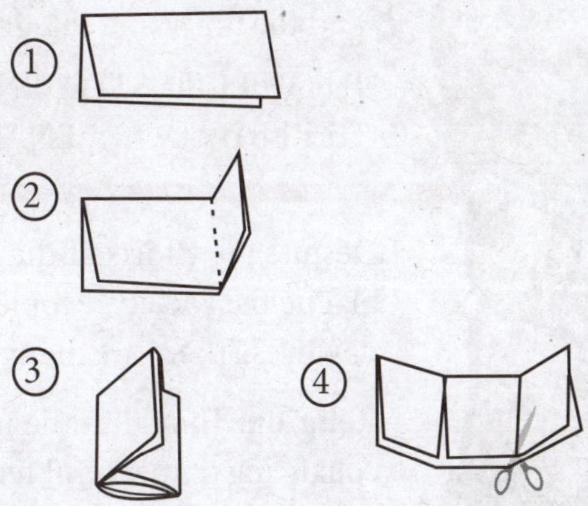

2. Democracy and Equality

Warm up

WE, THE PEOPLE OF INDIA, having solemnly resolved to constitute India into a SOVEREIGN SOCIALIST SECULAR DEMOCRATIC REPUBLIC and to secure to all its citizens:

JUSTICE, social, economic and political; LIBERTY of thought, expression, belief, faith and worship; EQUALITY of status and of opportunity;

and to promote among them all FRATERNITY assuring the dignity of the individual and the unity and integrity of the Nation;

IN OUR CONSTITUENT ASSEMBLY this twenty-sixth day of November, 1949, do HEREBY ADOPT, ENACT AND GIVE TO OURSELVES THIS CONSTITUTION.

Despite the efforts of the government, the laws and rights laid out, inequality continues to plague the society. People still face discrimination and unequal treatment in their day-to-day lives. There are many reasons for the existence of inequality in the society today.

Religion: Though India is a diverse country with a long history of different religions coexisting on peaceful terms with each other, the recent times have witnessed a growing religious intolerance that, in most instances, breeds violence and hostility. Some trace this divisiveness back to the British policy of divide and rule.

Gender: Throughout the world, women have had to face different types of discrimination and atrocities. In the typical patriarchal society, where men have social, cultural and political power, women have always been **relegated** to the background.

Economic status: Poverty does not allow the people to fully avail of the basic amenities that are available. Healthcare, education and jobs are areas where this can be prominently observed. Poor people cannot afford the medical facilities of private hospitals, and hence, have to seek medical care from government hospitals, which are on one hand affordable, but on the other hand, are overcrowded with an obvious shortage of healthcare facilities to tend to the large number of patients.

Caste system: Though the Constitution abolished the caste system in 1950, it continues to be practised in the rural and urban areas alike. People have been unable to change their mindset. However, with education and urbanization, change is inevitable. 'Dalits are not allowed to drink or take water from the same wells, offer prayers at the same temples, wear shoes in the presence of an upper caste or drink from the same cups in tea stalls', said Smita Narula, a senior researcher with Human Rights Watch. The oppressed classes in India are relegated to the lowest jobs and live in constant fear of being publicly humiliated. The term Dalit was coined by the lower caste people to express that they were not allowed to be a part of the larger society. Dalit means 'broken'.

relegated: to put someone in a lower or less important position

Equality in the Constitution

The Constitution of India begins with a Preamble. Equality is one of the ideals, listed in the Preamble, that our country strives to achieve. We see inequality all around us, not only in terms of the rich and the poor but also in other forms of differences.

Let us look at the provisions for equality that are given in the Indian Constitution.

Right to Equality in the Constitution

There is a detailed explanation of the various aspects of the right to equality in articles 14, 15, 16, 17 and 18.

FACT CHECK

Equality first formally became a part of the *Declaration of Rights of Man and Citizen,* adopted in France after French Revolution of 1789.

Equality before Law: Article 14 ensures that every citizen shall be likewise protected by the laws of the country. It means that no one is above the law and that all citizens as well as non-citizens who are living in this country shall be treated equally by the law, irrespective of any distinction in caste, creed or religion.

Social equality and equal access to public areas: Article 15 of the Constitution of India states that no person shall be prejudiced on the basis of colour, caste, creed, language, etc. Every person shall have equal admittance to public places like public wells, bathing ghats, museums and temples.

Equal treatment in matters of employment: Article 16 of the Constitution of India mentions that the state shall treat everyone equally in matters of employment. No citizen shall be discriminated against on the basis of race, caste, religion, creed, descent or place of birth with respect to any employment or office under the state. All citizens of India can apply for government jobs.

Abolition of untouchability: Article 17 of the Constitution of India abolishes the practice of untouchability in India. This practice has been declared as a crime and anyone found practising it is punishable by law.

Prohibition of the state from granting any titles: Article 18 states that the citizens of India are not allowed to accept titles from a foreign state. Titles like *Rai Bahadurs* and *Khan Bahadurs* given by the British government have also been abolished.

What's in the picture?

Look at this graphic and talk about what it means.

Universal Adult Franchise

In India, there is universal adult franchise, which means that all citizens of India who are 18 years and above are given the right to vote without any discrimination. This ensures equal participation of all citizens in the democratic process of the country. It also gives a sense of dignity and empowerment to the poor, minorities and other backward classes as they have an equal say in matters of their country. One vote one value is an important principle of democracy.

Apart from the Constitution, the Indian government also tries to implement the democratic principle of equality. It makes several laws to ensure equal opportunities to the people and promote social equality. The government also introduces schemes from time to time for the same purpose.

Mid-Day Meal Scheme

Mid-day meal

The government of India introduced the mid-day meal scheme in order to provide cooked lunch to all school children up to Class VIII in all government and government-aided schools. This scheme has been instrumental in increasing attendance in schools. The meals that are provided to the children are a big incentive for poor parents to send them to school. This assures them of at least one meal a day. Earlier, children were forced to drop out of school in search of work so that the family income could be increased. The scheme has also helped in promoting equality in two ways. Firstly, children from different castes and class backgrounds sit together to have their meals. Secondly, the lunch is mostly cooked by unprivileged people. It gives them an opportunity to earn a decent living. In 2007, an amendment was made to the scheme to provide mid-day meals even during summer vacations in drought-affected areas. From time to time, changes are introduced in the scheme to widen its scope and improve the standard of the food being served.

Green Earth

The Environment Protection Act was passed by the Parliament of India in 1986 in order to protect and preserve the human, animal, natural and built environment.

Case Study

The Sukanya Samriddhi Yojana is a scheme introduced by the government. It was launched by Prime Minister Narendra Modi, on 21 January 2015, under the 'Beti Bachao, Beti Padhao' Campaign. This scheme was launched to meet the expense of the girl child's higher education and marriage. It primarily ensures equitable share to a girl child in the resources and the savings of a family. The issue of the girl child being discriminated against has been an unfortunate part of the Indian society. Reports of female foeticide and abuse of girls are common knowledge. Government schemes like this not only help the cause of securing the life and future of girls but also work towards bringing about a significant change in people's mindset.

Q. What are the aims of the Sukanya Samriddhi Yojana scheme?

Apply it!

8 DECENT WORK AND ECONOMIC GROWTH

Read the following article on treating all jobs as equal and not looking down on any profession.

Dignity of labour is the philosophy that all types of work should be given the same amount of respect, despite the nature of the work. No occupation should be considered superior to others. Gandhiji believed a lot in the dignity of labour, both in word and in deed. He had said, 'No matter how insignificant the thing you have to do, do it as well as you can, give it as much of your care and attention as you would give to the thing you regard as most important, for it will be by those small things that you shall be judged'.

- What do you understand by dignity of labour?
- What can you infer from reading the lines spoken by Gandhiji?
- Dignity of labour is not yet fully achieved in the Indian society. Explain with two examples.

The Challenge of Democracy

In the Indian society, there are numerous instances of inequality. Should equality be understood in terms of being rich and poor, living in a big or small house, or should it be understood in terms of being treated equally before the law and getting equal opportunities? The Preamble of the Indian Constitution clearly states that it shall provide 'equality of status and of opportunity'. Here, status does not mean the standard of living but our status as the citizens of this democratic country. Discrimination exists even today and different communities have to raise their voices to be treated equally. The extent to which citizens comprehend the meaning of democracy has evolved tremendously over the years. Many communities that were previously not aware of their rights have now started voicing their demands for equality. As the different governments accommodate the demands of the people in some measure, they also face criticism and charges of being biased towards them. The idea of democracy has, thus, become more elaborate and refined in the process. The goal of bringing more and more people within the purview of democracy will take a long time to achieve, but it is not wholly unachievable.

Skill Builder

21ST CENTURY SKILLS

Critical-thinking skills: In India, there have been instances where food served during the mid-day meals was found to be contaminated, leading to the hospitalization of many school children. What alternatives would you suggest?

Life skills: Is it fair on the part of the government to launch special schemes for the girl child? Why are there not so many promotional schemes for boys? Is the government biased towards girls?

Information literacy: Compare and contrast any non-democratic country of the world to your own country. List out at least three differences in both the systems.

World Connect

Around the world, countless people are subjected to some form of inequality or the other. The most prevalent form of inequality is the divide between the rich and the poor. In America, homelessness has become a matter of grave concern. The U.S. Department of Housing and Urban Development, in its Annual Homeless Assessment Report to Congress, 2007, had put the number of Americans who are homeless as 7,50,000. About 21 per cent of all children live in poverty—a poverty rate believed to be higher than what is prevalent in other rich nations. Affordable housing, comprehensive healthcare and homeless assistance programmes are some of the policies the government is working on to improve the conditions of the poor in America.

Wind up

- Democracy & Equality
  - Equality, irrespective of difference in religion, gender, economic status and caste system
  - Constitution
    - Equality before law
    - Social equality and equal access to public areas
    - Equal treatment in matters of employment
    - Prohibition of the state from granting any titles
    - Abolition of untouchability
  - Universal Adult Franchise
  - Mid-day meal scheme

Exercises

A. Fill in the blanks.

1. The Constitution of India begins with the ....
2. Dalit means ....
3. Article 17 declares the practice of .... to be a crime.
4. Equality before law is enshrined in .... of the Constitution.
5. One .... one .... is an important principle of democracy.

B. Choose the correct answers.

1. In some rural areas, they are still discriminated against.
   a. Dalits b. Brahmins c. adults d. upper caste people
2. The mid-day meal scheme applies to
   a. all educational institutions b. government schools
   c. private institutions d. public and private schools
3. Private hospitals are
   a. overcrowded b. expensive c. inexpensive d. seasily accessible
4. Right to equality is discussed in these articles of the Indian Constitution.
   a. 14–18 b. 16–18 c. 17 and 18 d. 16 and 18

C. Write the article of the Indian Constitution to which these provisions belong.

1. Untouchability has been abolished. ....
2. All the people have equal access to public places. ....
3. All citizens can apply for government jobs. ....
4. Titles given to individuals have been abolished. ....

D. Answer these questions in brief.

1. What do you understand by equality?
2. How does the constitution of India promote equality?
3. What are the reasons for inequality in India?
4. What are the challenges that democracy in India faces?

E. Answer these questions in detail.

1. Which article of the Constitution abolishes untouchability? Why is it important?
2. What is universal adult franchise? Why is it considered to be a democratic principle?
3. How does the caste system lead to inequality?
4. List two advantages of the mid-day meal scheme.

F. Read this passage and answer the questions.

Poverty does not allow people to fully avail of the basic amenities that are available to others. Healthcare, education and jobs are areas where this can be prominently observed. Poor people cannot afford the medical facilities of private hospitals, and hence, have to seek medical care from government hospitals that are, on one hand, affordable and on the other hand, can be overcrowded with an obvious shortage of healthcare facilities to tend to a large number of patients.

1. Why are people not able to access private healthcare?
2. How can we solve this problem?

Think Big

English fun

Write an essay on the topic 'Dignity of labour'. Do you think all workers need rights to protect and safeguard them?

8 DECENT WORK AND ECONOMIC GROWTH

Learning Tools

Fill up the boxes in your own words to summarize what you have learnt in the chapter.

Define:

Democracy: ....

....

Equality: ....

....

Constitution: ....

....

Universal adult franchise: ....

....

Mid-day meal scheme: ....

....

Reasons for inequality	Equity in the constitution
....	....
....	....
....	....
....	....
....	....
....	....
....	....
....	....

Web links:

https://www.un.org/en/global-issues/democracy

https://www.un.org/sustainabledevelopment/gender-equality/

Last accessed on 31 August 2021

3. The State Government

Warm up

The Constitution of India consists of three lists to divide power and responsibilities among the central and the state governments. The state list consists of 66 subjects. Some of them are police, agriculture, monuments, libraries, public health and sanitation, places of pilgrimage, fisheries, markets, toll taxes, etc.

Look at the political map of India. Have you observed that some places on the map are marked with a yellow dot? Some of them are the state capitals and others are union territories. The main difference between the states and the union territories is that the states have their own state government, whereas the union territories are administered by the central government. They do not have a separate government and a chief minister.

Let us understand in detail why some states need a separate state government.

India is a large and diverse country. The needs of the people, their issues and the problems that they face also differ from region to region. One government at the national level would not be able to manage such a variety of issues. So, India chose to be a **federal** country, which implies that it has governments at two or more than two levels. The creation of government at the state level helps each state to be governed in a better manner.

Levels of Government

The government in our country functions at three levels, namely the central, the state and the local levels. The central government, or the union government administers the entire country. It takes decisions that affect the whole country. Each state has a state government to look after its concerns and issues. It shares the burden of the central government as specific problems of the states are taken care of at this level. The central government is able to concentrate on issues that affect the whole nation. Since the country is vast and every small area, whether village or town, can have a number of problems, there is a third level of government. This is known as the local government. For urban areas, the local government is known as the municipality, and for rural areas it is called the panchayat.

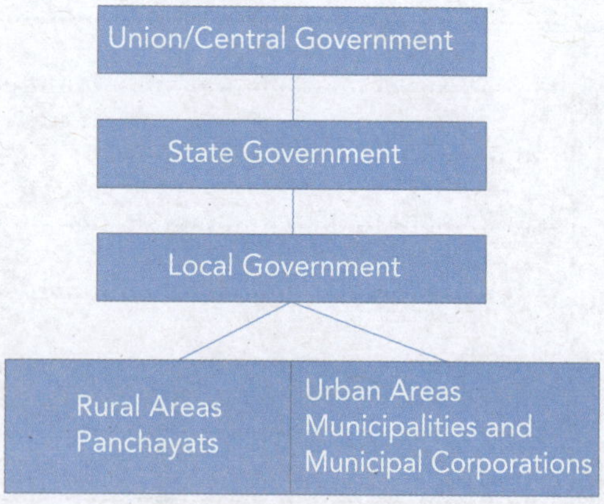

Levels of government

federal: having or relating to a system of government in which several states form a unity but remain independent in internal affairs

Geography skills

Working from this map, locate five state capitals and five union territories on an outline map of India.

Political map of India

Organization of the State Government

The three levels of government each perform similar functions. Only the scale of their responsibilities is different. The union government makes laws for the entire country and takes care of external affairs.

Governments at all levels organize their work under three broad heads—the legislature, which makes all the laws, the executive, which implements the laws, and the judiciary, which interprets and applies the laws.

This organization of work is also called separation of powers. It helps the system function smoothly without any duplication of work. Powers and responsibilities are clearly separated. The state legislature has two houses: the Legislative Assembly and the Legislative Council.

How is the Government Formed?

When a political party is able to win more than half the number of total constituencies, it is said to have won by a majority. This party wins the election and can form the state government. A government is elected for a period of five years, after which elections are held again. All other candidates, who win from their constituencies but whose political party does not get a majority, are said to be in the opposition. In case no political party is able to win a clear majority, the party with the highest number of seats has to tie up with other parties in order to reach the mark of more than half to form a coalition government.

For the purpose of elections, each state is divided into a number of smaller divisions called constituencies. A number of candidates from different political parties from each of these constituencies contest in elections. One candidate is elected from each of these. Thus, he or she becomes a member of the Legislative Assembly and is called a Member of the Legislative Assembly or an MLA. The minimum age for becoming an MLA is 25 years.

FACT CHECK

Constituencies are made on the basis of population and not on the basis of area.

Legislative Assembly

In India, most of the state legislatures have only one house, which is the Legislative Assembly or the Vidhan Sabha. This is called a unicameral legislature, where the assembly is empowered to take decisions and make laws.

All the MLAs, whether from the ruling party or the opposition, meet in the Legislative Assembly. The Legislative Assembly is the place where all debates and discussions regarding the running of the state take place.

Work of the Legislative Assembly

The Legislative Assembly is the highest authority in the state to make laws. The Legislative Assembly carries out extensive debates on proposals to make new laws for the state. The MLAs discuss all aspects of the proposed laws and evaluate the need to make changes to the existing laws. All subjects listed under the state list in the constitution can be considered by the Legislative Assembly. If the need arises, then the Legislative Assembly can also make laws on the subjects of the concurrent list.

Chief Minister

Once the election process is over, the elected MLAs of the ruling party elect their leader as the chief minister. People of the state do not directly elect the chief minister. The chief minister selects the ministers. The chosen MLAs now have a dual responsibility—as an MLA and as a minister.

The ministers take charge of the different ministries of the government. All the elected MLAs, including the opposition, constitute the legislature. The chief minister and his or her team of ministers are a part of the legislature, but they now also form the executive. All the ministers together form the Council of Ministers.

The chief minister heads the government at the state level. The governor of the state formally appoints the chief minister and other ministers in a ceremony. The governor is the head of the state, and he or she is a very important link between the central and the state government.

Role of the Opposition

All laws made by the legislature are implemented by the executive through the ministries and the departments. In the Legislative Assembly, the members of the house engage in discussions about all the aspects of a proposed law. Opposition members play a crucial role in keeping the ruling party alert by pointing out the flaws in their functioning. They also question the ministers, and thus, make the executive answerable and accountable to the legislature. This is a feature of democracy that shows us that no post or level in a hierarchy is given absolute power.

The Vidhana Soudha, the seat of the state legislature of Karnataka

Apply it!

In a democracy, leaders keep changing. Do you think this is good or bad for the state?

Legislative Council

The State Legislative Council, also called the Vidhan Parishad, is the permanent house of the state. There are very few states in India that have a Legislative Council or Vidhan Parishad. These states have a bicameral legislature or a legislature with two houses. They are Andhra Pradesh, Bihar, Karnataka, Maharashtra, Telangana and Uttar Pradesh. The members of the house have a six-year term. They are known as Members of Legislative Council or MLCs. To become a member of the Legislative Council, a person must be at least 30 years of age and a citizen of India. These members are not directly elected by the people. They are chosen from local government bodies, like municipalities and corporations, and some are nominated by the governor on the basis of their contribution to various fields like literature, science, arts, medicine, social work, etc. As a house of the legislature, the Legislative Council debates and discusses the proposed laws. It can also suggest amendments or changes to the proposals of the Legislative Assembly. Thus, it becomes an important part of the law-making organ of the state.

Green Earth

Suggest at least five steps to your state government that you can take in order to make your state a clean and green state.

Judiciary

The Supreme Court is the highest court in India. However, at the state level, we have the High Court, which is the highest judicial body in a state. Below the High Courts are the District Courts, which are subordinate to and under the control of the High Courts.

Skill Builder

Critical-thinking skills: Should there be a difference in the role and functions of the state government of a small state as compared with a large state. Why/Why not?

Life skills: In 2015, Chennai experienced unprecedented rain and floods. Life was thrown out of gear for the people. Prepare a comprehensive list of things that the government of your state should send to Chennai as aid in a similar situation. How can you contribute?

Collaboration: Form five groups in your class. Form a political party with your group members, and draw up a list of issues you will take up to win maximum votes in the state elections.

World Connect

In the United States, the state government also holds legislative, executive and judicial powers within the state. The state legislature is headed by the Senate, and its members are called senators. The state executive is headed by an elected governor. In the state judiciary, the method of appointment of judges or the structure of courts in the judiciary varies from state to state, with most states having one trial-level court and an intermediate appeals court.

Wind up

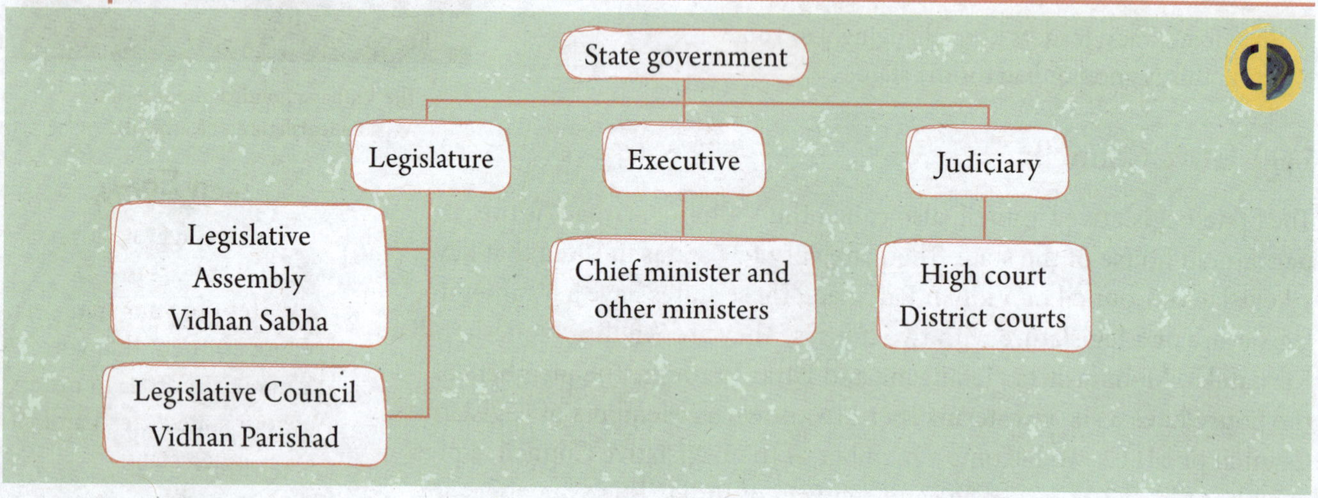

Exercises

A. Choose the correct answers.

1. The state Legislative Assembly is also called the
   a. Lok Sabha b. Rajya Sabha c. Vidhan Sabha d. Vidhan Parishad
2. The governor appoints the
   a. MLA b. chief minister c. governor d. minister
3. The members of the Legislative Assembly have a term of
   a. four years b. five years c. six years d. seven years
4. Laws made by the legislature are implemented by the
   a. judiciary b. executive c. chief minister d. prime minister
5. India chose to be a federal country because of its
   a. area b. population c. diversity d. all of these

B. Correct these statements by changing only the underlined word.

1. Coalition means India has governments at more than two levels.
2. Union territories have their own government and chief minister.
3. The party with the most number of seats is called the opposition.
4. The president appoints the chief minister and other ministers.

C. Write one word answers.

1. The head of the state government: ....
2. The minimum age for becoming an MLA: ....
3. The link between the central and state government: ....
4. The state legislative council is also called: ....

D. Answer these questions in brief.

1. How is a chief minister selected?
2. What is the role of the opposition in a state government?
3. List two responsibilities of a governor.
4. Who is elected directly by the people, an MLA or a minister?

E. Answer these questions in detail.

1. Explain the dual responsibilities of the ministers.
2. How does separation of powers help in the smooth functioning of the state government?
3. Why is it important to create governments at different levels?
4. How does the Constitution ensure division of powers between the different levels of government?

Think Big — Art integration

Collect and paste a picture of the legislative assembly of your state. Write a few lines about it on coloured paper, and present it in class.

Learning Tools

Create your own study guides by compiling the necessary information for swift recap.

Main ideas	Why it matters	Important terms and names
....	....	....
....	....	....
....	....	....
....	....	....
....	....	....

Web links:

https://powermin.gov.in/en/content/powers-state-government

Last accessed on 31 August 2021

4. Government and Public Welfare

Warm up

The world is currently fighting COVID-19, a deadly new virus that has claimed crores of lives globally. What started in China has caused a global upsurge because of its highly contagious nature. The World Health Organization declared it a global pandemic in 2020 and half way through 2021, the world has seen no respite, with the second wave in India affecting more lives than the first.

The Indian Constitution declares India to be a welfare state. In political science, the word 'state' is used to refer to a country. A welfare state is a state whose prime responsibility is to make policies and run the administration, keeping the welfare of the people as its topmost priority.

An important function of the government is to look after public welfare and make policies in order to develop a variety of fields such as transport and communication, technology, trade and commerce, education, healthcare, jobs and rural and urban housing.

Development of Transport

A DTC Bus, Delhi

An efficient transport system is a basic requirement for any place. To ensure that people are able to commute to their place of work and back home is crucial for smooth working of an economy. Thousands of people travel on roads everyday through different means of public and private transport. It is important that they reach their destination on time so that work can progress in a **systematic** manner and output can be maximized. Similarly, all kinds of goods are taken from one place to another, both within the cities and into the city from other distant places. An efficient infrastructure plays an important role in an effective transport system in any nation.

People use public or private transport. Public transport is operated by the state government or by private enterprises running on fixed routes. Public transport vehicles have high capacity and are used for the transit of masses. Since private transport is operated by individuals, they can chart their own route.

systematic: done or acting according to a fixed plan or system; methodical

Transportation in India

India is a densely populated country, and there is a rising demand for better public transport facilities. People commute to their workplaces, business centres or educational institutions, causing heavy traffic on the roads, especially during the peak hours in the morning and evening. Often, heavy traffic jams occur on the roads, causing further delay and adding to the chaos on the roads. The existing system always seems to fall short of the requirement.

Public transport in India includes buses, both state-owned and privately-owned, metros in cities like Mumbai and Delhi, trains and auto rickshaws. It is the responsibility of the government to provide a sound public transport system. It provides state buses, both intrastate and interstate. To maintain roads in good condition and build highways and expressways to ensure free flow of traffic are also some of the responsibilities of the government.

Public Transport

Although public transport is known to be convenient, cost-effective, environment-friendly and a source of revenue for the government in India, it is not efficient. Buses are overcrowded and do not have fixed timings. Passengers mostly comprise poor people who cannot afford to spend a lot of money on commuting every day.

What's in the picture?

What do you see in the picture? What could be the reason for this?

An effective public transport system forms the backbone of developing cities, being the only medium available for people and goods to move throughout the city. However, development in the Indian public transport system has a long way to go. It is often criticized for inadequate transport infrastructure, lack of adequate resources to upgrade the existing transport systems, overcrowded and undependable service and congested roadways. Poor transport systems suppress economic growth and development. Many thousands of people are killed or are grievously injured every year, in road and rail accidents. Steps have been taken to ensure that public transport in India runs on CNG, which is a clean fuel. Government-sponsored state transport corporations have introduced various facilities like low-floor buses and air-conditioned buses to encourage private car owners to use them more in an effort to help decongest the roads. Mumbai introduced air conditioned buses in 1998, Bangalore introduced Volvo B7RLE intra-city buses in January 2005 and Chennai houses one of Asia's largest bus terminuses, the Chennai Mofussil Bus Terminus.

FACT CHECK

BEST buses of Mumbai are the oldest operating bus service in India.

Green Earth

In 1998, the Supreme Court of India gave a ruling that by 2001, all public transport in the city of Delhi, which included buses, taxis and auto rickshaws were to be converted to CNG. This was a far-reaching step in combating the increasing levels of vehicular pollution in Delhi.

The government has introduced the Road Safety Week to be celebrated in India from 11th–17th January every year in order to spread awareness about safety on roads.

Private Transport

> **Apply it!**
>
> Think and make a list of all the different means of transport used by students to reach school.

The downside to public transport is that cars and motorcycles can, at most instances, be more flexible, and offer an easier form of travel to the commuter. The number of private vehicles on Indian roads have steadily gone up in the last few years. The main reason for this has been the lack of dependable and comfortable public transport facilities. Without a realistic public transport alternative to driving, people would not be easily swayed into reducing their **carbon footprint**.

A survey conducted by the Ministry of Road Transport and Highways, Government of India, in 2014-2015, showed that the number of registered motor vehicles per 1000 persons went up from 1,630 in 2001 to 3,861 in 2015 or by 137 per cent.

Role of the State Government

The state government is responsible for registering vehicles, issuing driving licenses and road permits, building highways, maintaining roads, collecting road tax and controlling vehicular pollution. It must provide better and wider signal-free roads, correct design faults in main roads and put better signage so that people can reach their destination even if they are new to the city. The people must also be encouraged to use public transport. To promote public transport, the state governments have pursued the construction of several rail-based systems like metro rail and monorail. However, in most instances, the finances required for metro projects are beyond the capacity of state or city governments.

Role of the Government in Education

Education is an important and integral part of nation building. It is necessary for the social, economic and political development of the country. School education, higher education, women's education and adult education are some areas that are regularly focused upon. Night schools are also operational to enable those people who, for a variety of reasons such as poverty and wage-earning activities during the day, are unable to avail of education facilities. The government is committed to bringing people within the ambit of education, and hence, introduces various schemes from time to time.

Samagra Shiksha Abhiyaan has been an ongoing programme in our country since 2000–2001. It emphasises the need for inclusive education. It not only refers to equal opportunities in education for all sections of the population but also creates conditions that improve day-to-day living. Many disadvantaged and minority groups like the children of workers and labourers, religious minorities, girls and children with special needs and learning difficulties are often not able to go to schools.

The mid-day meal scheme was introduced by the government in order to provide cooked lunch to the students of all government schools. The children from economically weaker families benefit immensely. The scheme was initially introduced in Tamil Nadu for the primary classes. With regular revision and additions in the scheme, it now benefits all states and union territories of India and has been extended to children up to class VIII.

In keeping up to date with the latest developments in technology, the government has also introduced DIKSHA, which is a portal for e-learning where resources and material are available to students and teachers alike. It takes learning closer to anyone who wants to learn even if they are physically not able to go to school.

carbon footprint: the amount of greenhouse gases , specially carbon dioxide, given off by something

Skill Builder

21ST CENTURY SKILLS

Life skills: The government has to ensure that people on the roads are safe. It has to enforce the rules through the fines collected for not wearing helmets and those collected for not following other traffic rules. How should citizens be made more responsible so that the government can concentrate on other issues?

Critical-thinking skills: Why do you think traffic signals are important? Can you mention what would happen if they were not there?

World Connect

The city of Tallinn is the capital of Estonia. It is a UNESCO Word Heritage site and is known for its beautiful architecture. The city government operates a system of public transport comprising buses, trams and trolley-buses. It also provides a local train service, connecting different parts of the city. In Tallinn, all public transport is completely free of charge.

Wind up

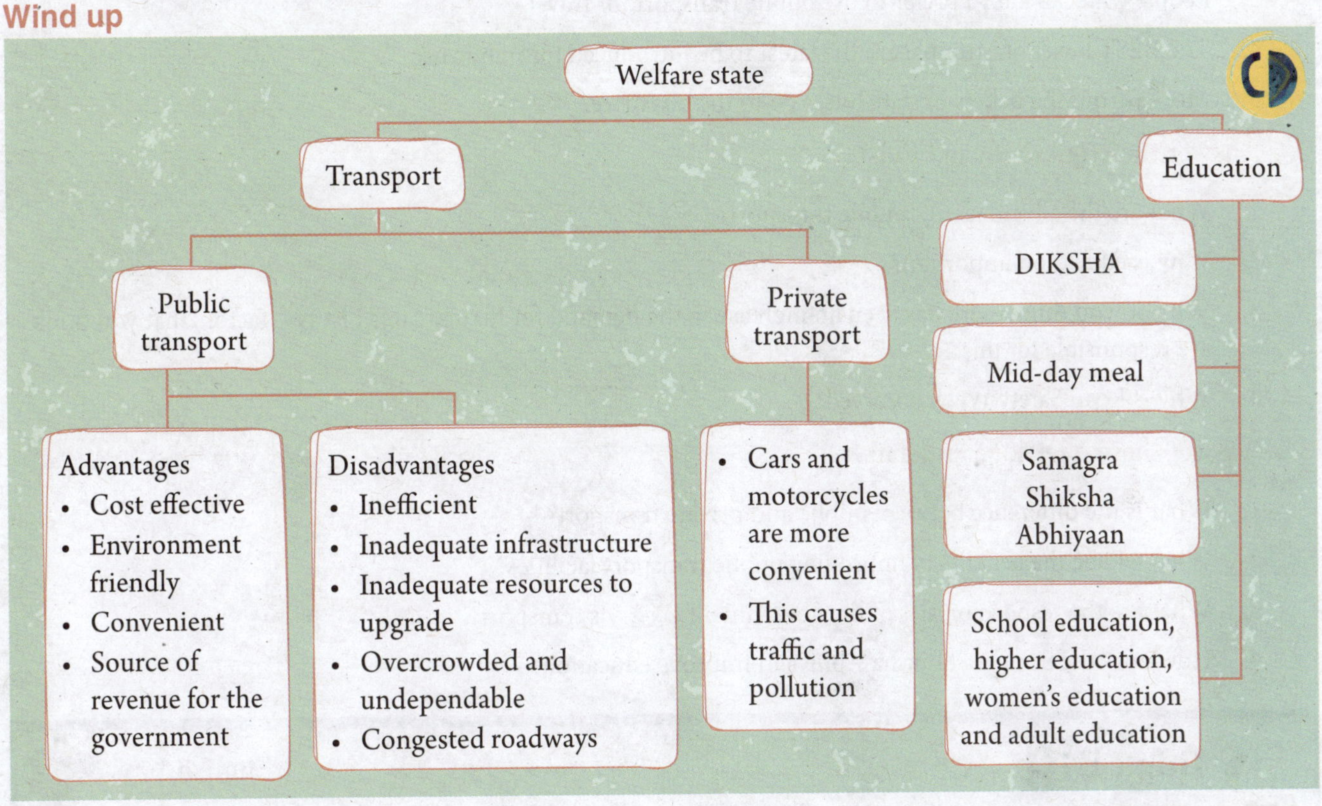

Exercises

A. Fill in the blanks.

1. .... and .... come under public transport.
2. The government is responsible for checking .... pollution.
3. Transport is essential for carrying .... and ....
4. National Road Safety Week is celebrated from ....
5. When trucks are allowed to transport goods in the whole country, it is called a ....

B. Choose the correct answers.

1. In political science, the word 'state' can be used to refer to
   a. a particular area   b. a country   c. a district   d. a village
2. Trains that run in cities like Mumbai and Delhi.
   a. Metro   b. Bullet trains   c. Superfast trains   d. Ultrasonic trains
3. Vehicles used to carry donated organs out of the state.
   a. Ambulances   b. Air ambulances   c. Fighter jets   d. Trucks
4. They are operational to enable people who are unable to avail education facilities during the day.
   a. School education   b. Women's education   c. Night schools   d. Creche facilities
5. Part of the responsibility of the government.
   a. Selling new cars   b. Collecting road tax   c. Issuing road permits   d. Maintaining roads

C. Correct these statements.

1. The mid-day meal scheme has decreased the number of children going to school.
2. All private transport in Delhi runs on CNG.
3. People who can afford prefer to use public transport for travel.
4. The BEST buses of Mumbai are the latest to be introduced for public use.
5. Money from the tickets in state buses go to the bus driver.

D. Answer these questions in brief.

1. What are the advantages of public transport?
2. Why is education important?
3. Why do you think there has been an increase in the demand for luxury cars? List two factors that you think are responsible for this.
4. Why is Road Safety Week observed?

E. Answer these questions in detail.

1. What is the difference between public and private transport?
2. What will be the benefits of improving public transport facilities?
3. What are the responsibilities of the government vis-à-vis transport?
4. How does the Samagra Shiksha Abhiyaan improve education?

Think Big

English Fun

Conduct a comparative study of a state-owned transport facility and a privately owned transport facility. Write about the time taken to travel, the waiting period, the length of commutes to the stand/station and the frequency of the service.

Learning Tools

Create a two-tab book by following these steps, and list important points you have learnt about transport and education.

1. Take a folded book and cut up the valley of the inside fold toward the mountain top. This cut forms two large tabs that can be used front and back for writing and illustrations.
2. The book can be expanded by making several of these folds and gluing them side-by-side. Use this book with data occurring in twos. For example, use it for comparing and contrasting, determining cause and effect, finding similarities and differences and more.

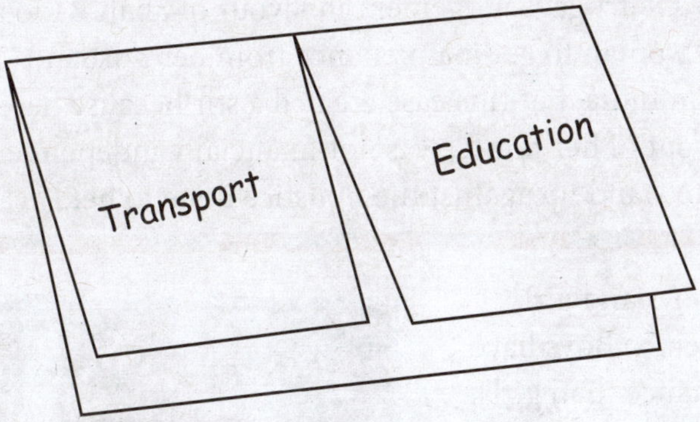

Web links:

https://www.india.gov.in/my-government/schemes

https://morth.nic.in/national-road-safety-policy-1

Last accessed on 31 August 2021

5. Gender Discrimination and Equality

Warm up

Shah Bano Begum was married to Mohammed Ahmed Khan and had five children. Her husband divorced her when she was 62 years old, married another woman and refused to give her alimony. Shah Bano filed a criminal lawsuit against her estranged husband. The Supreme Court gave judgement in favour of Shah Bano and upheld the right of a divorced woman to get maintenance from her husband. There are countless such stories in India, but this case created a stir because here was a woman who had been thrown out of her house, was not financially independent, was being victimized, but chose to stand up against the injustice done to her.

All a round the world, boys and girls have been treated differently. Boys have been given more importance than girls. Many times, this led to unfair treatment to girls and women. This is called gender discrimination. This distinction begins at home, with families preferring a son over a daughter or favouring sons more than daughters. Traditionally, women were expected to take care of the home and children, while the men were expected to provide for the family. These are called stereotypes and define how men and women are expected to behave in a society. Men were supposed to go hunting and perform tasks that were physically challenging. Women were considered to be delicate and unsuitable for heavy physical work. Largely, most parts of the world have a **patriarchal** society, which implies that men are considered superior and have control over the lives of the women in their family.

Women in science

Today, although women participate fully alongside men in all fields, the traditional views of society still curb their independence and freedom. Women around the country are still facing many obstacles and injustices every day.

Safety

Safety is one of the biggest issues faced by women in India today. Female infanticide and female foeticide prevail till today. Infant girls are killed soon after birth as their families only want boys.

Between 2001 and 2011, the ratio of children to the total population has declined, and the decline is sharper in female children. According to the 2011 Census of India, there are only

patriarchal: relating to or denoting a system of society or government controlled by men

about 940 females for every 1000 males. Crimes against women like domestic violence, assault, dowry are common and the sad truth is that society tends to blame the women in such situations. Every day, women face some form of harassment or the other, be it eve teasing, molestation or sexual harassment.

Education

In India, boys are looked upon as children who will grow up and contribute to the family income. They do not have to leave their parents' house after marriage, as per customs and traditions. In fact, when a boy gets married, he brings home another family member—his bride. Sons are seen as support for the parents in their old age, and hence, are preferred. Often, parents do not want to spend money on a girl's education as the girl leaves the household and when she earns, her income goes to her husband's family.

> **FACT CHECK**
>
> The Khasi community in the north east of India is matrilineal in nature. The youngest daughter inherits the property and it becomes her responsibility to care for her parents in old age. The sons leave the house after marriage and move in to their wives' household.

Housework

This traditional preference for boys and perception of women only as homemakers has only led society to perceive women as dependents. From childhood, girls are taught that it is their responsibility to cook, clean and do other household chores. Though housework is physically demanding and requires a lot of effort and labour, it is undervalued. Being a caregiver or a homemaker is considered to be equivalent to not doing anything. The main reason for this is that it does not bring in any remuneration. When women choose to have careers, both the burden of the work at home and the demands of the career fall on them.

Apply it!

Conduct a ten-step 'PRIVILEGE RACE' in your playground.

Gather all the students in your class and stand at the starting line. One student stands at the finish line and reads a list of statements. As the student reads each statement, take a step forward if the statement applies to you or it is correct. If it does not, stay put.

Use the following statements for this:

- You are expected to help with the dishes or housework at home.
- You are encouraged to excel in sports and athletics.
- You feel that you are respected wherever you live.
- You are not afraid to be stopped by police.
- You are not afraid of walking down a quiet lane after dark.
- Your parents have already saved enough money for your higher education.
- You have never felt discriminated against because of your gender.
- You have never been asked to help with the household chores.
- Your family has never undermined your studies.
- Your family has never insisted that you learn how to cook.

At the end of the race, reflect on the different ways boys and girls are brought up in India.

Career

In order to encourage women to take up jobs outside their homes, the government has introduced the scheme of *anganwadis* in the rural areas. In urban areas, any place of work with more than 30 women employees must have a child carecentre. This is to help women leave their small children under the care of professionals. When they know their children are being taken care of while they work, they can concentrate better on their jobs. This initiative of the government is a step towards providing equal opportunities to women in the workforce. This not only allows professionals to entrust their children to these workers but also provides employment for many women from the rural areas. Also, in many rural areas, young girls drop out of schools to take care of their younger siblings. *Anganwadis* prevent such instances and promote education of girls.

FACT CHECK

Mary Anne Evans was an accomplished novelist and writer in 19th century England. She wrote under the pen name of George Eliot and authored seven novels. She used the male pen name as she wanted to be taken seriously in the world of writing.

Gender Discrimination Around the World

According to the UN, 40 per cent of young women in South Asia and Sub-Saharan Africa are married by their eighteenth birthday. Even in developed countries, women are at a disadvantage when it comes to salary, especially at their workplace. There are still great disparities between the laws which are applicable to men and women, in matters concerning marriage, divorce, custody of the children in case of a divorce, inheritance of property and many others. Only a change in the mindset and attitude of societies around the world can address the issue of inequality.

Skill Builder

21ST CENTURY SKILLS

Critical-thinking skills: What qualities should women possess so that they are considered to be capable of handling tough jobs in the armed forces?

Information literacy: What is the difference between female infanticide and female foeticide?

World Connect

International Women's Day, which is celebrated on 8th March every year, was first observed in 1914. Special days dedicated to women were observed in different parts of the world before 1914, but since 1914, this was instituted as an annual feature.

Wind up

- Gender discrimination
  - Safety
    - Female infanticide and foeticide
    - Eve teasing, molestation and sexual harassment
    - Domestic violence, assault, dowry
  - Education
    - Boys contribute to family income, girls leave the house; so, families invest only in the boys education.
  - Housework
    - No respect for homemakers
    - Girls are expected to do all the house work
  - Career
    - *Anganwadis* and child care centres

Exercises

A. Choose the correct answers.

1. All the housework done by women is not valued because
   a. they do not go out for it
   b. they do not get paid for it
   c. their work is considered easy
   d. Both b and c
2. From childhood, girls are taught that it is their responsibility to do this for the family:
   a. cook
   b. drive
   c. study
   d. teach
3. International Women's day is celebrated on
   a. 8 May
   b. 8 March
   c. 8 August
   d. 18 August
4. According to the UN, 40 per cent of young women in South Asia and Sub-Saharan Africa are married by their
   a. nineteenth birthday
   b. seventeenth birthday
   c. eighteenth birthday
   d. sixteenth birthday

B. Fill in the blanks.

1. According to the Census of India, 2011, there are only about .... females for every 1000 males.
2. Any place of work with more than 30 women employees must have a ....
3. .... refers to killing of the girl child.
4. .... refers to killing of the unborn girl child.

C. Write T for true and F for false.

1. In India, boys are looked upon as children who will grow up and contribute to the family income. ☐
2. Society perceives women as dependents. ☐
3. According to the UN, 40 per cent of young women in South Asia and Sub-Saharan Africa are married by their sixteenth birthday. ☐
4. From childhood, boys are taught that it is their responsibility to cook, clean and do other household chores. ☐
5. Childcare centres not only encourage women to work, but also provide equal opportunities for women in the workforce. ☐

D. Answer these questions in brief.

1. Are boys and girls treated the same everywhere?
2. What are the reasons for discrimination against women in society?
3. Why do families prefer baby boys to baby girls?
4. What is a stereotype?

E. Answer these questions in detail.

1. What steps have been taken by the government in order to empower women?
2. Why do families prefer educating the boy child and pay less attention to a girl child's education?
3. Explain how women have come to be treated more equally now.
4. How do *anganwadis* or day care centres help raise the status of girls and women?

Think Big

Integrate with Maths

Take an interest in the finances of the house. Find out what services are used in the house on a day-to-day basis, like domestic help, service from someone who irons the clothes, gardener, driver, etc. Find out how much money is given to them as salary. Now calculate how much money is saved by women who do all the housework themselves.

Learning Tools

Use this foldable to recall whatever you have learnt about gender discrimination and equality under the headings safety, education, housework, career.

1. Fold a sheet of paper in half.
2. Fold this long rectangle in half.
3. Fold both ends back.
4. On the side, make vertical cuts through one thickness of paper, forming four tabs.

Use this book for data occurring in fours.

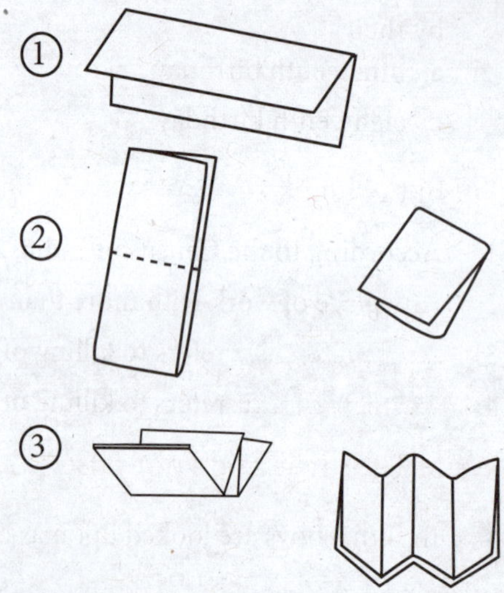

Web links:

https://www.savethechildren.org/us/charity-stories/how-gender-discrimination-impacts-boys-and-girls

https://www.unicef.org/gender-equality

Last accessed on 31 August 2021

6. Role of Women in a Changing World

Warm up

Kamala Harris is the Vice President of the United States of America. She is of Indian and African-American origin. She is an established politician in the US and commands a lot of respect. She is a symbol of the changing role of women in the modern world.

In the 21st century, women have made progress in various walks of life. Although gender stereotypes and prejudices against women still exist, education and broadmindedness make way for a better future. Professions and careers that were till now seen as suitable only for men have seen a considerable increase in the number of women, who have not only joined in but have seen tremendous success. Women are making a mark in aviation, banking, athletics, technology, entertainment, education, business, food and beverages, art, literature, medicine and many more fields.

Role of the United Nations

Vijay Laxmi Pandit

The United Nations has lent support to the cause of women's equality from the year 1945 when it came into existence. In its **landmark** Universal Declaration of Human Rights, which was adopted on 10 December 1948, it declared that, 'All human beings are born free and equal in dignity and rights', and that 'everyone is entitled to all the rights and freedoms set forth in this Declaration, without distinction of any kind, such as race, color, sex, language, religion, … birth or other status.'

The UN also embraced the feminist ideology with the General Assembly declaring the year 1975 as the International Women's Year. The first World Conference on Women was organized and held in Mexico City. Since then, the conference has been organized regularly. Vijay Laxmi Pandit became the first woman President of the United Nations General Assembly in 1953. In 2010, the UN achieved another milestone in this journey by creating a dedicated wing for all women-related issues called UN Women. The International Day for the Elimination of Violence against Women is observed on 25 November each year.

Changing times

Women's organizations: There are many organizations all over the country that do **commendable** work in empowering women. They have not only helped rehabilitate women who were victims of crimes but also have promoted entrepreneurship among them. These are mostly non-profit, non-governmental organizations, which fulfil their social

landmark: an event or discovery marking an important stage or turning point in something; commendable: praiseworthy responsibilities by providing opportunities, conducive environment and new avenues for women to earn their living respectably and become financially independent. We will learn about two such organizations.

The Army Wives Welfare Association, or AWWA, was formed for the wives and children of army personnel. It has played a significant role in helping war widows get back on their feet. Due to its efforts, the wives of army personnel can contribute suitably to the society, as per the area of their expertise and skills. The AWWA plans various activities and programmes for the welfare and development of women including organizing fairs and melas, setting up vocational training centres, women's hostels and shopping complexes.

Shri Mahila Griha Udyog Lijjat Papad is a cooperative set up by seven women in Girgaon, Maharashtra. They started the organization with a modest sum of ₹80 on 15 March 1959, and today, they run a business worth more than 6.50 billion rupees. It is a cottage industry that does not require a big industrial set-up. The membership is restricted to women. It has brought revolutionary changes in the lives of women, raising their self-worth and giving them a respectable place in the society by making them financially independent. The cooperative produces papad, flour, spices and many other things. Thirty to thrity-five per cent of the production of Lijjat Papad is being exported to countries like the United States, the United Kingdom, the Middle East, Singapore, Hong Kong and Holland.

What's in the picture?

What do you see in this picture? Do you think women's independence empowers the nation?

Moving towards Gender Equality

Today we see girls and women excelling in fields that were previously not considered to be their strength. Defence services are considering giving combat roles to women officers. Seats have been reserved for women in the legislatures so that women can be represented.

Women police officers

The Indian Army

Saina Nehwal

Women Empowerment Schemes

Several schemes have been introduced by the government in order to empower women.

- The Women Helpline Scheme **envisages** provision of 24-hour emergency and non-emergency responses to all women affected by violence.

envisage: contemplate or conceive of as a possibility or a desirable future event

- The Ujjawala scheme, for prevention of trafficking and rescue, **rehabilitation** and **reintegration** of victims of trafficking and abuse, has five components. They are prevention, rescue, rehabilitation, reintegration and **repatriation**.
- Swadhar Greh, a scheme for women in difficult circumstances, is an initiative by the Haryana government to set up homes for women and girls rescued from trafficking or domestic violence and abuse.
- One Stop Centre Scheme is a first of its kind set up in 2015 in Chhattisgarh, for the rehabilitation of women subjected to violence.

Green Earth

In 1999, a woman named Julia Butterfly Hill, an activist, author and poet, founded an organization called Circle of Life in the US, a world community of people, who joined hands to protect the environment. For 738 days, she lived in a 180-feet high canopy of an ancient redwood tree to help make the world aware of the plight of ancient redwood forests.

Apply it!

5 GENDER EQUALITY

This is Malala Yousafzai, a Pakistani girl who stood up for the right of girls to get education. She was shot by the Taliban but survived miraculously. She was awarded the Nobel Peace prize, and this is an excerpt from her speech.

'There are still conflicts in which hundreds and thousands of innocent people have lost their lives. Many families have become refugees in Syria, Gaza and Iraq. There are still girls who have no freedom to go to school in the north of Nigeria. In Pakistan and Afghanistan, we see innocent people being killed in suicide attacks and bomb blasts.

Many children in Africa do not have access to school because of poverty. Many children in India and Pakistan are deprived of their right to education because of social taboos, or they have been forced into child labour and girls into child marriages.'

1. Which award was conferred on Malala?
2. What did she fight for?
3. Which social issues is she referring to in her speech?

Malala Yousafzai

Skill Builder

21ST CENTURY SKILLS

Critical thinking skills: Many celebrities lend their name to various causes. How do you think this helps the cause? Make a list of at least five celebrities whose names are associated with some social, cultural or health issues.

Life skills: Imagine yourself as the CEO of a leading company. Write about how you will ensure gender equality in your organization.

Creativity: Make a poster on women empowerment. You can draw something, write a poem or a story or compose something related to women empowerment. Decorate the poster and display it in class.

rehabilitation: the action of restoring someone to health or a normal life through training and therapy; reintegration: the action or process of integrating someone back into society; repatriation: the return of someone to their own country

World Connect

We all know Mother Teresa as a great human being who touched and influenced millions of lives with her selfless service to humanity. Her benevolence and kindness were recognized by Pope Francis, the spiritual head of the Catholic Church, who has conferred Sainthood on Mother Teresa.

Wind up

- Women in a changing world
  - Role of the United Nations
    - UN Women
    - International Day for the Elimination of Violence against Women
    - Vijay Laxmi Pandit – the first woman President of the UN General Assembly
    - First World Conference
    - Lent its support since inception
    - International Women's Year
  - Women's organizations
    - Army Wives Welfare Association
    - Shri Mahila Griha Udyog Lijjat Papad
  - Women empowerment schemes
    - Women Helpline Scheme
    - Ujjawala Scheme
    - One Stop Centre Scheme

Exercises

A. Choose the correct answers.

1. This government has set up homes for women and girls, rescued from trafficking or domestic violence and abuse through the Swadhar Greh initiative.
   a. Haryana b. Punjab c. Chhattisgarh d. Maharashtra
2. The International Women's Year declared by the UNs.
   a. 1975 b. 2016 c. 2018 d. 1986
3. The Mahila Grah Udyog Lijjat Papad is a
   a. company b. co-operative c. corporation d. cottage-industry
4. The One Stop Centre Scheme to help women has been set up in
   a. Mumbai b. Chhattisgarh c. Haryana d. Maharastra

B. Correct these statements.

1. Shri Mahila Griha Udyog was set up in Karnataka.
2. The Shri Mahila Griha Udyog Lijjat Papad co-operative produces papad, flour, spices and many other things.
3. The Universal Declaration of Human Rights was adopted on 15 December, 1955.
4. Sarojini Naidu was the first woman president of the UN General Assembly.

C. Answer these questions in brief.

1. Discuss two ways in which women have progressed in the 21st century.
2. Why was the AWWA formed?
3. When is the International Day for the Elimination of Violence against Women observed every year?
4. Where was the One Stop Centre set up?

D. Answer these questions in detail.

1. Name the women empowerment schemes that you have learnt about in this chapter. How do these schemes help women and girls?
2. The UN has actively promoted gender equality. Support the statement with examples.
3. Write a note on two women empowerment schemes you have learnt about in this chapter.

Think Big — Integrate with technology

Given below are some names of women who helped shape the world. Form groups of five and prepare a presentation on any one of them.

1. Emmeline Pankhurst
2. Amelia Earhart
3. Sirimavo RD Bandaranaike
4. Valentina Tereshkova
5. Betty Friedan
6. Gloria Steinem
7. Margaret Thatcher

Learning Tools

Based on what you have studied in the chapter, write your own notes on the following.

Women of the 21st Century

....
....
....
....

Role of the UN in supporting women

....
....
....
....

Strong women leaders of today

....
....
....
....

NGOs and associations that work towards gender equality

....
....
....
....

Women empowerment schemes

....
....
....
....
....
....

Web links:

https://interactive.unwomen.org/multimedia/infographic/changingworldofwork/en/index.html

Last accessed on 31 August 2021

7. Media: A Pillar of Democracy

Warm up

What are the different means of communication that can be used to communicate with people in different countries?

In today's world, communication has become crucial. The word media comes from the word medium. It is a name given to different ways of communicating with people and spreading information. Media can also be used for communication between two individuals.

Mass media: Mass media can be defined as a variety of media technologies, such as the television, newspaper and the Internet, that spread information to a large number of people. Communicating with a large audience using technology is called mass communication.

Social media: It refers to virtual communities or networks, such as Twitter, Facebook and YouTube, that allow people to share and exchange information. Social media also acts as a platform where a large number of people can create and share ideas in the form of pictures and videos.

What's in the picture?

Do you think content on social media should be controlled and censored?

Media Technology

Information through different forms of mass media reaches millions of people with the help of technology. Technology changes with time, and it is very important for the media to keep up with the ever-changing technology. In order to remain up-to-date with the latest advancements in the field of technology, media requires money. The cost of production of programmes is very high. One of the ways in which mass media makes money is **advertising**. Based on the type of technology used, mass media can be categorized as print and electronic media.

Green Earth

Tamil Nadu Newsprint and Paper Limited is a company based in Tamil Nadu, committed to the cause of protecting the environment by adopting technologies that reduces pollution and minimizes wastage of resources. By using **bagasse** as the primary raw material, TNPL protects around 40,000 acres of forest cover from depletion annually. (Study conducted by Ms. Swati P Anavatti, Assistant Professor, Kala Institute of Management and Research, affiliated to the Mumbai University)

advertising: a promotional activity about a certain product, mostly done to increase its saleability

- Print media refers to newspapers, magazines, pamphlets, journals and books.
- Electronic media refers to the Internet, television, radio and mobile phones.

Media and Democracy

It is said that media plays the role of a **watchdog** in a democracy. It provides information about the policies of the government to the citizens. It also acts as a link between the government and the people. The policies of the government are explained to the people through various mass media, such as newspapers and news channels. The people can understand these policies and decide if they are good or bad for them. However, it is the responsibility of the media to disseminate a balanced information that has not been influenced by a single person's opinion or a political party.

Shaping public opinion: Media has been correctly called the fourth pillar of democracy. The smooth and efficient working of a democracy depends on the active public participation in the working of democratic institutions. People participate directly in the elections by voting for the candidates of their choice, and they take part in the government indirectly by taking interest in the activities of the government. People should be able to form negative or positive opinions about the work done by their elected representatives. Media plays a crucial role in making the news available to people, which makes it easier for common people to agree or disagree with the viewpoints presented, and thus, to shape their opinions. Media also helps by presenting different **perspectives** of an issue, which gives it clarity.

Setting the agenda: Setting the agenda means deciding what is newsworthy. The 'breaking news' on television programmes and the headlines in newspapers often grab the maximum attention of viewers and readers. People give more attention to the news stories that are highlighted. It is the duty of the media to focus on news that is important and not on issues of little importance.

Creating awareness: In today's fast-paced world, people are busy with their domestic and professional lives. Many do not get the time to gather information about what is happening around them. Mass media is the only way through which people can be made aware of the latest happenings and developments around the world. Prime time slots, news coverage in a short span of time, reporters who report from different parts of the country and short bulletin repeated during the day make it easier for people to watch at least one news programme.

Trial by media: When the media tries to interfere or influence the verdict of a court, it is called trial by media. It is the responsibility of the media to use this power in a proper way. While it is important to make people aware of the reality, the media should not interfere in the proceedings of the court and respect the criminal justice system of a country.

Mass media creates awareness about events

watchdog: in media, it refers to an organization that checks if the policies of the government violate any democratic principles; perspectives: a view or prospect

Independent Media

Albert Camus said, 'A free press can, of course, be good or bad, but most certainly without freedom, the press will never be anything but bad.'

Reports in the media need to be balanced as they influence the perspective of a large number of people. Often, the media is dependent on big business houses who invest in the latest technologies so that channels and newspapers can stay ahead in stiff competition for viewership and readership. This affects their independence because they cannot report anything that goes against the interest of the organizations that are providing them the financial support.

Balanced report: It is the coverage of an issue or an event in a fair and objective manner. The duty of the media is to report and not pass any judgements. It must allow the people to form opinions on their own. If a news report is biased, it cannot be called a balanced report. The report must present and discuss all the points of views and leave it for the readers to decide their position.

Paid news: When an influential person or organization tries to pay for the news that paints them in a good light or hides certain facts, it is called a paid news. This is an unethical way of influencing the opinion of the people. This has come under widespread criticism from institutions like the Election Commission of India and the courts because paid news can sway the public in favour of the corrupt and undeserving candidates during an election.

Apply it!

From today's newspaper, try to find out one news report that you feel is balanced. Stick it in the notebook.

Skill Builder

21ST CENTURY SKILLS

Information literacy: Chart the history of the 'Freedom of the Press' in the form of a timeline. Can you cite some current instances around the world, where freedom of the press has been curbed?

Life skills: Fake news nowadays travel as fast as real news. List a few steps you can follow to decipher between the two.

Critical thinking skills: The world has been brought closer by social media, but it often comes under criticism. What are some of the disadvantages of the social media?

World Connect

Code of Ethics for the Republic of China Radio Broadcasting in Taiwan

Journalists in the Republic of China have to follow a Code of Ethics. Radio programmes must keep in mind the socially accepted norms and be in good taste. No private interest should be taken into consideration. All programmes should be sensitive to the issues of gender, race, religion and profession. All information about law, medicine and technology should be presented carefully and accurately.

Wind up

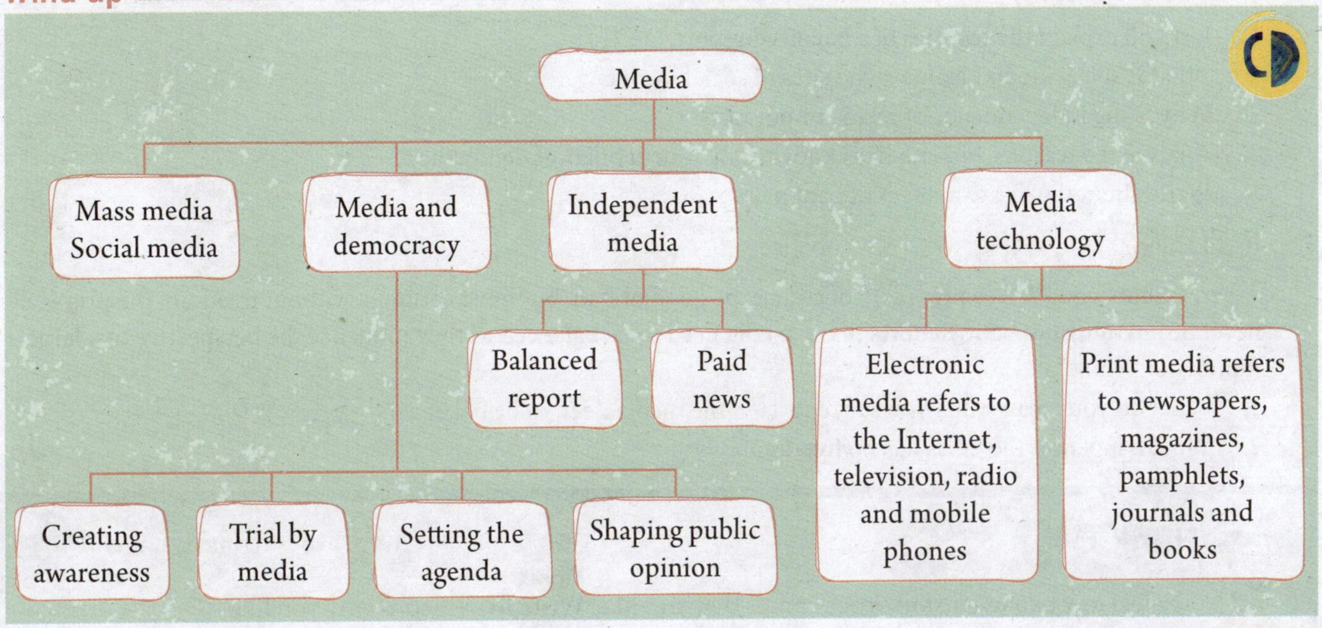

Exercises

A. Choose the correct answers.

1. An independent media
   a. is free of influence and bias
   b. is owned by big business houses
   c. is influenced by organizations
   d. influences the court's verdict
2. A type of electronic media
   a. Newspaper
   b. The Internet
   c. Journals
   d. Magazine
3. When media gives prominent coverage to some news, it is setting the
   a. agenda
   b. headline
   c. public opinion
   d. verdict
4. An email is a type of
   a. print media
   b. electronic media
   c. new media
   d. free media

B. Write T for true and F for false.

1. Balanced reporting always ends with passing a judgement. ☐
2. It is difficult to communicate through the Internet. ☐
3. A telephone is just a means of making a call. ☐
4. Paid news is not considered a positive development. ☐
5. During prime time, very few people tend to catch the programmes. ☐

C. Answer these questions in brief.

1. How does media depend on technology?
2. How does media set the agenda?
3. What is electronic media?
4. What is print media?

D. Answer these questions in detail.

1. List and explain the features of a balanced report.
2. What is social media? Name some sites of social media.
3. Why is the independence of media important?
4. Analyze the reasons why media is known as a 'fourth pillar of democracy'.
5. Write about the disadvantages of paid news.

E. Read the passage and answer the questions.

Albert Camus said, 'A free press can, of course, be good or bad, but most certainly without freedom, the press will never be anything but bad.' Reports in the media need to be balanced as they influence the perspective of a large number of people.

1. What do you mean when you say reports in the media need to be balanced?
2. What happens if the press has no freedom?

Think Big — Integrate with language

Select any two television programmes that you like. Write five reasons why you like it.

Learning Tools

Complete the following chart, and create a study guide for yourself on the chapter learnt.

Mass Media

....

....

....

....

....

Media and democracy

....

....

....

....

....

Independent media

....

....

....

....

....

Media technology

....

....

....

....

....

Define:

Mass media: ....

....

Social media: ....

....

....

Web links:

advocateshah.com/blog/what-is-freedom-of-press-the-fourth-pillar-of-democracy/

Last accessed on 31 August 2021

8. Advertising

Warm up

In British India, products were advertised mostly by foreign companies who used images of Indian gods, goddesses and kings to promote their products among the Indian people.

Advertisements have always been a popular way of reaching out to the consumers. An advertisement is a notice, picture or film that tells people about a product, job or service. It is a form of communication that aims to influence people to buy the product or services. Companies come up with innovative and creative ideas to capture the imagination of the people and make their product sell more than others in the market.

Advertisements showing different brands

Professionals in the field survey the market to see which kind of products are in greater demand. Advertising agencies design campaigns for the products. This is a very tough job, as selecting taglines, designing mascots or creating visuals that would be appealing and cater to different classes of society requires a thorough understanding of the people who make up the society. It has to be kept in mind that the advertisement should be able to impress the people so much that they feel like trying out the new product in place of the old trusted brand.

Brands

All of us need a variety of products in our day-to-day lives. These range from personal care products to household and electrical appliances and office-, school- or work-related articles. There are certain established companies in every field, which have been making those products for a very long time, and their products are trusted by customers. They have become established brands. Their names invoke trust in the customers as well as a promise of quality. Sometimes, companies make use of distinct symbols, logos and slogans to make an impression on public memory. This gives them an image and helps the brands to develop. We often associate different brands with their television jingles, hoardings put up on strategic points in the city or advertisements in newspapers and magazines.

FACT CHECK

Alauddin Khalji, a ruler of the Delhi Sultanate, was an efficient administrator who introduced a practice called *dagh*, which involved the branding of horses with a hot iron. This was done so that the imported and expensive fine breed horses in the military of the Sultanate would not be replaced with horses of lower breed by any corrupt official.

Making of Advertisements

These are some of the steps followed by the advertisement agencies to create advertisements.

- Select a product that is to be launched.
- Determine the class of people who would be the likely customers (rich people if it is a high quality expensive product).
- Design an ad campaign with the target group in mind.
- Conduct a survey of the market to see the brands that already exist and their loyal customers.
- Come up with strategies to counter the competition and reach out to the people.
- Sometimes, door-to-door campaigns are carried out in order to test the product as well as advertise it among the people before a formal launch of the product.
- Free samples of the product are also distributed and feedback is taken so that when the product is formally launched in the market, it is already successful among the target group.

Advertising and Money

The cost of advertising has increased substantially in the recent times. If a product has to be advertised on the television, the rates depend on the time slot. If it is the prime time then the rates are the highest. The newspaper remains a preferred medium for people who want to advertise.
A matrimonial ad in an English newspaper can cost up to Rs 800, for a five-line ad. For a front page ad, the cost can go up to several lakhs. You can get an estimate of the revenues that newspapers earn simply from advertisements.

Advertisements in a newspaper

Case Study

Amul Butter Girl

It is the moppet who put Amul on India's breakfast table. The Amul ad campaign has found place in the Guiness Book of World Records for the longest running ad campaign ever.

It began in 1966 when Sylvester da Cunha, the then managing director of the advertising agency ASP, wanted something that would win every housewife's heart, and hence, chose the image of a little girl. Thus, the popular Amul moppet was born, winning hearts of all age groups instantly. Over a period of time, Amul came to be known for its role of a social observer, and people started enjoying the starkly stated ads, which were often humorous puns on the reality. The tagline 'utterly butterly delicious' also saw some apprehension initially. Verghese Kurien, the head of Amul, said, 'I think it's utterly mad; but if you think it'll work, go ahead.' Some also said that it was grammatically incorrect, but as they say, the rest is history!

Influence of Advertisements

Advertisements make everything appear very desirable and essential. Here, the consumers have to exercise their wisdom and judgement in choosing the products carefully and not being lured by the glitzy and glamorous advertisements. In order to influence people, companies often make tall claims and glorify their products to the extent of being untrue. They resort to this so that they can stay ahead in the stiff, competitive market and make large profits.

What's in the picture?

How does this advertisement influence people? Find out ways in which you can recycle water at home.

Advertising and Social Message

As society evolved, advertising has also acquired a new role in spreading awareness about issues ranging from safety to rights and duties of citizens to prevention and eradication of diseases. The government also uses advertisements to convey social messages. Advertisements have emerged as a powerful medium of spreading information among the people. Many times, celebrities are included in the campaigns in order to reach out to a wider audience of all age groups. Traffic rules, safety and precautions while driving are some other areas that bank on creative advertisements to reach out to people.

Advertising and Democracy

Apply it!

What are some popular campaigns endorsed by celebrities?

Democracy and equality go hand in hand. It has been observed that advertising gives an unfair advantage to the agencies and companies that can afford the high cost of creating an ad for their product. This goes against the interests of small businesses, hawkers, vendors and poorer sections of society, who sell their wares without any advertisements or with very small budget ones, if at all. This brings in the question of equality. Branded goods are valued more by people than the local ones. This creates a divide in the society. The young generation is brand-conscious, and children often compete with each other on the basis of branded shoes, clothes, gadgets, stationery and other items they possess. At the same time, we must remember that opportunities exist for everyone, and society is a complex fabric made up of all kinds of people from different sections. So, it would not be wrong to say that all sellers find buyers.

Skill Builder

21ST CENTURY SKILLS

Critical thinking skills: Why should ad campaigns not be like election campaigns? Give reasons.

Creativity: Imagine yourself to be a small-time businessman. You do not have money to invest in an expensive advertisement. How would you create an advertisement with things available at home?

Life skills: Does advertising have adverse effects on the environment, when it comes to print media?

World Connect

Online advertising has emerged as an important form of advertising in the recent times. It involves a publisher, who designs and integrates the advertisements into its online content, and an advertiser, who provides the advertisements to be displayed. This new form is being used widely by different industries for promotions. The world appears to be truly connected in this trend as online advertising is gaining ground very rapidly across different countries.

Wind up

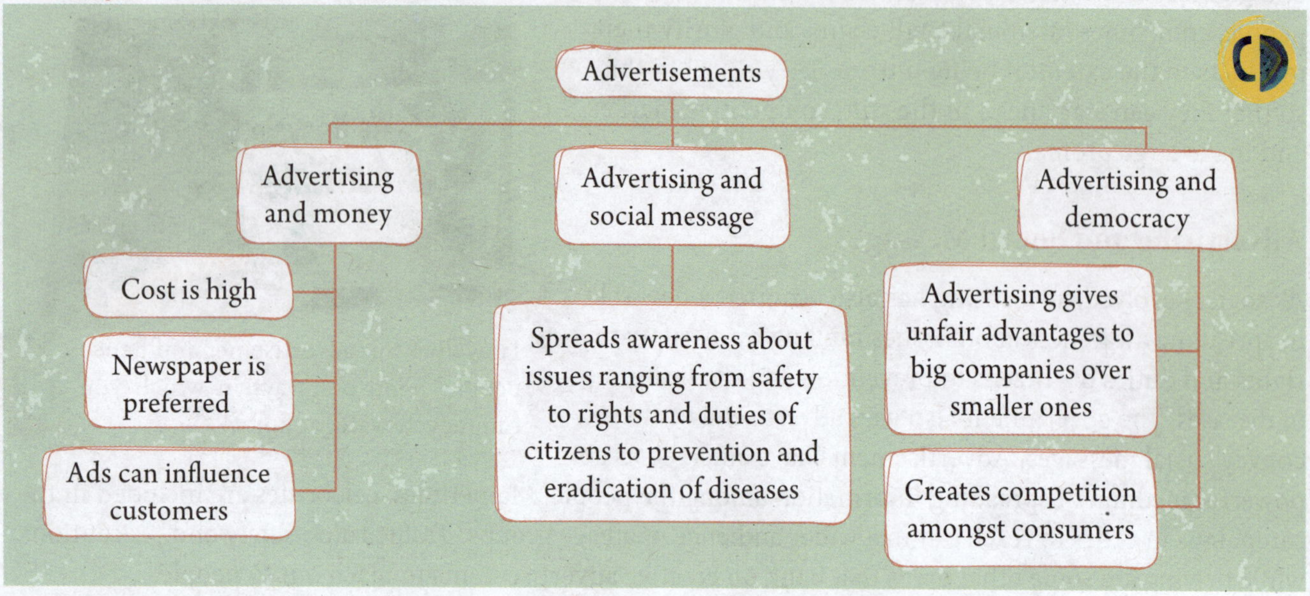

Exercises

A. Choose the correct answers.

1. This has also acquired a new role in spreading awareness about issues ranging from safety to rights and duties of citizens to prevention and eradication of diseases.
   a. Marketing b. Production c. Advertising d. None of these
2. A preferred medium for people who want to advertise
   a. social media b. newspaper c. television d. radio
3. Big companies advertise in
   a. hoarding boards b. newspapers c. radio d. notice boards
4. Social messages spread awareness about issues like
   a. selling of a product b. prevention of diseases c. new gadgets d. latest fashion

B. Correct these statements.

1. Advertising is a new industry.
2. Locally made goods are more expensive as compared with branded ones.
3. Ads are only meant for entertainment.
4. There has been only a marginal increase in the cost of advertising.
5. Free samples are distributed because the company has too many of them.

C. Answer these questions in brief.

1. What do you understand by brands?
2. Why do companies invest in advertising?
3. Advertisements are accused of creating a divide in the society. Explain.
4. List two ways in which you think advertisements influence buyers.

D. Answer these questions in detail.

1. What steps would you follow if you were to create an advertisement for a product?
2. Advertisements are instrumental in creating social awareness. How?

3. How do brands establish themselves?
4. Is it true that advertisements favour the rich? Give two reasons for your answer.

Think Big

Design thinking

Design an advertisement for an article of your choice. You must make it visually appealing and think of a catchy slogan or jingle for it.

Learning Tools

Create your own study guides by compiling the necessary information for swift recap.

Main ideas

....

....

....

....

Why it matters

....

....

....

....

Important terms and names

....

....

....

....

Web links:

https://www.britannica.com/topic/advertising

Last accessed on 31 August 2021

9. Markets

Warm up

Amazon was founded in the year 1994. It gradually rose to become a well-established brand in the sphere of entertainment, online market, e-commerce and live streaming. Today it has become a household name.

We depend on a variety of shops to fulfil our daily needs. These range from groceries, bakeries, and dairies to vegetable and fruit shops. Have you wondered how these products reach the shops? Market refers to any place where buying and selling take place. Markets include the sale of goods as well as services. If you want the services of a plumber or a carpenter, you pay the person for the service provided. Thus, the plumber or the carpenter sells his service and gets the money as a source of livelihood. Therefore, we can conclude that markets are a great source of livelihood to millions of people across the world.

Market System

The key players in the whole system of markets are the producers, the sellers and the consumers.

Goods that reach the markets for consumption by people are sourced through the farms. The raw materials are obtained from the farmers who grow them and sent to the industries or factories that process the raw materials into finished products. Some raw materials are not produced at a farm and can be sourced from mines. All the producers, consumers and sellers are dependent on each other.

Types of Markets

Markets can be divided into two categories—wholesale markets and retail markets.

Wholesale markets: In wholesale markets, goods are bought and sold in large quantities or in bulk. Goods are cheaper as they are bought from the producers directly. Instead of stocking their wares in showrooms, wholesalers usually have godowns from which they operate. Thus, the investment amount decreases as there are no shops to maintain.

A wholesale market

Retail market: The retail market is the one where goods are bought and sold in smaller units. They cater to people living in the neighborhood and sell things in small quantities. They charge a little more than the wholesalers because when the retailer buys goods from the wholesaler, and he adds his own margin of profit to the original cost of the product.

Selecting Markets

When we need something, we buy it from the market. We choose the market as per our requirement. There are many factors that impact a customer's choice of markets. Some of these factors are:

- The item that needs to be bought
- How much money would we like to spend on the item
- Best deals or bargains available for the item
- Convenience of shopping
- Proximity to the market
- Brands and quality of the products sold

A retail shop

Understanding a Chain of Markets

The goods we buy from the market actually reach us after a long journey. It starts from the producers or farmers, from where the raw materials are processed and bought by the wholesalers. They, in turn, supply the goods to shopkeepers in different areas to make those goods available to people. These shopkeepers are called retailers. From retailers, customers are able to buy a variety of goods. This journey of goods from the producer to the customer is called a 'chain of markets'. People between the producer and the customer are called traders. If you observe carefully, buying and selling take place at multiple levels. Every time the goods reach a new trader in the chain of markets, the price of the item increases.

Escalation of cost:

- When the farmer sells the onions to a local mandi, the price of onions per kilogram is Rs 2–4.
- The local mandi is the wholesale market of the vegetables.
- From here, the onions are transported to a nearby town and city wholesale markets.
- As the transportation cost, tax and the profit margin of the village wholesalers is added to the amount, they sell it at Rs 4–8 to the town wholesaler.
- The town wholesaler adds his share of profit to the cost and sells it at Rs 10–12 to the retailer.
- The retailer adds his own share of profit and sells the onions to the consumers at Rs 18–20.

Weekly Markets

In many areas, a day of the week is fixed when goods are sold on the pavements and roadsides. Lakhs of people earn their livelihood by selling a wide range of goods, such as fruits, vegetables, plastic ware, clothes, bangles, etc. There are lots of stalls in these markets, with snacks and other popular street food. The markets attract huge crowds as they are set up in the evening and continue till late in the night. They are bustling with people as the prices of goods in these markets are generally low. People also bargain with the sellers to further bring down the price. The sellers are also able to bring down the price because they do not have to invest or spend money on buying, renting or maintaining a shop. After the market day is over in a place, they carry their wares in small **minidors** and sell them on the next day in a different location. This is also called '*tehbazaari*'.

Hawkers and vendors are also an integral part of the markets. They move from place to place and make goods accessible to people. Fruit and vegetable sellers and ice cream vendors are common everywhere. Although they lead to traffic congestion on the roads when people stop or pull over to buy things from them, people who are aged or have medical problems, can conveniently buy from them as they come to the doorstep to sell their goods.

Weekly market

What's in the picture?

Do you think hawkers make enough money to live comfortably?

Shopping Malls

Shopping malls are usually closed, centrally air-conditioned areas that offer a variety of brands, both Indian and foreign. They have become very popular in the last decade due to various factors:

- Malls provide a comfortable shopping experience as they are closed, climate-controlled places.
- Facility to park vehicles of the customers is available, and this gives an edge to the malls over other markets as they are usually very crowded and do not offer a parking space.

Shopping mall, Delhi

- Entertainment and recreational activities attract crowds as people like to spend their leisure time taking part in them. They have become ideal places for book launches, music and dance concerts, theatre performances, street plays, awareness campaigns, movie promotions, etc. Kids' zones provide play areas for children and food courts offer a wide variety of snacks and beverages.
- Although the goods sold in the malls are generally expensive and shopkeepers do not bargain, the discounts offered attract many people. The cost of buying or renting a showroom in a mall is very high, and the owner has to invest in the infrastructure and facilities due to which the cost of products goes up.

Permanent Local Markets

A market comprising shops selling groceries, bread, milk, dairy products, fruits and vegetables, a bakery, street food stalls and two or three cloth shops describe a typical permanent local market. This type of market caters to the people in the vicinity of the market, who depend on it for the fulfilment of their everyday requirements. Most of the shopkeepers have owned shops in these markets for generations together, and the local people know them well. This is a factor that goes in favour of these shops. The goods sold in the market could be both imported and Indian.

With consumer awareness programmes, people have become aware of factors like maximum retail price, manufacturing and expiry dates of products, ingredients, etc. These programmes are run by the government in order to make consumers aware of their rights and prevent exploitation of the consumers by the producers. Consumer Rights Day is observed on 24 December every year.

minidors: a small three-seater autorickshaw used as a load carrier

Apply it!

Let us read about an interesting wholesale market in Delhi. It is called the Ghazipur Flower market, or popularly, Phool Mandi. Here, flowers come from all over India and foreign countries like China, Bangkok, Holland, Thailand etc. A typical day in the market begins at 4.00 am, when flowers arriving from various sources are collected, and the sellers set up their shops. In the next hour, many retailers from different parts of the city buy flowers in bulk at wholesale prices. This includes the florists we commonly see in the city. After this, small vendors, people who deliver flowers to homes and shopkeepers, take the flowers. In this mandi even the exquisite flowers are sold at one fourth of the rate in retail. So, this mandi is not only pocket friendly but also environment friendly as the fragrance of lovely flowers greet you as you come here to buy your favourite flowers.

Why is there a marked price difference between retail and wholesale?

Online Shopping

A recent development has been the rapid increase in the use of the Internet for shopping. There are many advantages of shopping online, and it has emerged as a very popular trend in the recent times. This allows people the convenience of buying a wide range of things without having to travel to the shops. It saves a lot of travel time and is ideal for the elderly and differently abled people to visit the markets. They also generate a lot of employment and millions of people are involved in the various stages and aspects of the online shopping network.

Green Earth

Most markets and stores in India have banned plastic bags. They provide paper or cloth bags at a nominal price.

Case Study

Judgment of a two Judge Bench in Maharashtra Ekta Hawkers Union v. Municipal Corporation, Greater Mumbai, (2004) SCC 625, decided on 9-12-2003.

Hawkers have a right under Article 19(1)(g) of the Constitution of India. This right, however, is subject to reasonable restrictions under Article 19(6). Thus, hawking may not be permitted where, for example due to narrowness of road, free flow of traffic or movement of pedestrians is hindered, or where, for security reasons, an area is required to be kept free, or near hospitals, places of worship, etc. The authorities also recognize the fact that if properly regulated, the small traders can considerably add to the convenience and comfort of the general public, by making available ordinary articles of everyday use, for a comparatively lesser price. The Court then enumerated the following restrictions and conditions, subject to which the hawkers could do business in Mumbai: (Maharashtra Ekta Hawkers Union case, (2004) 1 SCC 625 at SCC pp. 635-37, para 14)

- In such a manner that the vehicular and pedestrian traffic is not obstructed and access to shops and residences is not blocked.
- Hawkers must not put up stalls or place any tables, stands or such other things or erect any type of structure.
- There should be no hawking within 100 m from any place of worship, holy shrine, educational institutions and hospitals or within 150 m from any municipal or other markets or from any railway station.
- There should be no hawking on footbridges and overbridges. Further, certain areas may be required to be kept free of hawkers for security reasons.
- However, outside places of worship hawkers can be permitted to sell items required by the devotees for offering to the deity, or for placing in the place of worship e.g. flowers, sandalwood, candles, agarbattis, coconuts, etc.

Q. Do you think these guidelines for hawkers are followed in cities and small towns in India?

Skill Builder

Collaboration: Discuss with your classmates which markets they most frequently visit. Analyse the reasons for this.

Life skills: Markets also provide services along with goods. Can you list at least five services, which we source through markets?

Critical thinking skills: Why do shops in malls earn more revenue than local markets?

World Connect

PASAR- The Traditional Markets of Indonesia

Traditional markets in Indonesia are called PASAR. This is essentially a food market and sells fresh fruits, vegetables, meat, fish, spices and dry food items. Across Jakarta, which is the capital city, similar things are sold in the PASAR, with variations according to the local population. For example, in places where the Indian community is in a majority, Indian spices would be found in greater quantities. Prices of the goods are not labelled on the goods and may vary from day to day. People can bargain to get the best price for their purchases. Everyday, men and women from the nearby areas come to the market to buy fresh food items, and thus, this place is not only a market but also a great way for the people to socialize. A visit to the place can give a glimpse of Indonesia's vibrant culture.

Wind up

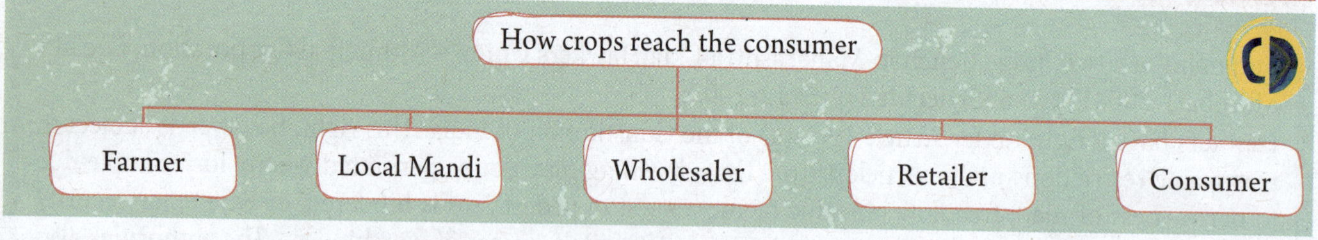

Exercises

A. Choose the correct answers.

1. These campaigns make people aware of the factors like maximum retail price and manufacturing date.
   a. Consumer awareness b. Consumer information
   c. Consumer benefit d. Consumer complaint
2. Key players in a market.
   a. Producer-consumer-seller b. Producer-consumer-government
   c. Producer-seller d. Magazine
3. In many areas, a day of the week is fixed when goods are sold on the pavements and roadsides. These are called
   a. online markets b. wholesale markets
   c. weekly markets d. daily markets
4. Comfortable and air-conditioned markets.
   a. Weekly markets b. Shopping malls
   c. Shopping hubs d. Shops

B. Identify the type of market.

1. Goods are sold in bulk. ....
2. Goods can be bought in smaller quantities ....
3. There is a fixed day in a week when this market is set up ....
4. People buy goods to meet their everyday needs ....
5. Big brands are sold in these ....

C. Fill in the blanks.

1. .... markets are usually cheaper than other markets.
2. Consumer Rights Day is observed on .... every year.
3. .... are usually closed, centrally air-conditioned areas that offer a variety of brands, both Indian and foreign.
4. Every time the goods reach a new trader in the chain of markets, the price of the item ....

D. Answer these questions in brief.

1. How do sellers in the weekly markets try to earn maximum profit?
2. What kind of goods are sold at a permanent local markets?
3. What is the chain of markets? How does it affect the price of goods?
4. Explain how consumer awareness campaigns have increased our knowledge about markets.

E. Answer these questions in detail.

1. Enumerate the reasons for the popularity of shopping malls.
2. With reference to hawkers and vendors, explain how the right to earn livelihood is an important fundamental right.
3. What are the advantages and the disadvantages of buying from the weekly markets?
4. Why has online shopping emerged as a viable option? List three reasons.

F. Read the passage and answer the questions.

Although the goods sold in the malls are generally expensive and shopkeepers do not bargain, the discounts offered attract many people. The cost of buying or renting a showroom in a mall is very high, and the owner has to invest in the infrastructure and facilities due to which the cost of products goes up.

1. Why are goods in malls costlier?
2. Why do people still shop from malls even though the prices of goods is high?

Think Big

Integrate with economics

Divide the class into groups of five. Prepare a menu card for the school canteen. The price of each item should be thought about carefully, depending on how you will source it. The prices should also be student-friendly.

Learning Tools

Use a chart to list the problems faced by different types of markets.

Problem	Solution
1.	1.
2.	2.
3.	3.

Web links:

https://www.managementstudyguide.com/what-is-market.htm

Last accessed on 31 August 2021

10. People for Equality

Warm up

'I have a dream. It is a dream deeply rooted in the American dream. I have a dream that one day this nation will rise up and live out the true meaning of its creed: We hold these truths to be self-evident: that all men are created equal.'

This is an excerpt from the speech given by Martin Luther King Jr. on equality and the rights of people.

Understanding Equality

The Constitution of India declares all the citizens to be equal, irrespective of their caste, creed, race or gender. The government also introduces various schemes from time to time so that this constitutional principle of equality can be implemented in the society. Universal adult franchise is guaranteed to all citizens of India who are 18 years and above. The right to equality is a fundamental right in the Constitution. However, we hear of stories and incidents of discrimination on various counts like caste, gender, economic status, religion, language and region.

FACT CHECK

In Sri Lanka, the Tamil minorities were discriminated against by the native Sinhala people. The Tamils were not allowed to speak or promote their language. Consequently, some of them formed an extremist group called the Liberation Tigers of Tamil Eelam (LTTE) to protest against Sinhala domination.

In the Bamiyan valley of Afghanistan, grand statues of Buddha made some time around the 6th century CE were destroyed by the Taliban regime in Afghanistan. They did so because these statues represent Buddhist beliefs. This act speaks of religious intolerance and demands religious equality.

Remains of the Buddhas of Bamiyan

The Taliban is an Islamic fundamentalist group in Afghanistan currently waging war within the country. The majority of the people in Afghanistan are Pashtuns, and there are a few minority communities. These minorities are treated in the most inhuman way. Public executions and amputations are common. Human rights violations have been taking place in large numbers. They propagate an extremist form of Sunni Islam and persecute people who follow different faiths.

People all over the world have raised their voice against racial, religious, linguistic and gender-related issues. Equality is a difficult ideal to achieve. Many people carried out struggles against the practice of unequal treatment and became prominent in history.

Rosa Parks fought against racial discrimination in America. Women in the Middle Eastern countries struggle to get equal rights and be treated with dignity and equality. Racial discrimination persists in many parts of the world.

Apply it!

Create a diversity logo and then display it or wear it! You can use a variety of images or photographs that you feel represent diversity. Then, write a short paragraph explaining why you chose this logo.

Struggle for Equality in India

There are many backward communities in India who have been struggling to get equal opportunities against injustice meted out to them by the society. Poor and uneducated people who do not have good jobs become easy targets of exploitation and unequal treatment. Women have to fight against harassment, both mental and physical.

A major source of discrimination continues to be the caste system, even though it has been abolished by law. Many backward and minority communities have been referred to as Scheduled Castes, Scheduled Tribes or Other Backward Classes, as certain benefits like reservation in education and jobs are given to them. People protest and agitate to get their demands heard by the government, and these protests sometimes turn violent and cause huge loss of life and property.

The struggle for equality should also be understood from the perspective of the displaced people and the hardships they face. Is the government to be squarely blamed for their plight? Is it not the responsibility of the government to provide development for all the people? Let us analyze these issues with the help of a story.

In 2016, a community of people living mainly in Haryana, the Jats, started an agitation demanding reservation in education, government jobs and other benefits given to the Scheduled Castes, Scheduled Tribes and Other Backward Classes. Though the agitation began peacefully, it soon took a violent turn with the services in the state getting affected for almost 10 days. A similar protest was also carried out by the Gujjar community of Rajasthan.

What's in the picture?

Observe the pictures given and discuss the different types of discrimination in our society with your classmates.

The Constitution—A Living Document

Our Constitution continues to support the struggles of different communities in different parts of the country. It is a silent but strong support system for people, as all the ideals that India strives to achieve are written there. The Constitution, thus, has real meaning in our lives and remains alive in the hearts of all the citizens of India.

Case Study

The largest Dam in India—Sardar Sarovar Dam

Let us follow the story of the biggest dam in India, called the Sardar Sarovar dam, built on the river Narmada.

Advantages: The construction of a dam is associated with development and progress in a society because a dam is a source of power generation or hydroelectricity. Dams lead to better water management and make irrigation of crops possible in areas where there is a shortage of other sources of irrigation, such as a river. They also help drought prone areas and make water available to the people.

Disadvantages: Construction of big dams involves human suffering and environmental damage. People who live around the site of construction are mostly poor people, tribals or *adivasis*. They do not have saved money and resources to fall back on, in case of any issues. When the construction of the dam begins, these communities are displaced as a large area is required to build the reservoir of the dam. Although they are promised relocation by the authorities, such procedures take a lot of time, causing inconvenience to the people.

They usually have emotional attachment to the place they live in as the lands are ancestral and have been with them for generations. They do not find work in the new place easily, and their children cannot get admissions in schools. It disturbs their whole life.

The ecosystems of forests or hills, where these dams are normally constructed, also get disturbed. Animals also have to leave their natural habitat. Thus, the development that the dam brings comes at a huge price, which is paid by innocent people.

Narmada River: Take a closer look at the map of India, and note the states that were directly going to be influenced by the construction of the dam on the Narmada River. These states had a conflict of interest on sharing of the cost of construction as well as the benefits from the dam. The poor people, mostly farmers, whose lands were going to be submerged were worst affected, irrespective of the state they belonged to.

There was not enough land within the states to rehabilitate the thousands of people who were displaced because of the dam.

The Narmada Bachao Andolan was the coming together of the affected communities, environmentalists and human rights activists. It soon became a movement to spread awareness about the damage being done to the river, considered scared like Ganga, in the Deccan regions of India. Its leaders were Baba Amte and Medha Patkar.

They highlighted the facts that fishing, which was a main source of livelihood for the people, would be affected due to the reservoir water becoming saline. Deposition of sediments could also lead to formation of raised land in the reservoir, causing the water levels to rise dangerously and flood the nearby areas. They organized protests and sit ins. Posters and slogans were raised to attract public and government attention to the issue.

Medha Patkar undertook a fast for about 22 days, which forced the World Bank to set up a commission called the Morse Commission to look into the matter. The World Bank stepped in as it had agreed to grant India a loan for the construction of the dam. In 1993 and 1994, Medha Patkar again undertook fasts, and as a result, the Court ordered the stoppage of work. It instructed the governments to first rehabilitate the people and restore their livelihoods.

The construction of the dam was eventually completed, and it gave the promised benefits to the people.

This study shows that the voice of the people is powerful in a democracy. If they get together, they can fight for their rights. The real success of democracy lies in the fact that communities that have suffered in silence till now are able to raise their demands. It must also be understood that all demands of the people are not justified, and the government has to strike a careful balance between genuine demands and those that want to extract benefits from the system.

Q. List the advantages and disadvantages of constructing the dam.

Skill Builder

21ST CENTURY SKILLS

Life skills: You and your friends are unequal, yet equal, in many ways. Discuss the ways in which all of you are equal to each other.

Critical-thinking skills: If dams are so beneficial, then why have struggles taken place around the issue of construction of dams?

World Connect

Vjosa is a big river in Europe. It flows through Albania. The government of Albania has proposed to build dams on the river to generate hydroelectricity. The people in Albania got together to appeal to the Prime Minister Edi Rama not to construct dams on the free river. The river is popular among the kayakers, which is boating on a raft boat. The people making the appeal included residents, artists, representatives from the European Parliament and environmental activists.

Wind up

Equality means putting an end to

- Classism
- Casteism
- Racism
- Gender discrimination
- Religious intolerance

Exercises

A. Choose the correct answers.

1. In India, a major source of discrimination continues to be the
   a. practice of dowry   b. caste system   c. practice of child marriage   d. practice of sati
2. The main source of livelihood for people near Narmada was
   a. farming   b. fishing   c. textile   d. handicraft
3. A neighbouring state of Gujarat that would also have been affected by the construction of the dam was
   a. Madhya Pradesh   b. Uttar Pradesh   c. Maharashtra   d. Andhra Pradesh
4. Along with Medha Patkar, a leader of the Narmada Bachao Andolan was
   a. Baba Amte   b. Anna Hazare   c. Medha Patkar   d. None of these

B. Fill in the blanks.

1. People are discriminated against due to .... and ....
2. The .... is an Islamic fundamentalist group in Afghanistan currently waging war within the country.
3. Universal Adult Franchise is granted to people who are .... years and above.
4. .... fought against racial discrimination in America.
5. Our .... continues to support the struggles of different communities in different parts of the country.

C. Correct the incorrect statements.

1. Medha Patkar supported the construction of the dam.
2. The World Bank refused to grant loans for the construction of the dam.

3. The Sardar Sarovar dam is built in Karnataka.
4. Large dams are always environment friendly.
5. The Bamiyan Buddhas were constructed by the Taliban.

D. Answer these questions in brief.

1. Why was the Narmada Bachao Andolan started?
2. Write a short note on women's struggle for equality.
3. Why are poor people discriminated against?
4. Why is the Constitution considered a living document?

E. Answer these questions in detail.

1. Why were the Bamiyan Buddhas destroyed? What kind of intolerance is this?
2. List the many reasons that cause inequality in India and the world.
3. Write a note on the struggle for equality in India.

Think Big — Art integration

List a few measures that can be followed to put an end to discrimination and inequality on a chart and decorate it. You can paste photos of events and happenings from around the world.

Learning Tools

A. Create your own study guides by compiling the necessary information for swift recap.

Main ideas	Why it matters	Important terms and names
....	....	....
....	....	....
....	....	....
....	....	....
....	....	....
....	....	....
....	....	

Web links:

https://www.equalityhumanrights.com/en/secondary-education-resources/useful-information/understanding-equality

Last accessed on 31 July 2021

Did you know there are four chemicals in your brain that affect happiness? They are dopamine, oxytocin, serotonin and endorphin. Let's figure out how to get them to work.

Our brain secretes **dopamine** after

- Completing a task
- Doing self-care activities
- Eating food
- Celebrating little wins

Our brain secretes **Oxytocin** after

- Playing with a pet or baby
- Holding hands
- Hugging members of your family
- Giving compliments

Our brain secretes **serotonin** after

- Meditating
- Running
- Sun exposure
- A walk in nature
- Swimming and cycling

Our brain secretes **endorphin** after

- Laughter
- Essential oils
- Watching a comedy
- Eating dark chocolate
- Exercising

Have you tried these? Overall, how happy would you say you are after trying these out?

THINGS THAT I LIKE ABOUT MYSE LF

What we think of ourselves also plays a role in determining our happiness levels. Fill up the following to reflect on your own self-talk and encourage yourself more.

1. ....

   ....

2. ....

   ....

3. ....

   ....

4. ....

   ....

5. ....

   ....

ASSESSMENT 1

History

Max Marks: 80

A. Multiple Choice Questions

10 × 1 = 10

1. Who wrote the book *Ain I Akbari*?
   a. Abdul Fazal b. Minhaj-ud-din Siraj c. Al Biruni d. Amir Khashru
2. Who was the earliest African traveller who visited medieval India?
   a. William Hawkins b. Thomas Roe c. Ibn Battuta d. François Bernier
3. The Rashtrakutas became powerful under the leadership of
   a. Gopala b. Dantidurga c. Nagabhata d. Rajpala
4. Kakatiyas ruled in
   a. Warangal b. Devagiri c. Kalyani d. Kanchi
5. Who was the founder of the slave dynasty?
   a. Qutubuddin Aibak b. Iltutmish c. Razia Sultan d. None of these
6. Tughlaqabad fort was built by Ghiyasuddin Tughlaq in the year
   a. 1348 b. 1425 c. 1321 d. 1328
7. Name the eldest son of Babur.
   a. Akbar b. Jahangir c. Aurangzeb d. Humayun
8. Who was in charge of the judicial department in Akbar's administration?
   a. Qazi b. Bakshi c. Sadr d. Diwan-i-Aam
9. Humayun's tomb is located in
   a. Agra. b. Patna c. Fatehpur Sikri. d. Delhi
10. Golden Temple is the worshipping place for
    a. Hindus b. Muslims c. Sikh d. Buddhists

B. Answer the following.

2 × 4 = 8

1. Name any four sources of the medieval history.
2. What was Tripartite Struggle?
3. Write any four economic measures of Alauddin Khalji.
4. 'The rulers of medieval India had a keen awareness about water conservation'. Explain the statement.

C. Answer these questions in brief. (Attempt any 2)

3 × 2 = 6

1. How did buildings and monuments help the study of medieval India?
2. Who founded Chola Empire? Write any two contributions of the Chola Empire in the medieval India.
3. Briefly explain Nagara style of temple architecture.

D. Read the following passage and answer the questions.

3

The Taj Mahal is an ivory-white marble monument located on the bank of the Yamuna in Agra. It was built by Mughal emperor Shah Jahan for his wife Mumtaz Mahal. It has been declared one of the Seven Wonders of the World and was designated a UNESCO World Heritage Site in 1983. Its construction employed around 20,000 artisans and its cost is estimated to be around 32 million rupees which in 2020 would amount to over 70 million rupees. It is considered to be the jewel of Muslim art in India and stands as a symbol of India.

1. Where is the Taj Mahal located and who built it ?

2. How many artisans worked for the construction of Taj Mahal?
3. When was Taj Mahal declared as World Heritage Site By UNESCO?

E. On an outline map of India locate and use different colours to mark the following kingdoms. 3 × 1 = 3

1. Rashtrakutas
2. Cholas
3. Palas

Geography

A. Fill in the blanks Any five (5)

1. A narrow belt on the Earth where life is found ....
2. Slate and limestone can metamorphose into ....
3. All the continents of the Earth were once a supercontinent called ....
4. The wearing away of rocks by agents on the surface of the earth is called ....
5. This gas makes up 78 per cent of the atmosphere ....
6. The area lying between the two tropics is called the .... zone.

B. Multiple choice questions Any five (5)

1. Which one of the following is a threat to environment?
   a. Growing population b. Growing crops c. Growing industries d. All of these
2. The lower most layer of the earth's surface is called
   a. the crust b. the core c. the roads d. the forest
3. This is a dormant volcano.
   a. Stromboli b. Mount Etna c. Mount Rainier d. Mount Vesuvius
4. Which of the following features is not formed by a glacier?
   a. Delta b. Moraine c. Cirque d. Pyramidal peak
5. Ozone is present in this layer of the atmosphere
   a. Thermosphere b. Stratosphere c. Troposphere d. Exosphere
6. The instrument by which air pressure is measured by
   a. barometer. b. thermometer c. seismograph d. anemometer

C. Answer these questions.

1. Explain the importance of tides giving any two reasons. 2
2. What is the extent of the troposphere? List any two important features of the troposphere. 1 + 2 = 3

D. Give reasons. 5

1. Lithosphere is important to us.
2. Extrusive rocks have small crystals.
3. Delta is formed at the mouth of the river.
4. Jet pilots prefer to fly their aircraft in the Stratosphere.
5. Shimla is colder than Delhi in summer.

E. Name and describe the pressure belts of the earth. 5

F. Draw a neatly labelled diagram of the water cycle. 5

Social and Political Life

A. Multiple choice questions. 8

1. Which one of the following is not a national party?
   a. BJP b. INC c. AAP d. BSP
2. Caste system was abolished by the
   a. Constitution b. government c. Parliament d. British
3. The minimum age of becoming an MLA is
   a. 18 years b. 21 years c. 25 years d. 30 years
4. Ministers are
   a. selected by the Chief Minister
   b. elected by the people
   c. appointed by the Union government
   d. selected by the President
5. The Road Safety Week is celebrated in India from
   a. 11th -17th January b. 11th-17th February c. 11th-17th March d. 11th-17th April
6. Which of the following is not a part of public transport?
   a. Buses b. Auto rickshaws c. Metro trains d. Scooters
7. Which of the following terms indicate a male dominated society?
   a. Female foeticide b. Female infanticide c. Patriarchal society d. Stereotypes
8. *Aanganwadis* help women as
   a. they pay all the women
   b. their children are taken care of while they are working
   c. they give loans to women
   d. they educate the women

B. Answer these questions.

1. The mid-day meal scheme has helped in many ways. Give any two points to support the statement. 2
2. In what ways does the opposition play an important role in the Legislative Assembly? 2
3. Write about 3 schemes introduced by the government in order to improve education in India. 3

C. Passage Based

This traditional preference for boys and perception of women only as homemakers has only led society to perceive women as dependents. From childhood, girls are taught that it is their responsibility to cook, clean, and do other household chores. Though housework is physically demanding and requires a lot of effort and labour, it is undervalued. Being a caregiver or a homemaker is considered to be equivalent to not doing anything.

1. From the passage pick out 2 lines which show the expectations of society from girls. 2
2. Why is a homemaker considered to be not employed? 3

ASSESSMENT 2

History

Max Marks: 80

A. Multiple Choice Questions

10 × 1 = 10

1. Guilds are the association of
   a. Craftsman b. Traders c. Labours d. None of these
2. Which city is known as the 'City of Thousand Temples?
   a. Tanjore b. Madurai. c. Machilipatnam d. Kanchipuram
3. These tribes worked in the tea estate of Assam.
   a. Bodos b. Bhils c. Munda d. Maharashtra
4. The Toda tribes are
   a. skilled craftsman b. Blacksmith c. Pastoral community. d. Potters
5. Name the worshipping place of Sikh religion.
   a. Gurudwara. b. Church c. Temple. d. None of these
6. Tukaram was a famous saint from
   a. Assam b. Rajasthan c. Maharashtra. d. Kerala.
7. The fusion of Hindi and Persian gave rise to a new language called
   a. Urdu b. Sanskrit c. Hindi d. Punjabi
8. Rajputs belonged to this caste.
   a. Brahmins. b. Kashtriya. c. Vaishyas d. Sudras
9. Which new dynasty developed in eastern part of the country?
   a. Cholas b. Palas c. Chahamanas d. Rashtrakutas
10. Which devotional path evolved since the 8th century?
    a. Bhakti b. Sufism c. None of these d. Both of these

B. Answer the following.

2 × 4 = 8

1. Name any two European countries that traded from Masulipatnam or Machilipatnam.
2. How did most tribals earn their livelihood?
3. Mention any four features of the miniature paintings of the medieval period.
4. Who were the major patrons of Kathak?

C. Answer these questions in brief. Attempt any 2.

3 × 2 = 6

1. Briefly explain the teachings of Kabir.
2. Name the Ahom king who ruled for as long as forty years. Distinguish between the kanri paiks and chamua paiks.
3. Write a note on the Bhils of Rajasthan.

D. Read the following passage and answer the questions.

3

Hinduism is the main and largest religion in India According to the 2011 Census of India, 966.3 million people identify as Hindu representing 79.8% of the country's population. India contains 94% of the global Hindu population, the world›s largest Hindu population. The Indian subcontinent is the birthplace of four of the world's major religions: namely Hinduism, Buddhism, Jainism, and Sikhism—collectively known as Indian religions that believe Moksha is the most supreme state of the *Ātman* soul. The vast majority of Hindus in India belong to Shaivite and Vaishnavite denominations. India is one of the three countries in the world Nepal and Mauritius being the other two. where Hinduism is the dominant religion.

The Vedic culture developed in India in 1500 BCE and 500 BCE. After this period, the Vedic religion merged with local traditions and the renouncer traditions, resulting in the emergence of Hinduism, which has had a profound impact on India's history, culture and philosophy. The name *India* itself is derived from Sanskrit *Sindhu*, the historic local appellation for the Indus River. Another popular alternative name of India is *Hindustān*, meaning the "land of *Hindus*".

India saw the rule of both Hindu and Muslim rulers from c. 1200 CE to 1750 CE. The fall of Vijayanagar Empire to Muslim sultans had marked the end of Hindu dominance in the Deccan. Hinduism once again rose to political prestige, under the Maratha Empire.

1. Name the religion that originated from the Indian subcontinent.
2. What is the meaning of Hindustan?
3. The fall of which kingdom marked Hindu dominance in Deccan

E. On an outline map of India locate and name the following temple towns from medieval India 3 × 1 = 3

1. Tanjore
2. Somnath
3. Madurai

Geography

A. Multiple choice questions (Any ten) 10

1. This forest trees are tall, straight and evergreen and have needle-like leaves. Name the tree
   a. Coniferous b. Tropical evergreen c. Temperate deciduous d. Temperate Evergreen
2. These towns are located at major crossroads of major roads or railways.
   a. Junction towns b. Residential towns c. Industrial towns d. Administrative towns
3. The chital, kingfishers and eagles are found in
   a. The Ganga-Brahmaputra Basin
   b. The Prairies
   c. The Velds
   d. none of these
4. Settlements that form along linear features such as banks of rivers, coasts or transport routes like roads or railways are
   a. Circular Pattern b. Linear Pattern c. Radial Pattern d. none of these
5. Tropical rain forests are also called the
   a. Selvas b. Pampas c. Prairies d. None of these
6. The grasslands of South Africa are called
   a. Velds b. Prairies c. Steppes d. Pampas
7. Sal and teak are found in
   a. Tropical Deciduous forest
   b. Temperate Deciduous forest
   c. Temperate evergreen forest
   d. Tropical Evergreen forest
8. Oxford and Cambridge in the UK and Santiniketan are examples of:
   a. Cultural and Educational Towns
   b. Religious Towns

c. Industrial Towns

d. Market Towns .

9. The Trans-Siberian Railway is the longest railway system connecting
   a. St. Petersburg to Vladivostok
   b. Halifax to Vancouver
   c. Buenos Aires with Valparaiso
   d. Sydney to Perth

10. Robins, snowcocks and ravens are birds found in
    a. Cold desert—Ladakh b. Hot desert--Sahara, c. Antarctica d. none of these

11. Amazon forest is located in
    a. the equatorial region between 10° N and 10° S
    b. region between 20° N and 20° S
    c. region between 30° N and 30° S
    d. none of these

12. The Ganga originates from this glacier in the Himalayas
    a. Gangotri b. Siachen c. Baltoro d. none of these

B. List four factors on which the location of human settlements depend. 2

C. Give one point of difference between: 1 x 3 = 3

1. Amazon Basin and Ganga-Brahmaputra Basin
2. Coniferous trees and deciduous trees
3. Mediterranean climate and tropical desert climate
4. Urban settlement and rural settlement

D. Give reasons: 5

1. In India, the Northern Plains are most suitable for the construction of railway lines.
2. The best places for fishing are Newfoundland, Canada and Japan.
3. The trees shed their leaves in the Tropical deciduous forests.
4. Most of the animals in deserts in deserts are nocturnal.
5. Tourism in summer is the main source of livelihood in Ladakh

E. Map work

1. On a map of the world, locate and name the following: 5
   a. A tropical desert b. A cold desert c. Selvas d. Coniferous forests
2. On a map of India, locate and name the following: 5
   a. The Ganga-Brahmaputra Basin
   b. Ladakh
   c. One administrative town
   d. One port town
   e. Hot Desert region

Social and Political Life

A. Multiple choice questions 8

1. She became the first woman president of the UN General assembly
   a. Indira Gandhi
   b. Vijay Lakshmi Pandit
   c. Sarojini Naidu
   d. Pratibha Patil
2. AWWA helps women by
   a. employing all of them
   b. organizing fairs of their crafts
   c. setting up hostels for them
   d. organizing trainings for them
3. One of the ways media earns money is through
   a. advertisements
   b. asking for donations
   c. grants from the government
   d. malpractices
4. Branded goods are considered better than local ones, often because
   a. of their quality
   b. of their designing
   c. of their value
   d. all of the above
5. Markets are best defined as
   a. places that are crowded
   b. places that are expensive
   c. places that are cheap
   d. places where buying and selling takes place
6. The journey of goods from the producer to the consumer is called
   a. retail markets
   b. wholesale markets
   c. chain of markets
   d. e markets
7. LTTE was an extremist group in
   a. India
   b. Afghanistan
   c. Pakistan
   d. Sri Lanka
8. Which of the following statements is false?
   a. Discrimination exists only in India
   b. Bamiyan Buddhas were destroyed by the Taliban
   c. Rosa Parks spoke against discrimination
   d. Women in middle eastern countries still struggle for equality

B. Answer these questions.

1. Give two instances to show that India is fast moving towards giving equal status to women as men. (2)
2. How do media impact the people? Give any two ways. (2)
3. Why are advertisements useful for the people and the companies both? (2)
4. List out 2 advantages and one disadvantage of a wholesale market. (3)

C. Passage Based 3

Our Constitution continues to support these struggles of the different communities in different parts of the country. It is a silent but strong support system for people as all the ideals that India strives to achieve are written there. The Constitution, thus, has real meaning in our lives, and remains alive in the hearts of all the citizens of India

1. Why is the Constitution called a living document?
2. In what way is it relevant to us?
3. List out any one ideal written in our Constitution.

Scale 1 : 16 670 000

Lambert Conformal Conic projection